NO MONEY DOWN

FINANCING

for

Franchising

ROGER C. RULE

The Oasis Press® / PSI Research
Central Point, Oregon

Published by The Oasis Press®/PSI Research

This publication is designed to provide accurate and authoritative information in regard to the subject matter covered. It is sold with the understanding that the publisher is not engaged in rendering legal, accounting, or other professional service. If legal advice or other expert assistance is required, the services of a competent professional person should be sought.
> — *from a declaration of principles jointly adopted by a committee of the American Bar Association and a committee of publishers.*

Editor: Constance C. Dickinson
Book Designer: Constance C. Dickinson
Compositor: Jan Olsson
Cover Designer: Steven Burns

Please direct any comments, questions, or suggestions regarding this book to
The Oasis Press®/PSI Research:

> Editorial Department
> P.O. Box 3727
> Central Point, OR 97502
> (541) 479-9464
> info@psi-research.com *email*

The Oasis Press® is a Registered Trademark of Publishing Services, Inc.,
an Oregon corporation doing business as PSI Research.

Rule, Roger C.
   No money down financing for franchising / Roger C. Rule
     p. cm. — (PSI successful business library)
   Includes index.
   ISBN 1-55571-462-5
   1. Franchises (Retail trade)—United States—Finance.   I. Title.
II. Series.
HF5429.235.U5R85   1998
658.8'708—dc21   98-45404

Printed in the United States of America
First edition 10 9 8 7 6 5 4 3 2 1 0

 Printed on recycled paper when available.

To my wife, Eileen,
and in memory of my mother, Margaret Evelyn,
with eternal love

Contents

Part III: Your Financing Resources

Appendices

Preface

The only people who never fail are those who never try.
— ILKA CHASE

Of all the facets of franchising, probably the least understood are the financing methods available to you, the would-be franchisee. Quite often, in your initial, novice search for comparing franchises of similar specialties and industries, you go to the library, bookstore, or trade show and find information on the many franchises available. The first things you check are the cost of the franchise fees and the required start-up costs. Next, you might typically compare royalty fees and cooperative advertising royalties from one franchise to another. From these early findings of how one franchise stacks up against another, you often decide on a franchise that best fits your budget. Normally, after this early analysis, you then go on to compare the other details, the secondary, nonfinancial statistics of one franchise to another — such as numbers of outlets, both company-owned and franchised; the age of the franchise; and other data.

One of the great missing links in this quick scanning between cost requirements and the other details is financing. Only a few source books address this, then usually only with a yes or no answer as to whether a franchisor offers financial assistance. *No Money Down Financing for Franchising* details all of the facets of financing that are available to you, the prospective franchisee, and provides step-by-step planning to successfully achieve it.

While the material in this book has taken several years to research, one of the most rewarding experiences has been learning from skilled and knowledgeable professionals and from the hands-on people in franchising: franchisees, the staff of franchisors, and their supporting lenders. Writing this book has provided such an opportunity. Although it is impossible to thank everyone who helped make this book possible, I would like to acknowledge these individuals:

Publisher: Emmett Ramey for publishing this book and Constance (C. C.) Dickinson for her untiring efforts both as senior editor and designer in pulling together all the material in an easy-to-understand format.

Accountants: Steve Akre (Management Advisory Services (MAS)), Ross Cofer, (Burnett, Umphress & Company, LLC), Carleton L. Williams (Detor & Williams Certified Public Accountants), and Steve Meester, CPA.

Attorneys: Kevin McBride, Robert Triantos, Ralph Ogden, and Jack Leebron.

Lenders: Diane Wissing (City Bank), Robert Lawton (Central Pacific Bank), A. Sean Aguilar (Arroyo & Coates), Ken Merport (The Foxboro Group), and Nick West (GMAC CM).

Educators: Richard G. Patterson, Romy Angle, Eric L. Saltzen, and Robert Fisk, Ph.D. (California State University, Stanislaus); and Robert T. Justis, Ph.D. (Professor, Louisiana State University, Baton Rouge).

For their contributions: Marcia McKinsey, Charles R. Suydam, and Lee Erickson.

And these franchises: A & W Root Beer, AAMCO Transmissions, Adia, The Athlete's Foot, Baskin-Robbins Ice Cream, Big-O-Tires, Blockbuster Video, Budget Rent A Car, Burger King, California Closets, Century 21 Real Estate, Chem-Dry Carpet Cleaning, Conroy Flowers, Culligan Waters, Dairy Queen, Domino's Pizza, Duncan Donuts, Fast Signs, Future Kids of America, Gingiss Formal Wear, Gloria Joan's Coffee Beanery, Gymboree, Holiday Inns, Jani-King, Jazzercise, Jiffy Lube, Kampgrounds of America, Kentucky Fried Chicken, Little Professor Book Center, Long John Silver's, MAAKO Auto Painting, Mail Boxes Inc., McDonald's, Merle Norman Cosmetics, Merry Maids, Midas Mufflers, Miracle Ear, Money Mailer, One-Hour Martinizing, Packy the Shipper, PIP Printing, Ponderosa Steak House, Precision Tune, The Pro Image, Ramada Inns, Round Table Pizza, Service Master, Sizzler's Buffet, Subway Sandwiches, Supercuts, T-Shirt Plus, Taco Bell, TCBY, Tony Romas, Uniglobe Travel, Video Data Services, Wallpapers To Go, Western Temporary Services, Wicks-N-Sticks, and Wienerschnitzel.

Franchising in the United States

There is now scarcely an outlet for energy in this country except business . . . .
— JOHN STUART MILL

Franchising is a method of sales expansion by a successful company wanting to distribute its product, service, or method of operation through retail outlets owned independently by others. The successful company allows these independently-owned retail outlets to use its trademarks, trade name, or marketing techniques, with defined controls, in return for payments of fees.

The latter type that distributes its method of operation is newer and called business-format franchising. It involves two separate business entities:

- The company, or franchisor, that developed the system and lends the use of its name or trademark; and

- An independently owned outlet, or franchisee, that buys the right to operate a business under the franchisor's name or trademark.

In addition, the International Franchise Association (IFA) defines franchising as a "continuing relationship between franchisor and franchisee in which the sum total of the franchisor's knowledge, image, success, and manufacturing and marketing techniques are supplied to the franchisee for a consideration."

A business-format franchising program has three major components.

- An identity. A trade name often identified by a symbol protected by registration such as a trademark or service mark for the exclusive use of the franchising system.

- A business format. A system of operating a daily business that a franchisor can transfer to individual franchisees.
- A continuous financial arrangement. An initial fee paid up front and supported by continuous ongoing royalties paid by the franchisee to the franchisor based on a percentage of sales revenues.

Statistically, franchising is a very popular and profitable way to do business. The U.S. Department of Commerce reveals franchise sales of products and services accounted for some $700 billion in gross sales in 1992. This is via some 100 different industry specialties in more than 565,000 locations across the country and represents approximately one-third of total gross retail sales in the country.

A Brief History

Franchising is not new. Its earliest forms were product or trademark franchising back in the 1800s. The I.M. Singer Company used the system to sell sewing machines by licensed dealers in the 1850s. While it is still used today by automobile dealers, service stations, and soft-drink bottling companies, among others, this older style of product or trademark franchising is on the decline. According to the U.S. Department of Commerce, the number of product franchises fell by 40 percent from the early 1970s to the mid-1980s.

However, the business-format system of franchising — where a franchise duplicates its business format — is flourishing. It represents more than 90 percent of all franchising operations in business today. It has been around, in significant numbers, only since the 1950s when motels and fast food restaurants started replicating themselves. And only in the last two decades has it made an impact as a popular expansion strategy for successful businesses. Take a look around and you will see that business-format franchising is on a dynamic upswing.

Some sources project that by the year 2010, franchise sales in this country may reach one-half of all gross retail sales. This growth is not limited to the United States. In recent years, it has expanded globally with another 32,000 franchise locations overseas in such diverse markets as Africa, the Caribbean, Europe, Israel, Russia, Micronesia, and Japan. The U.S. Department of Commerce, which tracks franchising trends for the federal government, claims that franchising is the wave of the future. There seems to be no limit. The late Ray Kroc, co-founder of McDonald's, which is one of the undisputed leaders in franchising with approximately 19,500 units worldwide and one opening every six hours, is quoted as saying, "Saturation is for sponges."

The Franchise Advantage

Franchising offers some strong advantages for both you, as a franchisee, and the franchisor. Besides obtaining fees from the franchisees, the franchisor is able to expand its business much faster and in far greater depth than by doing so on its own. This quick access to new markets is further enhanced because a franchisor is not limited to its corporate resources of either personnel or expansion capital.

From the franchisor's standpoint, the system represents an efficient method of rapid market penetration and distribution without the expensive capital costs normally associated with company-owned expansion. Since franchisees are independent owners of their businesses, they supply nearly all the capital to set up their outlets, contracting with the franchisor for the idea, identity, perfected business format, and, in many cases, product. Through contract obligations, the franchisee must maintain consistency and quality control, with restrictions on what they can sell and how they can operate, to come across as a company-owned, chain-type outlet. Thus, in addition to the positive cash flow, the franchisor can maintain significant control of its image and the profitability of its outlets.

When comparing company-owned chain operations with corporate franchisors of equal size, expansion for the chains is extremely slow. Most medium-sized companies can add only a few units a year at best, when capitalizing the expensive labor, construction, equipment, fixtures, and inventory costs associated with expansion from their own capital and financing. In franchising, on the other hand, expansion is not capitalized by the franchisor but is paid for by you, the franchisee.

For the franchisor, it is the same as having a business partner who pays for everything when adding a unit, as well as an additional $5,000 to $40,000 for the privilege. This is reminiscent of Tom Sawyer's principle for white washing the fence. In Mark Twain's book, *The Adventures Of Tom Sawyer*, Tom talked Huck Finn and his friends into white washing his aunt's fence for him, not only saving himself from the work but also charging his friends for the opportunity to do it for him.

At the same time, you, as the franchisee, gain many advantages in addition to the opportunity to own a business that has a minimum risk of failure. As well as the right to sell a proven product or service that is recognizable by the general public and is competitively priced, you receive supervision and assistance from a proven parent company. In addition to management assistance, the franchisor furnishes you with an ongoing support system through training, advertising, marketing, and product and service testing and improvement. Most franchisors have strong purchasing power through volume buying, and the savings are passed on to you through central purchasing. Often, the ongoing support includes central data processing, field evaluation of franchisee operations, field training, inventory control, a franchisor newsletter, regional and national conference meetings, a telephone toll-free number for immediate answers, and an Internet home page for advertising and directing customers to local franchisees.

Franchisors, as proven businesses, have already tested their products or services, made their mistakes, worked out their best business solutions, and established their reputations. For you, as a franchisee, a lot of the guesswork is removed; you have the freedom of being on your own, but you do not have to feel you're going it alone. Statistics prove that you are more likely to succeed as an owner of a franchise than as an independent, small business owner.

According to the U.S. Department of Commerce, 80 percent of all non-franchised small businesses fail, many within their first year of business. In contrast, less than 3 percent of all new franchises are discontinued in their first year of business, and approximately 90 percent are still operating after ten years. According to the *Franchise Bible*, by Erwin J. Keup, the statistics are even better, with less than 2 percent of new franchises discontinued over a three-year period. A small business not in a franchise system is four and one-half times less likely to succeed than one that is. The few small businesses that are not franchised but do succeed earn only 80 percent as much as their franchised counterparts.

If you are seeking to become your own boss, you can hardly ignore the overwhelming advantage the franchise system offers. This is often referred to as "the franchise advantage" and takes its basis not only from the statistics but also from the advantages offered by the franchisor/franchisee relationship.

The advantages of a franchise system over a company-owned chain operation can be divided into separate advantages for each player, the franchisor and the franchisee. But, the real success of the franchise system lies in the many mutual advantages they both enjoy.

- Franchising affords more rapid market penetration and distribution.
- More efficient buying power exists because volume prices for the entire franchise system are passed on to the franchisees. This increased buying power results in lower costs, more competitive consumer pricing, and improved profit.
- Franchise owners experience more pride of ownership due to their capital investment and profit potential than do managers of company-owned chains. Also, there is little or no turnover in franchising.
- Greater consistency and better quality control are created, in part, by more experienced managers but primarily by the network operations manual, training, and contract agreements.
- More advertising dollars exist, whether from advertising royalties or from cooperative, or co-op, advertising, that cover local as well as regional and often national levels.
- The franchisor is provided a consistent cash flow from royalties, which in turn creates a steady cash flow available for franchisee support and assistance.
- The greater research and development support contributed by the franchisor is supplemented by the experience and creativity of franchisees, who have a self-interest in making suggestions to constantly improve the system.

Franchising Popularity

Why is franchising so popular? Franchising allows the successful franchisor to expand rapidly with financing contributed by franchisees. This popularity has moved middle-sized companies into the national marketplace. Its highly successful expansion capability separates franchising from any other marketing system.

What adds to the popularity of this system is the fact that most industries in business-format franchising are in the service sector, one of the largest and fastest growing sectors of the economy. According to the U.S. Bureau of Labor Statistics, nearly three-fourths of the American work force is employed by service-producing industries. The service sector has generated 14 million jobs over the past 25 years, while the combined total for manufacturing and agriculture has remained about the same.

The franchising business fits in well with today's economy because of the minimal requirements for training and inventory. For example, you, as a prospective franchisee of a service franchise, can be trained in just a few weeks, sometimes in a matter of days. This minimal training is a win-win situation, as it keeps franchisors' costs low and affords franchisees the ability to turn a profit more quickly. In addition, inventory requirements are kept to a lower limit which requires less up-front money needed by prospective franchisees which, in turn, means more people can qualify as franchisee candidates.

Franchising Trends

Riding on the wave of franchising's popularity are some intriguing economic trends. On a national level, there is a major economic trend toward franchising. Andrew J. Sherman in his book, *Franchising and Licensing: Two Ways to Build Your Business* gives ten reasons for this trend. Here is a brief summary of those ten reasons.

- After its first 40 years, there is a changing of the guard in franchising. Well-trained executives ready to take over and improve the already strong in-place management systems are replacing the entrepreneurial and high-risk-oriented founders.
- The new generation of franchisees is improving in their level of sophistication and financial strength due to an influx of well-trained executives who are leaving corporate jobs because of swings in the economy.
- There is a new involvement by large corporations to franchise previously independent industries such as real estate, insurance, and banking.
- There is a surge of growth by U.S. franchisors into the international market, which is a wide-open field with strong acceptance by international consumers.

- There is a new trend toward combination services provided in a single franchise, such as pizza and chicken, caused by mergers of franchisors, resulting in increased efficiency, both from the franchisor's administrative end and the franchisee's operational level.
- There is increased interest by commercial banking and venture capitalists, which is making more capital available to franchising through both lending and investing.
- There is a growing involvement by colleges and universities that are recognizing franchising as the system of the future for retail and service expansion.
- There are intensified efforts by franchisors and local governments to increase the role of minority groups in franchising.
- There is more widespread recognition and support for franchisees by franchisors through regional and national conferences, seminars, and advisory councils.
- The IFA has predicted that the strong existing franchise industries will continue to expand and that special personal service industries will boom in the future.

Franchising and You

After seeing the popularity and advantages of franchising, you have probably already made your decision to become a part of franchising. The most common stumbling block is the capital requirement and this book will assist you in financing it. If complete ownership is not a requisite, then it is very possible to structure your financial needs with no money down. But if it is important for you not to give up any ownership, this book will direct you towards other possibilities of 100 percent financing available through some franchisors and still other sources with no money down.

How This Book Can Help

If you are thinking of going into business for yourself to benefit from the franchise advantage, the decision between whether to buy a franchise or to open your own independent small business is obvious. To get you started down the right road to no money down financing, you need to determine your capital investment requirement in selecting your franchise, to develop a document to use as a financial request, and to tackle the specific types of financing sources available. To assist you in achieving these goal, the book is divided into three parts.

Part I covers the financial preliminaries or prep work. Be ready to

- Discover your own credit rating and see yourself as lenders see you;

- Establish your capital investment needs; and
- Ascertain the amount of funds you may have to seek.

Part II covers all of the information you need to prepare a complete and lengthy professional franchise business plan for your loan request or investor proposal. Each segment is highlighted with examples of a completed franchise business plan, so you can see how it can be done.

Part III prepares you for making the best presentation of your franchise business plan to financiers and investors and covers the types of financing resources available to you, including:

- The many sources of equity financing used in franchising;
- Methods available for third-party debt financing; and
- Financial assistance offered by the franchisors.

Financial assistance from franchisors ranges from simply directing you to commercial lenders who have made loans to franchisees within the franchisor's system to providing you with 100 percent in-house financing at the top end of the scale. The franchisors that offer assistance comprise only about 20 percent of the complete domain of franchises.

If financing is necessary for you to get started, begin with those franchises that provide it. Appendix F has an up-to-date listing of these franchisors. *The Franchise Redbook*, to be published in October 1999 by The Oasis Press, will offer even more complete financial assistance information. However, if franchisor financing appears necessary and you start with Appendix F and the suggestions in Chapter 14, you'll be 80 percent ahead of the game in your search.

Finally, this book's purpose is to supply you with all the information currently available to actively seek and acquire financing for your franchise venture, including the options for no-money-down financing.

Good luck and happy financing in your quest to own, open, and operate your chosen franchise.

Part I

Your Financing Preliminaries

Chapter 1

Your Financial Picture

The successful businessman sometimes makes his money by ability and experience; but he generally makes it by mistake.
— GILBERT K. CHESTERTON

If you are going to apply for a franchise, it is essential to first make a financial assessment of yourself so you can see what the franchisor will see when reviewing your file. The franchisor's view will become apparent when you develop your financial profile. You will undergo this same exercise to understand your capital needs and assess your financing goals for discussions in later chapters. For now, the first step in developing your financial profile is a credit check.

Your Credit

To check your credit, call your local credit bureau and request a copy of your credit report. The local credit bureau is probably an affiliate of one of the three major credit-reporting agencies: CBI/EQUIFAX, TRW, or Trans Union. The Yellow Pages usually list these under credit-reporting agencies.

Reading a credit report can be quite complicated if you are inexperienced at it. Although their formats vary, all credit reports have the following salient data at the top of the forms:

- Name to whom the report is addressed
- Date of request

- Date of completion of report
- Applicant's name
- Applicant's present and previous addresses with length of stay at each
- Marital status and number of years married
- Number of dependents
- Present and previous employers and numbers of years with each
- Social security number
- Date of birth

Below that is the body of credit history in columnar format. On forms from CBI/EQUIFAX, the first column on the left is an association code, 0 to 9, coded on the back of the form. These simply identify the account as joint, co-maker, or individual. The next column has:

- Account name
- Date reported
- Date opened
- Highest credit limit in terms of dollars
- Balance owed and amount due if any
- Number of payments
- Current status rating
- Number of months of history reviewed
- Number of times past due, more than 30, more than 60, more than 90, date last past due, and remarks

The current status rating, coded on the back of the form as current rating, indicates type of account with a letter code:

- O – Open account
- R – Revolving
- I – Installment
- M – Mortgage
- C – Credit Line; followed by a numeric code 0–9:
    - — 0, too new to rate
    - — 1, pays within 30 days
    - — 2, pays between 30 and 60 days
    - — 3 through 8 get progressively worse until
    - — 9, bad debt, collection account, charged off, skip

At the bottom of the report, any judgments or other remarks may appear.

TRW forms are similar. In the column on the left, times past due is subdivided into three columns of 30, 60, or 90+ days with an additional column for payment status and the words As Agreed or Pd As Agrd entered, unless delinquencies are reported. An updated version has a payment profile showing the numbers 1 through 12 for each month of the year. A C indicates current and an *N* represents no activity, such as for a revolving account that is not used during this report period.

The right column on Trans Union forms details the payment pattern separated into number of days, 30–59, 60–89, and 90+, with a type of account and manner of payment (M.O.P.) rating on the far right. Like CBI/EQUIFAX, type of accounts are indicated as O, R, I, M, and C. The M.O.P. rating codes are as follows:

Manner of Payment (M.O.P.) Rating Codes

Number	Code
00	Too new to rate
01	Pays within 30 days or not more than one payment past due
02	Pays between 30 and 60 days [after bill is due]
03	Pays between 60 and 90 days [after bill is due]
04	Pays more than 90 days [after bill is due]
05	Pays in more than 120 days or four payments past due
06	No code
07	Making regular payments under wage earner plan
08	Repossession
08A	Voluntary repossession
08D	Legal repossession
08P	Payment to a repossession account
08R	Repossession redeemed
09	Bad debt, charged-off account
9B	Collection account
9P	Payment to be charged off
UR	Unrated
UC	Unclassified
RJ	Rejected

A rating from 03–09 can cause you a problem in getting a business loan. Lenders look for quick payers and consider borrowers with all 01s as having a track record which is a strong credit rating.

If you or any recent lenders have requested a credit report in considering a new loan, this shows up also. If several requests are noted, a lender may ask you to write an explanation as to why you are tendering other requests.

After you review your own credit report, you may disagree with its accuracy. If you wish to dispute something, pull your files and send copies of evidence with a letter of explanation. Mail these return receipt requested so you have proof the letter is received. The credit reporting agency then forwards a copy of your explanation to the company in question, which may either agree with you and change the report or retain its same position. In either event, the credit bureau is required by law to report back to you within 30 days or remove the disputed material from your credit report. If the company you dispute does not agree with your explanation to the credit-reporting agency, you have the right to have your version of the problem entered into the credit records. If you know you are right and it's important to straighten out the matter, you may want to contact an attorney to send a strong letter to the company that erroneously reported the problem.

Your Financial Statement

Once you have established that your credit is acceptable to a franchisor and you still wish to buy a franchise, the franchisor will want you to complete your financial profile by submitting a financial application. With this document, your prospective franchisor will evaluate your net worth and your liquid assets. In many states, if you are married, this includes your common or community property with your spouse. You may have an accountant prepare this, but you can obtain a typical personal statement form from any bank, which is not difficult to complete yourself.

On the next page is a typical blank balance sheet. In completing this form, remember that assets are anything you own or are due to you. Often the largest asset for most individuals is their home, followed by their automobiles. List your home and any other real estate holdings at their appraised value, although you do not need to get an appraisal at this time. Show values of your automobiles or boats at their book values. If you have marketable securities, such as stocks or mutual funds that can be immediately liquidated, these can be shown as liquid assets on the form similar to cash on hand, savings and checking accounts. The cash value of whole life insurance is also a liquid asset. You may have nonmarketable securities such as stock ownership in a privately owned company that has value but cannot be easily liquidated. There is an appropriate place on the form to display these by cost and present value.

Accounts receivable are assets that are owed to you. These are value that you will realize when paid but are currently classified as assets, which does not help toward liquidity but does for net worth. Other assets to list are valuable art; jewelry; furniture; coin, stamp, or gun collections; and any vast assemblance of expensive equipment such as computers, tools, and photography equipment. Set the value of the latter items realistically as the price you could sell them for, not what you paid for them.

Offsetting assets are liabilities. This is a group of all creditor claims and financial obligations against your assets. These are secured notes payable, and loans for automobiles, boats, furniture, and equipment, as well as unsecured notes payable, such as any signature loans or short-term loans that are arranged without collateral. Also under liabilities are accounts payable, unpaid bills, all other debts, revolving accounts, and credit card balances.

Your net worth is simply the difference between your assets and liabilities.

Additional pages to the form ask for annual income, including your spouse's, and miscellaneous information as support detail for the assets and liabilities. For instance, your home value may be $195,000 and your

Balance Sheet

Date: _____

Assets

Current Assets:

Cash (on hand and in banks)	_____
Accounts receivable	_____
Interest receivable	_____
Inventory	_____
Supplies	_____
Prepaid expenses	_____
Other	_____
Total current assets	_____

Fixed Assets:

Real estate	_____
Vehicles and equipment	_____
Furniture, fixtures, and signage	_____
Total fixed assets	_____

Other Assets:

Franchise fee	_____
Personal equipment and furniture	_____
Other	_____
Total other assets	_____

Total Assets _____

Liabilities And Equity

Current Liabilities:

Accounts payable	_____
Current maturity long-term debt	_____
Accrued taxes	_____
Other	_____
Total current liabilities	_____

Long-term Liabilities

Long-term debt	_____
Other	_____
Total long-term liabilities	_____

Total Liabilities _____

Total Equity (Net Worth) _____

Total Liabilities and Equity _____

mortgage may be $125,000. The difference, $70,000, is your equity and is probably one of the larger components of your net worth.

Preparing your personal financial statement establishes a record of your net worth. It assists you in deciding how much you can afford for a franchise. The franchisor will be assessing your ability to afford its initial or original investment, not just its initial fee. If, for example, the original investment is listed as $85,000 for a particular franchise, the franchisor is looking for this, prorated to a minimum of 50 to 60 percent of your net worth. In terms of dollars, you need about $142,000 to $170,000 of net worth.

For an original investment of $85,000 and a 50 percent net worth, the net worth needed is $170,000; for a 60 percent net worth, the net worth needed is $142,000. In this example, a prospective franchisee that has $34,000 cash, will probably be eligible for a loan for the difference:

$85,000 – $34,000 = $51,000.

Once you apply for a franchise, the franchisor requires you to complete an application besides the financial statement that encompasses a myriad of other information, such as for example, employment history, a credit check, and bank and personal references.

Compiling your financial statement before you even decide which franchisors you are going to approach serves to let you know what you can afford and speeds up the process when you do decide. If you expect to go forward and be a successful franchisee, it is imperative to make an honest evaluation of your financial statement. Do not overstate your assets and understate your liabilities; your financial success depends on it. Buy what you can afford. If you do not overpurchase or overestimate your net worth, you can weather the cash flow problems in the early stages when times are the roughest.

Now that you have assembled your financial profile, the next step is to establish the investment requirement to determine if you are going to need any outside financial assistance. Chapter 2 addresses your investment requirement.

Understanding Your Investment Costs

There is only one success — to be able to spend your life in your own way.
— CHRISTOPHER MORLEY

After establishing your financial profile, you have some idea of your own equity position for your journey forward in acquiring a franchise. From this point, you are now ready to find out the total investment needed for buying and opening your franchise. Once you know the investment requirement and compare it with your equity, you can then determine your financial needs for a loan or capital infusion by others.

When buying a franchise, two components control a major share of the investment requirement. First is the fixed requirement dictated for the specific franchise you select. When you study most of the reference materials of the various franchise corporations, you find a price range for the original investment, often referred to as the initial investment. Several factors affect this range. Sometimes the initial franchise fee varies and is listed as a small range within the original investment as a set of high to low figures.

The second component is the variable requirement that consists of variable costs associated with location that can drastically affect the wide range of the original investment. It is this location component that makes up the major cost impacting your investment requirement and is the most difficult to establish. The purpose of this chapter is to assist you in closely analyzing these two components to determine the total investment requirement before you make the commitment to buy a franchise.

The best starting point is your prospective franchisor's estimates of the required initial investment, as set forth in item seven of the Uniform Franchise

Offering Circular (UFOC), or disclosure document. The franchisor bases the cost for opening a franchise on its previous and current experience of typical units. This is usually exhibited as a high to low range, but if it is just one number, it represents a median cost for all franchisees. The biggest mistake made in buying a franchise is underestimating total start-up needs. Check out this one area more than any other in your research process.

The table below shows a diversified group of franchise industries with comparisons of their estimates of average start-up cash requirements and their average total investment requirements. The difference between the figures in the two columns is frequently the amount being sought for financing.

Franchise Industries Start-up Costs and Investment

Type of Industry	Number of Franchises	Average Investment	Average Start-up Costs
Accounting, consulting	8	$ 35,600	$ 17,800
Automotive	72	282,400	141,200
Auto rental	7	973,500	649,000
Business support centers	5	487,400	203,500
Children's products and services	35	391,200	202,700
Convenience stores	10	406,400	127,000
Dry cleaning and laundry	6	430,500	257,800
Employment services	26	129,200	86,100
Food, fast service	198	615,400	236,700
Health care	20	308,400	154,200
Hotels and motels	10	7,783,200	4,864,500
Maintenance services	73	30,000	25,000
Pets' products and services	15	172,500	89,400
Real estate	7	65,500	39,200
Restaurants, full service	46	1,225,000	818,800
Retail, nonfood	58	266,726	138,200
Travel agencies	10	95,000	56,900

The franchisor gives average start-up costs because the total investment required is impossible to state in the disclosure document. The franchisor cannot control the many arbitrary variables. For example, the amount of financing for any one franchisee depends on the franchisee's assets and credit worthiness. It also depends on variances in cost estimates caused by differences in geographic areas for overhead expenses as well as differences in lease versus mortgage payments. If a facility is purchased, other financing variables come into play, such as how much a lender will loan for real estate and how much, if any, for fixtures.

While the franchisor cannot state these estimates with specific accuracy, you as the prospective franchisee still must address the issue to get a true and clear estimate of what your total investment is going to be. You can arrive at this more successfully if you solicit the help of a good certified public accountant or business accountant to develop a worksheet for your investment requirement or your cash investment needs. This starts with an accurate forecast of your earnings that estimates your revenue, expenses, and costs.

Your accountant can assist you in compiling a forecast to predict the potential earnings. This typically includes an estimate of revenue from sales, a budget of estimated fixed and variable expenses with a prediction of costs of goods, and a forecast of both profit and cash flow needs. Cash flow covers your ongoing payments of franchise royalties.

Estimating Revenue

For the best estimates of income, you can turn to your prospective franchise system. Contact the franchisor and request sales figures for an average outlet. Separately, whether or not your response is satisfactory, turn to item 20 of the franchisor's disclosure document that lists the past and current franchisees and their addresses. Contact several and attempt to document their monthly sales revenue.

If for some reason this information cannot be given to you, at least obtain sales averages by products, product mix, or service mix. Compare your findings with your accountant's knowledge of sales in an average month for comparable businesses in your area. Make some allowances for possible fluctuations in your market, such as seasonal differences and demographics. These are covered in more detail in Part II.

Predict the number of customers and the number of sales per customer you expect to have each month. Estimate the revenue they will generate by multiplying the number of customers by the number of sales per customer by the average sales price. For a new business, this figure should be very conservative and increased modestly each month throughout the first year using realistic expectations — usually a fixed percentage determined with the help of your accountant and franchisor.

If you have different products that create a variation of prices, or price ranges, you can find out how the typical mix sells by percentages from other franchisees. You can make up your own spreadsheet of monthly sales. You can categorize the inventory into two, three, or four range groups, adding the monthly revenue of each group to get the total monthly revenue, or you can forecast sales on a pro-rata basis breaking them down into one basic average. It works out the same; the former method is more useful for other projections later. Your accountant can help with this once you have reliable figures from the franchisor or the other franchisees.

Estimating Expense

To estimate expense, start with some basic statistics from businesses in the same industry. Often, your business accountant can assemble some realistic estimates of expenses for your line of business. From here, you can begin your own research and refinements of the figures.

Turn to your prospective franchisor as a source by first examining its disclosure document. If you have sent applications to more than one franchisor in your field, review item seven of the disclosure documents for each of them. As you narrow the field to one, compare the franchisor's estimates with your accountant's. Unless the franchisor's numbers are unusually low or different, give it the benefit of the doubt at this point; using its numbers as a basis. Nevertheless, have your accountant review them as an additional safety measure.

Your accountant should be able to help you prepare this budget with relative ease, when supplemented with the costs particular to your franchise as detailed in the disclosure document. The other expenses are routine for most accountants, given personal input from you.

Fixed Costs

While the disclosure document reveals most of the variable cost projections, you and your accountant must speculate the local fixed ones, for example, lease payments, insurance, salaries, automobile expenses, and telephone and utilities costs.

Lease or Rent Payment

You probably already know what this cost will be. If you haven't selected your site yet, you will need to develop a number for this budget item — you can revise it when you know your actual lease or mortgage payment. You can contact a real estate agent or check the classified section of your newspaper for sites similar to what you need in size, zoning, and site location.

Property Taxes, Insurance, Utilities, and Maintenance

If you are leasing your facility, check with your commercial real estate broker or property owner to find out the monthly taxes, insurance, and typical maintenance. For utilities, if your facility is not new, you can contact the local utility companies and determine the previous average monthly utility bills. If it is new, your accountant probably has a good idea of this if the site is local or within proximity to his or her other clients. If the building is used, get a history of maintenance from the proprietor or previous tenants.

Payroll

The disclosure document will indicate the number of personnel needed for your franchised outlet, both part and full-time, managerial, secretarial, and other types of personnel. What it does not indicate are the wage rates prevailing in your geographic area. Again, ask your accountant who, from experience with other clients, can give you ideas of these numbers. For your salary, it is helpful to make up a family budget; you probably realize the need to keep expenses to a minimum during the start up of a business. Austerity is going to be your catchword for the first year. When compiling your family budget, include such items as:

- Automobile insurance
- Automobile maintenance
- Automobile payments
- Clothing
- Educational expenses
- Food
- Gifts
- Home maintenance
- Homeowner's insurance
- Life insurance
- Medical and dental expenses not covered by insurance
- Medical insurance
- Miscellaneous
- Mortgage payment or rent
- Property taxes
- Utilities

If you classify everything else under miscellaneous, watch those expenses closely for three months and reclassify recurring expenses in their own category.

Employee Taxes and Benefits
Your accountant can compute this easily, but the rule of thumb is to use 20 percent of the payroll amount.

Telephone
The amount of this expense depends on the nature of your business, the number of telephones in your franchise, and the number of long-distance calls that you need to make. Your accountant can give you some idea of what you can expect in the way of an expense for this business. A standard for a small business that does not have extensive telephone use is to use the local telephone company's actual monthly charge for the basic rate, then double that basic rate for your monthly estimate to cover long-distance calls you might make to suppliers. Most franchisors have a toll-free number for you to call, usually referred to as the hotline support service.

Other Insurance
Consult the franchisor's disclosure document and the franchise agreement to confirm the types of insurance and amount of coverage you are required to carry. State law may have some requirements also. Typically, you need business liability, comprehensive fire and damage, and workers' compensation insurance. Contact your insurance agent to get the exact premiums to budget the payments in the appropriate month.

Legal and Accounting Expenses

You probably do not have ongoing regular attorney fees, but it is necessary to budget a figure anyway. A common plan is to budget the equivalent of three or four appointments a year. Ask your attorney for a typical appointment charge and set it up for the first month of each quarter. Your business accountant also should give you a fixed monthly fee for specified services. There may be a higher year-end extra, depending on the way it's structured. You can set up the monthly fee and add in the additional year-end charge in the month it is due.

Miscellaneous Expenses

Although every expense imaginable should be predicted, as in your personal budget, there always seems to be some expense each month that creeps into the accounts to be paid. To cover this, most businesses set up a flat-rate expense, say $200 or so, for miscellaneous expenses. If it becomes obvious that some expense continually shows up in this category, include it as a regular line item in the monthly chart of accounts.

Variable Costs

While each of these variable costs is a percentage of the gross sales or revenue earned, enter their total as one computation for quick spreadsheets.

Costs of Goods Sold

On financial statements, this is referred to as cost of revenue earned. Depending on the nature of your business, if you are buying and selling products or buying supplies to manufacture items for sale, it is essential to determine the cost of goods sold, which is the cost per unit of each item sold. An estimate of this should be available from the franchisor and other franchisees. If you are buying some items from suppliers designated by your prospective franchisor, the costs involved should still be a percentage of sales. Attempt to accurately calculate the total cost of goods sold as a known percentage of gross sales.

Supplies

To get an idea of this expense, add it to your list with the other areas to investigate when contacting the franchisor and other franchise owners. They can probably tell you to use a percentage based on gross sales. The more sales you have, the more supplies you use. A typical small business can use as much as two percent of gross sales for business supplies. Again, your accountant can probably give you an estimate from experience with other clients.

Commissions

If commission salespeople sell the products or services, compute their commission as a percentage of the gross sales. Whatever gross revenue you are projecting for any particular month, simply compute the commissions as percentages and enter the calculations as the expense for that month.

Advertising

If required, your first advertising cost estimate will be for the franchisor's advertising royalty, which is typically two percent of gross sales. It is usually paid along with your franchise royalty. Set up an additional amount for local advertising and promotion that you will generate and control. This too is usually budgeted as a percentage of gross sales. Contact your prospective franchisor and other franchise owners to get an idea of what they spend. In particular, ask them what a good first-year estimate should be. If you cannot obtain a good estimate from them, check with your accountant or local media to get an average of what similar businesses spend on local advertising.

Royalties

Similar to the advertising payment to the franchisor, the royalty is typically a straight percentage of gross sales that is usually paid monthly. If the sales for the month are $25,000 and the royalty is five percent, estimate $1,250. The key to estimating this expense, and that of advertising, obviously depends on the accuracy of the estimated sales revenue. You can monitor these closely and modify the expenses that are a function of revenue in the ongoing attempt to improve accuracy in your budget forecast.

Ongoing Costs to Estimate for Operations

Item	Estimated Cost
Accounting fees	_____
Advertising royalties	_____
Commissions	_____
Employee taxes and benefits	_____
Equipment rent, lease, or purchase	_____
Facility and equipment maintenance	_____
Franchisee advertising	_____
Interest payments	_____
Legal fees	_____
Licenses	_____
Other insurance	_____
Payroll and your salary	_____
Promotion	_____
Property taxes and insurance	_____
Purchase of materials and supplies	_____
Rent, lease, or mortgage payment	_____
Royalties	_____
Taxes	_____
Training	_____
Travel	_____
Utilities and telephone	_____
Total	_____

Profit Forecast

If you have projected the estimate of revenue on a month-to-month basis and compiled the estimated expenses on a month-to-month basis, then the profit is simply the difference between the two amounts.

Profit = Revenue – Expenses

Obviously, when the actual number for revenue is higher than the actual number for expenses, the profit is positive. The way you want it to be! The opposite means a shortfall. Not only do you lose money, you also have to put more capital into the business to pay the bills.

Most new businesses find themselves in a shortfall circumstance for the first few months, anywhere from three to nine months. The month in which the loss becomes a profit is the month of the break-even point. The cumulative shortfall before your break-even point needs to be considered in the total investment for starting your business, which is what you will look into next.

Total Original Investment

Item seven of the franchisor's disclosure document shows the total costs of opening a franchise unit. These costs include:
- Initial franchise fee
- Any other initial fees
- Real estate and construction or lease expenses
- Leasehold improvements
- Equipment and fixtures
- Office furniture
- Freight and installation
- Sales taxes
- Opening inventory
- Security deposits
- Utility deposits
- Signage
- Supplies
- Training expenses
- Grand opening
- Working-capital requirement
- Accounting and legal fees
- License and permit fees
- Insurance
- Advertising
- Miscellaneous expense

The total of these costs is what you will need to open the business and continue operating until the break-even point when profits are realized. Of all the costs listed, it is most important to carefully review the working-capital requirement because it is easily underestimated and often discovered too late.

Forecasting Your Working-capital Requirement

Working capital is defined as total current assets minus total current liabilities. Current assets are defined as those assets that can be converted to cash within one year, and current liabilities are those obligations that must be paid within one year. For franchises, current assets for working capital are cash, the cost value of inventory, and accounts receivable; and current liabilities for working capital are accounts payable, short-term notes, and income taxes. The difference between your current assets and current liabilities is your working capital. It is your working capital that is considered the basis for determining the short-term financial health of your business.

However, the working-capital requirement for your franchise is the amount of available funds you will need to support the new business and you and your family until the business gets to the break-even point and begins to make a profit. While the break-even point, as defined by standard accounting practices, is the point in time when profit turns from negative to positive (loss to gain), this is not to be confused with the cumulative break even of the business. A business is considered to break even when the cumulative total of the gain (positive) equals the cumulative total of the loss (negative). For the working-capital requirement, it is the shortfall sustained to the break-even point that is evaluated — not the cumulative break even of the business.

To establish your working-capital requirement, a forecast of your break-even point is an essential tool. Your business reaches the break-even point when the revenue equals the total costs — fixed and variable. Remember, fixed costs are those that are not a function of sales but are substantially the same month to month, such as rent, salaries, automobile payments, and insurance, to name a few. Variable costs are those that change directly proportional to sales and are a percentage of sales. For example, advertising payments, royalties, costs of sale, inventory changes, and commissions are all variable costs.

Your franchise becomes successful after it reaches the break-even point — when the revenue exceeds the total costs. This excess is profit. Before the break-even point, when total costs exceed revenue, you have a loss, or shortfall. In determining the shortfall, estimates must be made of the revenue and the fixed and variable costs.

Normally in a break-even analysis, accountants combine the shortfall and profit columns displaying the shortfall in parenthesis as a negative. In the example Break-even Analysis, the two columns are separated to graphically demonstrate where one ends and the other begins, to emphasize the break-even point. The total shortfall in the example is $8,125, which is most but not all of the working-capital requirement. Added to this amount should be the other initial expenses not included in the budgets, such as needed cash on hand, early rent before opening, and any out-of-pocket costs during pre-opening and training. All of these need to be included to arrive at your total working-capital requirement.

Working-capital requirement = Shortfall + Pre-opening expenses

---

Break-even Analysis

Month	Revenue Forecast	Fixed Costs[1]	Variable Costs[2]	Short-fall	Monthly Profit
July	$ 20,500	$ 7,250	$ 15,375	($2,125)[3]	$ 0
August	21,000	7,250	15,750	(2,000)	0
September	22,500	7,250	16,875	(1,625)	0
October	24,000	7,250	18,000	(1,250)	0
November	26,000	7,250	19,500	(750)	0
December	27,500	7,250	20,625	(375)	0
January	29,500	7,250	22,125	0	125[4]
February	31,000	7,250	23,250	0	500
March	32,000	7,250	24,000	0	750
April	34,000	7,250	25,500	0	1,250
May	36,500	7,250	27,375	0	1,875
June	38,800	7,250	29,100	0	2,450
	$343,300	$87,000	$257,475	($8,125)	$6,950

1. Fixed costs and living expenses for franchisee's family.
2. Variable costs, figured at 75% of revenue.
3. Parentheses are used in accounting to represent negative numbers.
4. The break-even point (shortfall) where profit occurs.

A franchise business forecast is often erroneously referred to as a business plan. It is more comprehensive than most forecasts in that it actually combines two projections — the income statement and cumulative cash flow. In the One-year Franchise Business Forecast example that follows, the revenue for the first month is estimated and increased by ten percent compounded for each successive month. Although all fixed costs are the same each month, the quarterly legal fees create a variance in the monthly subtotals.

All variable costs are a function of sales. In this forecast they total 75 percent of gross sales and break down as follows:

- Cost of goods sold – 55 percent
- Supplies – 2 percent
- Commissions – 8 percent
- Royalty payments to the franchisor – 6 percent
- Co-op advertising paid to the franchisor – 2 percent
- Local advertising – 2 percent

It is typical with most new franchises not to show a profit until the sixth month of business. In a cash-and-carry business the cash flow line is a cumulative total of profit — in the example, it is negative through the ninth month. Somewhere between the fifth and sixth months the profit goes from negative to positive — as indicated in the fifth month of the forecast where the $10,002 shortfall indicates the the worst-case month.

This cumulative negative cash flow projection is the shortfall portion of the working-capital requirement for the franchisee. For the total working-capital requirement, the pre-opening expenses must be added to the short-fall. However, in the real world most consultants advise franchisees to set aside an additional 50 percent as a safety margin. If the pre-opening expenses in this example were zero dollars, the working-capital requirement would come to $15,000.

Once you have an idea of the total investment required for opening a franchise and have compared it with your assets, you will have a good idea of the amount of capital you will need to raise through financing.

One out of five franchisors provides some financing assistance. Explore this option first, but keep in mind several other sources exist that allow you to get into a franchise business without a cash investment. While later chapters and the appendices cover these sources in detail, the next step toward successful financing, regardless of the sources approached, is to develop a professional franchise business plan. This is the subject of Part II.

One-year Franchise Business Forecast

Month:	1	2	3	4	5	6	7	8	9	10	11	12
Revenue Earned (gross sales)	24,000	26,400	29,040	31,944	35,138	38,652	42,517	46,770	51,446	56,590	62,250	68,475
Cost of Revenue Earned (cost of goods sold, variable costs)												
Goods	13,200	14,520	15,972	17,569	19,326	21,259	23,384	25,724	28,295	31,125	34,238	37,661
Supplies	480	528	581	639	703	773	850	935	1,029	1,132	1,245	1,370
Commissions	2,400	2,640	2,904	3,195	3,514	3,864	4,252	4,677	5,145	5,659	6,225	6,848
Royalties	1,440	1,584	1,742	1,917	2,108	2,319	2,551	2,806	3,087	3,395	3,735	4,109
Co-op advertising	480	528	581	639	703	773	850	935	1,029	1,132	1,245	1,370
Local advertising	480	528	581	639	703	773	850	935	1,029	1,132	1,245	1,370
Total Cost of Revenue Earned	18,480	20,328	22,361	24,598	27,057	29,762	32,737	36,012	39,614	43,575	47,933	52,728
Gross Profit	5,520	6,072	6,679	7,346	8,081	8,890	9,780	10,758	11,832	13,015	14,317	15,747
Operating Expenses (fixed costs)												
Lease or rent	1,200	1,200	1,200	1,200	1,200	1,200	1,200	1,200	1,200	1,200	1,200	1,200
Property tax and insurance	150	150	150	150	150	150	150	150	150	150	150	150
Maintenance	50	50	50	50	50	50	50	50	50	50	50	50
Utilities	300	300	300	300	300	300	300	300	300	300	300	300
Payroll	5,000	5,000	5,000	5,000	5,000	5,000	5,000	5,000	5,000	5,000	5,000	5,000
Employee benefits	1,000	1,000	1,000	1,000	1,000	1,000	1,000	1,000	1,000	1,000	1,000	1,000
Telephone	80	80	80	80	80	80	80	80	80	80	80	80
Janitorial	200	200	200	200	200	200	200	200	200	200	200	200
Other insurance	300	300	300	300	300	300	300	300	300	300	300	300
Legal fees	100	0	0	100	0	0	100	0	0	100	0	0
Accounting	120	120	120	120	120	120	120	120	120	120	120	120
Miscellaneous	300	300	300	300	300	300	300	300	300	300	300	300
Total Operating Expense	8,800	8,700	8,700	8,800	8,700	8,700	8,800	8,700	8,700	8,800	8,700	8,700
Operating Income	(3,280)	(2,628)	(2,021)	(1,454)	(619)	190	980	2,058	3,132	4,215	5,617	7,047
Cash Flow (cumulative)	(3,280)	(5,908)	(7,929)	(9,383)	(10,002)	(9,812)	(8,832)	(6,774)	(3,642)	573	6,190	13,237

Part II

Your Franchise Business Plan

Chapter 3

A Professional Presentation

The worst crime against working people is a company which fails to operate at a profit.
— SAMUEL GOMPERS

Now that you have identified your working capital requirement in terms of dollars needed to start your business, you are ready to put together a professional loan request or investment offering. While for years it was acceptable to assemble a minimal loan or investment package, in the last few decades, it has become necessary to write a complete business prospectus. This is simply termed a business plan. This started out as a requirement for large businesses but, because of heightened competition in the information age, it is now the standard for small businesses as well. In its complete form, a business plan is for business improvement, a management tool for measuring the efficiency of both start-up and ongoing businesses for current and future planning. Today, it is essential to prepare a business plan for financial requests.

Many how-to books and software programs are on the market for writing business plans, but as of this writing, none address the specialized adjustments required for franchise businesses. A franchise business plan is a shorter version of the nonfranchised business plan; nevertheless, before you tackle the subject, it is helpful to first understand the popular formats in the world of business for nonfranchised businesses.

In surveying many successful business plans, you will find that no one format fits them all. Depending upon the nature of the business, certain topics take precedence over others. Often owners write their company's business plan since they know the most about their business operation and management, and they have learned what elements to include to make the best impression.

Here are some typical business plan outlines for nonfranchise businesses that have been accepted.

Nonfranchise Business Plan Outlines

Nonfranchise Business Plan A
- Business summary
- Company history
- Industry analysis
- Manufacturing plan
- Production and personnel plan
- Products or services
- Research and development
- Competition
- Marketing and sales
- Management team
- Financial analysis
- Appendices or exhibits

Nonfranchise Business Plan B
- Executive summary
- Company review
- Products
- Market analysis
- Marketing plan
- Production plan
- Management team
- Financial history and forecast
- Risks and potential problems

Nonfranchise Business Plan C
- Abstract
- Company overview
- Founders and directors
- Products and services
- Market analysis
- Financial information

Nonfranchise Business Plan D
- Executive summary
- Investment proposal
- Business objectives
- Services or products
- Markets
- Competition
- Company and management
- Financial forecast
- Advantages to the investor
- Appendices

Nonfranchise Business Plan E
- Executive summary
- Company description
- Industry analysis
- Market
- Competition
- Marketing and sales plans
- Operations
- Management and organization
- Financial history and forecasts
- Long-term plan
- Exhibits

Nonfranchise Business Plan F
- Executive summary
- Company description
- Industry analysis
- Market
- Competition
- Marketing and sales strategies
- Management and operations
- Financial information
- Long-term plans

Many successful business plans have used the outlines above. Currently, the most popular is Plan F. Although your outline is going to be a modified version for franchising, review these and as many other outlines as you can find. This research will serve as a background check to see if there may be some specialized categories to insert besides the basic ones proposed here for your franchise business plan.

You can see by these outline variations, it makes a difference whether your business is a start up or a continuing business, and what particular industry yours is in, such as automotive, dry cleaning, convenience stores, or quick service restaurants, to name a few. Nevertheless, a common thread runs through them all. While a business plan can be a way to set the direction and improve the efficiency of a company, usually its main goal is to obtain financing. Notice Plan D above, which has both a section entitled investor proposal and a section entirely devoted to advantages for the investor. Obviously, this plan is written specifically for finding and acquiring financing — as is the franchise business plan developed in chapters 3 through 11.

Unlike the plan outlines above, however, a franchise business plan must combine components of both your business and the franchisor's business. Your business plan, in effect, is a merging of elements of both companies. These chapters explain how to do this and create a complete and comprehensive franchise business plan.

The Franchise Business Plan

A complete franchise business plan for a new start-up franchise should feature at least eight basic sections.

- Abstract. The abstract in your franchise business plan is briefer than an executive summary.
- Business Summary. The franchise business summary retrieves the omitted subjects of a conventional executive summary and combines these with elements of the traditional company description. Nothing is left out, just rearranged.
- Franchise Overview. The franchise overview replaces the usual industry analysis.
- The Market. Treatments of the market and the competition combine to form the market section.
- Marketing Plan. Marketing and sales strategies are conventionally included together in the marketing plan.
- Management Qualifications. Essentially the same as in traditional business plans, this section describes your management staff and your operation framework.
- Financial Pro Formas. Also a traditional section, it groups together your financial projections for the first year and for a longer range of three or five years.
- Exhibits. This final section is where you put supporting documents needed to evaluate your business plan — either to support information in other sections or to provide auxiliary information not covered.

If your franchise is well known or dominant in its industry, the above outline works better than a nonfranchised business plan. A professionally written franchise plan has these basic sections, which are sometimes referred to as chapters. When your business plan is written to obtain financing, it should also include a specific section, or chapter, tailored either as a loan request or as an investment offering proposal.

The abstract section serves as a prologue, and the plan usually ends with a section of exhibits. Although, to avoid one huge exhibit section at the end of the plan, you can insert some of the exhibits in the sections where they apply. Some business plans are nearly 100 pages long, but they should never include unimportant information for the sake of bulk alone. Today, it is considered better to keep the length to 50 pages or fewer, and 30 to 40 is the more recommended length for the franchise business plan.

Franchise Business Plan Outline

Title Page

Table of Contents

I.   Abstract
   A. Financing needed
   B. Business synopsis
   C. Intended use of funds
   D. Market findings
   E. Financial forecast

II. Business Summary
   A. Franchisee summary
   B. Company description
   C. Mission
   D. Products or services
   E. Location and territory
   F. Management
   G. Business objectives
   H. Developmental progress
   I. Financial status
   J. Keys to success

III. Franchise Overview
   A. Franchise summary
   B. Franchise background
   C. Industry analysis [if appropriate]
   D. Franchise products or services.
   E. Franchise market segments
   F. Franchise customer profile
   G. Reasons for choosing this franchise

IV. The Market
   A. Exclusive territory
   B. Market description
   C. Market size and trends
   D. Competition description
   E. Market share

V.   Marketing Plan
   A. Marketing summary
   B. Franchisor marketing plan
   C. Franchisee marketing plan
   D. Marketing budget or advertising plan
   E. Sales force and forecast

VI. Management Qualifications
   A. Management summary
   B. Organizational structure
   C. Management team
   D. Personnel plan
   E. Franchisor management experience

VII. Financial Pro Formas
   A. Financial summary
   B. Important assumptions
   C. Break-even analysis
   D. Pro forma income statements
   E. Pro forma statement of cash flows
   F. Pro forma balance sheets
   G. Business ratios

VIII. Loan Request or Investment Offering

IX. Exhibits

Beginning with the title page, each section and subsection (segment) of the franchise business plan outline will be covered in order. In Chapter 9, you will use most of the decision making data you assembled in Chapter 2 for developing your financial pro formas.

Each element in the development of your franchise business plan is highlighted with examples in shaded boxes of a complete business plan drawn up for a fictitious company, MegaBucks Smith and Associates — a franchisee of MegaBucks International.

That First Impression

The saying, "There's no second chance to make a good first impression," is highly appropriate when it comes to the opening sections of your business plan and its overall appearance. With current desktop publishing, business plans are looking more professional — companies are competing for neatness and an impressionable presentation that sets them apart.

Format

As to format, the norm is to bind your business plan in booklet form with high quality materials. Better ones have quality report covers in dark or rich colors and are labeled on the front. The title page serves better than a label if laminated or positioned behind a windowed cover or behind a full clear cover. Many types of bindings are available at copy centers: ibico and GBC® presentation bindings, Wire Bind™, and Velobinder® are a few of the better ones. Some businesses go the extra step to have printed covers or printed binding strips. Three-ring binders have been used for years and are still acceptable, but you improve your odds for making that favorable first impression by using the latest and most professional-looking, high-tech materials available.

Page Layout

Make sure the layout of each page is balanced and artistically pleasing, with a lot of open or negative space — paragraphs, lines, and characters should not be too closely spaced. With desktop publishing, many types of letter styles (fonts) are available. The text is generally easier to read if the font used has serifs, for example New Courier, New Times Roman, or Charter and the margins justified. For a professional quality, use a sans-serif font, such as Arial, Modern, or Univers, for titles, sideheads, tables, and outlines. Choose one of each and stay consistent throughout the presentation.

Using the latest software printing design tools such as boxes, borders, shadow lines, and enlarged and bold characters, can add a professional look if correctly done without drawing attention to their use and stealing the show from the material itself. Color printing, judiciously placed, is being used more all the time.

Tabs and Titles

Each subject, with titled heading, should have its own section and be separated with indexed partitions keyed to the table of contents. Tabbed index partitions make it easier to locate information, especially during a presentation, than fumbling through page numbers. Another feature is to use colored partitions, preferably muted or soft colors that coordinate with the color of the cover and with the colors of any charts or graphs inside. Instead of custom tabs, some plans are assembled with printed tab indices with miniature plastic covers, but if you have access to preprinted laminated tabs, they are preferable. A recent innovation is hidden tabs that protrude past the pages but not the cover.

Within each section, set off subsections with crossheads — such as those used within the chapters of this book — usually set bold in a contrasting font and justified to the left margin.

Color and Charts

Charts, graphs, and illustrations are commonly acceptable if appropriate to the text. Color is often better than black and white; however, choose reds and blues, not chartreuses, yellow-oranges, or some other unusual color. In fact, if you are going to use extensive colored charts and graphs, choose a theme of three or four rich colors and use them consistently throughout the work. Reserve photographic prints for the exhibits. Even then, they should be presented in protective sheets and labeled or captioned. If needed in the main body of the business plan, pictures look more professional when converted to color copies with titles and captions in font styles consistent with the rest of your presentation.

Printing

Use laser or ink-jet printers to print on paper of stationery quality. Paper should be the brightest white you can find, laser quality, or one of the muted color résumé stock in soft gray or ivory. Staying consistent by using the same type of paper for text, graphs, charts, and illustrations yields a quality professional look. Using bits and pieces of different paper gives the impression the plan was thrown together.

Proofreading and Copyediting

Have your figures checked by an accountant and the text proofread by an editor or proofreader. An accurate, easy-to-read, and well-organized text will convey professionalism and credibility. Too often this important step is avoided or forgotten and, despite all the work that has gone into creating an impressive presentation, typos, missing words, poor sentence construction, and figures that don't add up become a significant, but negative, part of that first impression made on a reviewer.

The Title Page

As the cover is opened, the title page can reveal letterhead stationery with your business data: logo, company name, address, telephone number, fax number, and Internet and e-mail address. It should also give the name of the person to whom the package is addressed, the name of the person who prepared the business plan, and the date it was prepared.

Title Page

MegaBucks $mith and Associates
77-6452 Alii Drive
Kallua-Kona, Hawaii 96740
(808) 555-1234 – FAX (808) 555-1111
e-mail: MegaBucksSmith@aol.com

Business Plan

Prepared for:

    Mr. Stephen Clayton
    Assistant Branch Manager
    Bank Of Hawaii
    75-5595 Palani Road
    Kailua-Kona, Hawaii 96740-9909

Prepared by:
    Lisa Soma
    June 2001

Table of Contents

The table of contents page usually follows the title page. Several professional formats exist; one of the more familiar is shown in the example. Under the heading Contents, make two columns, one for subjects and one for page numbers or indexed sections opposite those. You may head the columns with subject and page number or section, but it is not necessary.

Table of Contents Page

Contents

Abstract	
Business Summary	A
Franchise Overview	B
The Market	C
Marketing Plan	D
Management Qualifications	E
Financial Pro Formas	F
Loan Request	G
Exhibits	H

The Abstract

While an executive summary in a nonfranchise business plan is often two or three pages, an abstract for a franchise business plan is typically no more than one page. Because partitions look awkward when separating a one-page section from others, it is not indexed in the table of contents and not separated like the other sections. You can place the abstract immediately behind the table of contents or, as is the practice of some businesses, insert it as a preface located between the title page and the table of contents. Either way is acceptable.

Like an executive summary, an abstract is the official opening of your franchise business plan, so make it as interesting and vibrant as possible. Aim for your target readers, both in tone and content. To grab and maintain the reader's attention is crucial, therefore, the abstract must be the most well-written part of your business plan. Lenders and investors generally have so many requests come across their desks they take time to read only the abstract before deciding whether to read further or go on to the next deal.

Your abstract is a concise statement of key information that leads into the rest of the business plan, so you will want to wait until the entire business plan is generated before you write it. That way you can present the essential points and emphasize the interesting findings that need to be stated. It does not hurt to attempt your abstract early if you remember to totally revise it after your research is completed, the facts are analyzed, and the balance of your business plan is written. You can use this same process for all the other opening summaries you will write. In your abstract, the reviewer is looking for specific elements of your proposal to be highlighted. These are:

- Financing Needed. The amount you are requesting should be presented in the first sentence of the abstract.
- Business Synopsis. This is a short description of the prospective business, ownership, products or services, and important points about your franchisor. This information should be covered within a few sentences in the first paragraph.

Abstract

MegaBucks Smith and Associates, owned and operated by Denver Smith, is seeking $60,000 for start-up capital to open a commercial real estate brokerage, under a franchise agreement with MegaBucks International. MegaBucks International is the number two commercial real estate franchisor in four countries, including the United States. The start-up funds will be used as a down payment on our commercial site and offices and on computers, copiers, telephone equipment, and office furniture to open business and start operations. Our location is 77-6452 Alii Drive, Kailua-Kona, Hawaii, a premium location with excellent parking, in the heart of tourist traffic between Kailua-Kona and the exclusive Keauhou neighborhood commercial and golf communities.

Our primary market is customers for offices, both medical and professional, and for commercial space for light retail shops and shopping centers. Currently in Kailua-Kona, the vacancy rate is less than three percent in these categories, which is well below the state average. Our multiple listing service shows sales of $50,000,000 a year in our area, and our market studies support our capturing 29% of this market within the first year with gross revenue of $14,500,000 and net revenue of $1,021,800.

Per our financial pro formas, with seven pre-sales and four top producers from other offices (two of the best salespeople on the Big Island), we will reach the break-even point during the sixth month. Profit before taxes will be $60,800 for the last six months, increasing steadily to an annual net profit of $420,000 for the fifth year after opening.

1st Paragraph:

Present the requested amount of financing.

Add a short description of your prospective business, ownership, and products or services. Insert influential points about your franchisor.

Include how the funds are to be used.

2nd Paragraph:

Describe your customer profile and your market.

3rd Paragraph:

State your break-even point and estimates of profit for the first and third or fifth years' forecasts.

- Intended Use of Funds. Include within the first paragraph a statement of how the funds are going to be used.

- Market Findings. The second paragraph should describe your customer profile and your market. Specifically mention your location, important demographic points, and estimated number of customers in your area.

- Financial Forecast. The third and last paragraph should project capable management, the break-even point, and financial estimates for the first year with a long-range, three to five-year forecast of pretax profit. Write the forecast so that investors or lenders feel they have an excellent chance of getting their money back.

Next Steps

Throughout the next eight chapters, you will identify the research, compile the findings, and summarize the logical conclusions of each of the sections of your franchise business plan. If you have already selected your franchisor, you are way ahead of the game because most franchisors can supply their new franchisees with much of this data. Chapter 4 covers this first section, the business summary.

The Business Summary

Every great man of business has got somewhere a touch of the idealist in him.
— WOODROW WILSON

In a nonfranchised business plan, the executive summary has some elements the more concise abstract of a franchised business plan does not cover. But, the more complete business summary contains those concepts omitted from the abstract and nearly everything in the conventional company description, as well. These aspects are introduced in the business summary, then developed in more detail later in your business plan.

As shown in the Franchise Business Plan Outline in Chapter 3, the business summary is comprised of:

- A franchisee summary
- Your company description
- A history of your past performance, if you have a continuing business
- Your mission
- An introduction of your products or services
- A preview of your location and territory
- An introduction of your management
- Brief business objectives
- Your developmental progress, if a start-up business
- Your financial status and the milestones you've achieved, if you have a continuing business
- The keys to success, factors that make your business unique

In the business summary section of your plan, it is very important to use specific language and pertinent highlights from your research findings to establish credibility for your plan. When you write, avoid flowery adjectives and generalized statements that are subjective.

Franchisee Summary

Start your business summary with a paragraph summarizing the basic information about your business. Like the abstract, write this important opening summary clearly and concisely, preferably after all of the material for the entire section is gathered, assembled, and logically reviewed. Emphasize three or four of the most important findings from the ten segments in this section that are special for your business — for example, your dba may be a national trademark; the identity of your major shareholders may be only you, as sole owner; the vesting may be a general partnership insuring your personal backing; or your location may be a significant factor for improving your odds of success.

Franchisee Summary

By focusing on our strengths and answering the needs of our customers, MegaBucks Smith and Associates will capture one-fourth of the commercial market — real estate listings, sales and leases — in the North Kona district by the end of our first year. We have an outstanding location with convenient parking in the heart of our territory and bring to the industry 140 years of professional, commercial real estate experience with an honest and personable staff. All sales people have been top producers in other real estate offices. We are implementing the model real estate organization for the new millennium with departmental specialists, under proven management with experienced marketing, using the most innovative promotional techniques.

The basis of our customer development program will be our computer database, second to none, constantly updated for a tenacious follow-up of all new leads and repeat and referral customers. Results of our pre-opening marketing efforts support our projections to capture a total of 29% of the commercial market in our territory, with an emphasis in professional offices and light retail space. After break-even, we will have a reasonable profit the first year, for a new business, with an average increase of 17% per year for the next five years.

Summarize the highlights of your company description, mission, products or service, and location and territory.

Company Description

Following the franchisee summary, under the heading Company Description, describe your company's:

- Legal or corporate name
- Fictitious business name (dba)
- Home state where incorporated, if applicable
- County or municipality where you have your business license
- Identity of the owners or major shareholders
- Type of vesting or business ownership
- Location
- Term of your franchise agreement
- Number of employees

Refer to your franchisor's disclosure document or UFOC for help because many include a written business description for a typical franchise outlet. If yours does, use it and add any missing information from the suggested list above. In addition, be sure to include any differences between the franchisor-provided description and your franchise business.

Company Description

MegaBucks Smith and Associates, Inc. is a Hawaii corporation, a privately-held subchapter S corporation, doing business as MegaBucks Smith and Associates licensed in the State and County of Hawaii. Denver Smith is the sole proprietor. The office is located at 77-6452 Alii Drive, Kailua-Kona, Hawaii 96740. The term of our franchise agreement, which started in May, is ten years with multiple ten-year renewable terms. At startup, our operation will have ten employees, including the owner, and will reach eighteen by the beginning of our second year.

List the company name, home state, municipality where your business license is registered, identity of owners and type of ownership, address, and number of employees.

Mission

Following your company description, write a brief paragraph capsulizing your mission statement. This simply states your business goals, your business offering, and your targeted market. Your mission should answer three questions: what are you selling, to whom, and why? Refer to your franchisor materials; most franchisors have already compiled a mission statement and make it available to you. Be brief here; many other areas exist in your business plan to explain the specifics in more detail.

Mission Statement

Our company's mission is to best serve our commercial real estate customers by fulfilling their needs through our tedious efforts, integrity, professionalism, kindly attitude, and incomparable follow-up — to build long-term, unbreakable customer relationships. For the first year the goal is to reach thirty key listings, ten major sales, and twenty leases — targeting customers for medical/professional offices and for light retail/shopping centers. For the first five years, the goal is steady expansion.

Write your mission statement in a brief paragraph.

Products or Services

In the next paragraph, give a general description of your products or services by number and types of lines, with the number of products or services in each line. Keep the description on an introductory level because you will cover this more thoroughly in the franchise overview section.

Services Description

Our product is service. Our market will be served by commercial real estate sales and lease agents with a combined experience of 140 years in listing, selling, and leasing all types of commercial space with specialties in professional offices and light retail stores.

Write an introductory description of your products or services.

Location and Territory

While your location is mentioned in your company description, this paragraph is used to identify the major advantages of your location. If your franchisor has completed a location data report (LDR) to support your site selection, refer to it for facts. Note, for example, whether you are centralized within the area of your market share or have favorable traffic flow, superior access, parking, or proximity to other successful, complementary businesses. State only two or three key items about your location here. In addition, concisely describe your facility, such as the building square footage, superior architectural or functional layout, service area size, warehousing, amount of parking, and drive-through convenience. Emphasize any location essentials that a reviewer should recognize as valuable. Next, give a brief introductory description of the size and location of your franchise territory. Later in the market section, you will go into more detail.

Location and Territory Description

Our air-conditioned 2,200 sq. ft. office on Alii Drive is centrally located, with convenient parking and an ocean view, midway between downtown Kailua-Kona to the north and the exclusive Keauhou district to the south. Our territory includes all of North Kona district, which covers the downtown Kailua commercial area as well as three major shopping centers and eleven neighborhood commercial centers.

Identify your location's physical points and two or three key features.

Include a short description of the size and location of your franchise territory.

Management

List your company officers and managers by title and name — functions are elaborated later. If you are the sole owner and operator of a new business, label yourself as president or chief executive officer. Briefly describe the background, education, or experience that brought you to the decision to open a franchise and why you feel it is a sound and timely decision. Keep it short; your résumé is inserted in another section. Also note the types of supplemental management support services furnished by your franchisor. Refer to item eleven of your UFOC for the complete list.

Management Description

Our president and CEO is Denver Smith, R, CCIM, resident broker, with twenty-five years of experience and winner of the MegaBucks Numero Uno Award, MBI's highest, eighteen times in twenty-three years for number one in gross sales revenue in the state of Hawaii. Mark McKinsey heads marketing. Besides having an M.B.A., he has been top producer in commercial units-sold for the past three years for Delta Commercial Real Estate in the California-Nevada region, which takes in northern California and all of Nevada excluding Las Vegas, Along with Mark, we have a specialist relocation director in Paulette Sia. Another top producer, our general sales manager, Steve Swan, was number one in sales for the last 5 years while with our largest local competitor. These are joined by proven excellent assistant managers: Barry O'Brien, commercial sales; Marcia Clay, offices; Judy George, retail; and David Wong, commercial leasing. Our in-house head bookkeeper, Lisa Soma, has had several years' experience as an office manager for Delta Commercial Real Estate in the downtown San Francisco office.

At MegaBucks International, we are backed by George Collins, our Regional Director, a noted speaker and real estate motivator, with many published motivational materials on commercial real estate sales and listings. Mr. Collins is our direct national managerial representative.

List your company officers and managers by title and name.

Briefly describe your background, the education or experience that qualifies you to operate your business.

Include the types of management support services provided by your franchisor.

Business Objectives

Your business objectives are [a description of how you will achieve] your business goals. Write them as solid statements which answer the how, when, what, and why questions in the mind of a reviewer: What do you plan to achieve (result)? Why are you going into business (purpose)? How you expect to obtain your goals (method)? When you plan to reach them (timing)? When writing your objectives, make sure to cover management, marketing, finances, and the bottom line objective, profit. Make these objectives specific, measurable, and consistent with the rest of your business plan.

Management Objective

For a new franchisee, a management objective is typically understood and may not need to be specifically addressed if the goal is to simply purchase the franchise, get the facility ready, and open for business. However, you may have some special management objective that is distinctive for your success; if so, state it here. The other types of objectives need more discussion and clarity.

Market Objective

Your marketing objective is an estimate of market share. This is a function of the demographics, the quantity and strength of the competitors, the proximity to other franchisees in your corporate franchise system, and the size of your exclusive territory or trade area. You can quantify this. For example, label your franchise outlet A. Assume you have two nonfranchised competitors in your trade area you call B and C. You have one other franchised competitor called D. If their strengths, compared to your operation, are: B is two times as large as yours, C is equal to yours, and D is equal to yours, the estimate can be figured as in the example.

Market Share Estimate Example

Business	Strength		Franchise Factor		One of Four Competitors		Market Share (numerator)
A (your business)	1 (equal)	×	1.2*	×	0.25	=	0.30
B (nonfranchise)	2 times	×	1.0	×	0.25	=	0.50
C (nonfranchise)	1 (equal)	×	1.0	×	0.25	=	0.25
D (franchise)	1 (equal)	×	1.2*	×	0.25	=	0.30
					Total Market Share (denominator)		1.35

Your Market Share: .3 / 1.35 = 22.2%

* As a rule-of-thumb, a franchised business has 20% more of the market than a nonfranchised business; this is an assigned factor of 1.2.

In this example, your market share is .3 out of a total of 1.35 or 22.2 percent. This is your expected objective. If your franchisor is a major franchise in the market, you might anticipate this to be as much as two times as strong, or 45 percent. While the strength factor given here for outlet B is two times, in reality, the strength of a powerful competitor may be as high as three times an average outlet.

In your business summary, you only need to state your market share findings. You will include supporting market share data in the market section of your business plan.

Financial Objective

In a brief statement, give the projected sales for the first year and for the third or fifth year, depending on your choice of three- or five-year projections. Also state the amount of the financial assistance you are seeking and the return for an investor or the term of payback for a lender. Information on how to complete projected sales and the investor return is provided later.

Profitability Objective

As the final objective, summarize your estimated profit in a narrative sentence or two — from your business forecast, Chapter 2. Include the estimate for your break-even month, along with the anticipated year-end profits for the first and for the later years you project — the full term of your three- or five-year projection. Do not exhibit the complete graphic business forecast in your business objectives summary. This merely describes, by narrative conclusion, the results from that business forecast. You are going to present a variation of the actual document in the financial pro formas section of your business plan.

Business Objectives

Our business objectives comprise five goals: 1) To finalize our lease and begin operations at the start of the year with a send-off of our new promotional campaigns; 2) To capture 29% of the market based upon our anticipated market share; 3) To recruit, hire, and train eight new salespeople by the end of the first year; 4) To reach gross sales of $1,050,000 the first month with a steady increase to $2,065,000 per the final month for the first year — a total of $14,500,000 gross sales and $1,022,000 net sales. By the end of the fifth year, forecast is $27,000,000 gross sales; $1,893,000 net sales. This assumes a two-year operating loan of $60,000 for our capital requirement: $30,000 for startup costs and $30,000 operating cash; 5) To obtain a net profit of $60,000 for the last six months of our first year (our projections show our break-even point will occur during the sixth month) and an annual net profit of $212,000 by our fifth year of operation.

Summarize your specific goals — dates, numbers, percentages. Be consistent with your business plan.

- State the anticipated date for your business to open.
- Estimate your market share.
- Project the sales for the first and third or fifth years of business.
- Include the break-even month and the anticipated year-end profits for the first and third or fifth years.

Developmental Progress

If your business is just getting ready to open, write a narrative of what is done, including the dates of completion, and what specific items are left to be completed. For an existing business, give the year the company started and the level of maturity of your operation, whether it is growing or stable.

Developmental Progress Description

We have acquired our MegaBucks franchise, negotiated our lease, and purchased our furniture and equipment. Remaining, we have to close on the transaction for our offices (in part from the operating loan) and implement our send-off promotions, which include press releases, a formal grand opening, and the customary pre-opening open house for preferred customers, related business consultants, and community leaders.

Specify those things that have been completed to start business and the things that are left to do.

Financial Status

If your business is a new start up, omit this topic. If yours is an existing business, then state in a descriptive narrative your previous year's financial history in terms of total revenue earned, or sales, and net income, or profit before tax.

Keys to Success

If your business is different from other franchised outlets within your franchise system — such as specific geographic or climatic advantages for your business or any other special differences that set it apart from others — describe those here, even if the reasons seem to have a specific place elsewhere in the business plan. It is acceptable to repeat some information in a business plan, especially important elements, because reviewers rarely read a business plan like a book from start to finish. They tend to skip around, first reading the portions that interest them the most. Because of this, you can repeat essential conclusions needed to support information in related discussions.

List only three or four keys to success. If you have several, choose the most convincing ones. For example, one of the keys could be your location; however, if it is, emphasize the particular reason why it is an advantage. If exceptional managerial talent is guiding your business, include a statement to that effect — later, you will include the details in the management qualifications section and your support documents in the exhibits. If the franchising system you are joining is exceptionally different from the competitors, this may be influential enough to add as a key to success in this summary even though it is repeated and expanded in the franchise overview. A good example of this is MAACO Auto Painting and Bodyworks, which at this writing has 489 outlets, while its closest competitor has only 48. In other words, the business summary is suppose to introduce major reasons that make your business different and give it a competitive edge.

Keys to Success Description

The keys to our success are strong management, departmental specialists, an excellent location, a constantly updated computer database to develop long-term customer relations, excellent marketing with strong promotional skills, and vast combined experience in our industry in general and the Hawaiian commercial market in particular.

Include three or four reasons, different from other franchisees within your franchise system, that will lead to your business success.

Revise Your Franchisee Summary

When you have completed all the components of this section, review them for the strongest points and write, or re-write, your opening summary — the franchisee summary — emphasizing the prominent findings.

Now that you have covered your franchisee business, you are ready to discuss your franchisor and the franchise system you are representing, which is the subject of Chapter 5.

The Franchise Overview

To be a success in business, be daring, be first, be different.
— MARCHANT

Once reviewers have read your preview about your business as a franchisee, their interest is piqued to learn more about your franchisor and the franchise's role in the industry.

For most franchisees, the franchise overview is the easiest section of the business plan to prepare if the material supplied by your franchisor is sufficient. You can refer to your franchisor's disclosure document (the UFOC) the location data report (LDR), the prospectus, sales brochures, and any other franchisor literature for most of the information you need to include. These resources — along with results from conversations with your franchisor and other franchisees — supply most of the data for the franchise overview section.

To get organized, make copies of original documents as worksheets, highlight the appropriate data, rewrite the needed portions, and merge the applicable information into your business plan categories. The franchise overview section should include the following segments:

- Franchise summary
- Franchise background
- Industry analysis (optional)
- Franchise products or services
- Franchise market segments
- Franchise customer profile

Franchise Summary

Begin your franchise overview with a summary paragraph of your franchise system — a short narrative description of the significant points discussed in this section. As in the previous opening summaries, write, or rewrite, it after completing the overview to emphasize the essentials of each segment.

Franchise Summary

MegaBucks International is the number two franchise in commercial real estate, with 965 outlets — 123 of which are company-owned stores. Headquartered in Kansas City, Missouri, MBI is registered in all but two northeastern states, and has been franchised for over thirty years. The company name is a registered trademark and is nationally known with major presence in Central, Southwest, West and Northwest/Hawaii regions. While MBI's services include all real estate listings, sales, and leases, its emphasis is on commercial properties, and it has been able to provide customer profiles for our franchise market. Nationally, MBI has grown 6% per year. We have found the nationally recognizable advertising, the regional structure, the field support services, the computer database, the helpful and truly interested staff, and MBI's franchise philosophy of doing business — to be consistent with our mission and needs.

Summarize the highlights of your franchise background, industry analysis, franchise products or services, franchise market segments, and customer profile.

Franchise Background

The next segment discusses your franchise background. This should cover the impressive details from items one through 23 of the UFOC: franchisor identification, affiliates and key-personnel identification, management, a description of the business, business experience, and franchisor history. For this segment you will examine items 1, 2, 5–9, 11–14, 19, and 20 of your UFOC. It is preferable to use the numerical order. Other item numbers not listed here are addressed in other areas of your business plan. The emphasis here is to describe your franchise's experience and history. As you are disclosing this coverage in your business plan, make sure it is permissible with your franchisor. If not, you may have to modify each to the extent that your franchisor approves. The assumption from this point forward is that you have permission to relay the foregoing facts.

Franchisor Identification

For the franchisor identification (UFOC, item one), include the legal name, address of principal place of business, fictitious business name statements, states registered, and nature of the business. Also give the year the business started, the year the company began franchising, and the total number of corporate employees.

Franchisor Officers, Directors, and Managers

From item two, itemize the key officers, directors, and management personnel by name and position. If the list is cumbersome, give only three or four and separate others simply by type of position and number of each. In the exhibits, also enclose summary résumés of personnel who are in direct line management with your outlet. These may be the CEO; CFO; managing director of franchisee operations; director of marketing and sales and both, if different; director of field support services, one or several if broken down; and your field representative; among others.

Initial Franchise Fees

From item five, state the initial franchise fee, other payments, and the payment structure.

Royalties and Other Fees

From item six, list the royalties and every other fee you have to pay in addition to the initial fees and payments. This entails advertising percentages, service fees, training fees, lease payments or rents, insurance requirements, audit and accounting costs, expenses relevant to participation in advisory councils, and any construction or improvement costs disclosed in the offering circular.

Original Investment

From item seven, report the franchisor's estimate of the cost for a franchisee to begin operations. Briefly explain the nature of the costs as presented in the disclosure. Besides the initial fee, this may involve costs for equipment and fixtures, working capital requirement, purchase, rent or lease, construction, parts, tools, materials and supplies, inventory, training for yourself and your employees, opening advertising and promotion, state and local licenses, and miscellaneous costs. If these are given in a high to low range, keep it simple and use the same figures.

Required, Controlled, and Specified Goods and Services

From items eight and nine, state the requirements and controls that your franchisor enforces regarding your goods and services.

Franchisor Obligations

From item eleven, explain the training program and training requirement to give the reviewer additional assurance that you are well-trained for the franchise system. Likewise, give a concise list of the field support services that your franchisor provides, which could include data processing, central purchasing, evaluation of operations, on-site training, store opening, inventory control, franchisor conferences, telephone hotline, and online support. Specify the significant effects that any of these may have on your specific franchise system.

Exclusive Territory

Item twelve of the UFOC should define your specific territory. If you have some exclusivity from other franchisees in your franchise system, mention the extent. Briefly identify the size and boundaries of your territory here. Another section of the business plan is reserved for your market potential and a map of your territory and sphere of influence.

Trademarks, Trade Names, Patents, and Copyrights

Look closely at items 13 and 14. If there are any trade secrets, special licensing, or trademarks that separate your franchisor from others, giving your system a special competitive edge, indicate those you are permitted to disclose. This also encompasses any special franchisor technology that you can divulge.

Franchise Sales, Profits, and Earnings

Item 19 of the UFOC gives you the basis for any earnings claims made by your franchisor about what you can expect to make. These are often supported by statistics of the percentage of existing franchisees that have achieved these claims. For the business plan reviewers, this section is especially valuable. Use actual numbers if you can, or averages, and separate sales, profits, or earnings into both forecasted and historical columns if both are available.

Other Franchisees

Through various sources, you can find franchisees listed by total numbers of outlets for the last three years. If these are further separated out by the numbers of company-owned and franchised outlets for the last three years, include these numbers and look at the trend to see if your franchisor is growing, stabilized, or declining. Most are growing. You can make calculations of the statistics to interpret the rate of growth of your franchise system. Find out the number of outlets that your franchisor plans to open within the coming year and the major areas planned for expansion.

If the rate of growth for company-owned stores is increasing, this can indicate a high level of commitment that the franchisor has in its own system. Item 20 of the UFOC also gives facts about past, current, and future franchises that may add more depth to this category. Besides total numbers, give the distribution figures and the numbers of the main areas of concentration. Show these per state, province, or country.

Franchise Background

MegaBucks International, Inc. (the franchisor) is a publicly held Delaware corporation, doing business as MegaBucks International (and MBI), headquartered at 1234 Walnut Street, Kansas City, Missouri, and is registered in forty-eight states excluding Maine and Vermont. MBI is in the business of distributing a service and method of operation through company-owned and independently-owned retail outlets using the franchisor's trademarks, trade name, marketing techniques, and business format. MBI started business in 1964 and opened its first franchise in 1967. Today, the current number of MBI employees is 114.

Officers and Directors of MBI are: John C. Reeves, CEO; David Preston, CFO; Marie Davies, Managing Director of Franchise Operations; Jack Devaney, Director of Marketing and Sales, Harriot Peterson, Director of Field Support Services; and George Collins, Director of Washington/Oregon/Hawaii Region.

The Initial Franchise Fee varies per territory per population density, ranging $25,000 to $50,000, and is paid in one payment before Grand Opening. The franchise royalty assessed per transaction is 7% of net sales (total commission) which includes a 1% reserve fund for national advertising and a 1% reserve fund for local advertising. Training for the franchisee is included in the franchise fee. Quarterly audits are paid by the franchisor. MBI requires that the franchisee names the franchisor as additionally-insured on all franchisee liability policies.

The average original investment to open an MBI franchise is $100,000 to $150,000. Costs for an original investment of $100,000 are: $25,000 for the Initial Fee; $18,000, furniture; $12,000, telephone system; $5,000, computer equipment; $20,000, working capital requirement; $5,000, first month rent; $4,000, licenses and legal; $7,500, advertising and promotion; and $3,500, miscellaneous.

For controls, MegaBucks International insists that each franchised outlet is subject to quarterly audits, unscheduled field efficiency inspections twice a year, approval for all advertising locally generated, and an honor code for the integrity of franchise system. Audits must show a specified number of minimum transactions (not allowed to reveal the number). Fines can be imposed for royalties not paid.

As to support, MBI requires an initial two-week training program for the franchisee. Up to three franchisee employees may attend with the franchisee at the latter's additional expense. MBI provides data processing and on-line support, central purchasing (business cards, letterhead, envelopes, uniforms, and other supplies), operations evaluation, grand opening, franchisor conferences, telephone hotline, and national and regional institutional advertising.

continued

Cover the important background details of your franchise system from your UFOC, highlighting the following categories.

Include your franchisor's name, address, states registered, nature of the business, year started, year franchised, and number of corporate employees.

Identify three or four key officers or management personnel; list the remaining positions by function or title only.

Put summary résumés of franchisor managers in direct-line management of your franchisee in the exhibits.

State the initial franchise fee and payment structure.

List the royalties and every other fee to be paid in addition to the initial franchise fee.

List the franchisor's estimated costs for a franchisee to begin operations and explain those that are vague.

State the requirements and controls your franchisor enforces for your products or services.

Briefly describe the training program and the field support services provided by your franchisor.

Franchise Background (continued)

MBI has no established exclusive territory system, as is the norm for most real estate franchisors. However, MBI does design a territory of emphasis and uses discretion in deciding whether to allow other offices within that territory. The franchisor has a mileage rule for the distance allowed between offices. This varies by population centers.

MegaBucks International and MegaBucks are registered trademarks of MegaBucks International, Inc. The operations manual of MegaBucks International is considered a trade secret.

The earnings claims made by our franchisor cover a matrix caused by four factor adjustments: size of office, population center, years in business, and geographic area. For a start-up franchise, with ten employees, in a populace of 100,000, in Hawaii, the franchisee is projected to have average first-year net commissions of $900,000 and an average year-end profit of $50,000 after all salaries have been paid including the franchisee's. Average annual increases for forecasts are 4%.

In terms of other franchisees in the system, MBI shows the following for the past three years:

	Number of Company-owned	Number of Franchised	Total Outlets
Last Year	123	842	965
Two Years Ago	101	784	885
Three Years Ago	176	683	859

It can be seen from the above table, that the total number of outlets is growing, as well as the number of franchised units. This is corroborated by the disclosure that MBI has published with projected-new-units for the end of this year to be: number of company-owned, 126; number of franchised, 902; for a total number of 1,028 outlets.

Currently, the major number of franchisees for MBI are concentrated in four U.S. regions: Central, 186; Southwest, 172; West, 364; Northwest and Hawaii, 156; with a sparse showing of others in all regions, excluding the states of Maine and Vermont.

Briefly describe the boundaries of your territory and the size in area.

List the trademarks, trade names, patents, or copyrights held by your franchisor that give you a competitive edge.

Show the earnings claims given for a typical franchisee.

Describe the growth trend of your franchise system and use statistics for the last three years to support your findings.

Show the main areas of concentration by density of franchisees.

Industry Analysis

A strong industry analysis can seem intimidating to develop and report. However, according to business consultants of the conventional business plan that, although unnecessary for a continuing business, is a definite necessity for a start-up business. While a new start-up franchisee is a new start-up business, usually the franchisor is a continuing business. For a well-known or dominant franchise, a strong franchise background, as described above, typically will suffice for the industry analysis.

On the other hand, if you are in a franchise that is breaking new ground in its industry or a not-so-popular franchise or a not-so-popular industry, then a detailed review of the industry becomes vital. In these cases, it may be worthwhile to research and assemble an industry analysis for your franchise business plan. Even if your franchisor doesn't contribute much, you might be surprised to learn that, armed with the resources presented here, you can gather everything you need for a thorough industry analysis from a well-stocked public library in just one day. But check first to see if your franchisor has the data needed to write your industry analysis. The three elements of an industry analysis are:

1. An industry description, including the
   - Economic sector's size and growth rate and
   - Industry's size and growth rate;
2. The industry's trends and impacts, sensitive to
   - Economic swings,
   - Seasonal effects,
   - Distribution and supply channels,
   - Geographic trends and differences,
   - Regulatory impacts,
   - Technological improvements; and
3. The industry's opportunities.

Sources for Industry Information

If your franchisor cannot furnish the necessary information, your best source is the public library. First, look for business and trade publications. Before you begin, it is helpful to know the numerical code for your standard industrial classification (SIC). Your franchisor should be able to give you this, but if not, you can find it through Dun & Bradstreet or Robert Morse Associates.

Many industries have active trade associations that publish statistics tracking their industry sales, profits, and economic trends. Refer to *The Gale Directory of Publications and Broadcasting Media* listing periodicals or *Information, USA* for association listings. For another index of business magazines and journals, try *Business Periodicals Index*. For two sources on most trade associations, consult the *National Trade and Professional Associations of the United States* and the *Encyclopedia of Business Information Sources*.

Besides business and trade publications, the government publishes other excellent sources of information. If you have access to a large city or university library, check to see if it is a depository of U.S. government documents. The *American Statistics Index (ASI)*, published annually with monthly supplements by the Congressional Information Service of Bethesda, Maryland, is a reference that provides an index of all statistical publications of the U.S. government. This publication lists the documents of the

U.S. Bureau of Labor Statistics and those of the U.S. Bureau of the Census entitled, *Current Industrial Reports (CIR)*. The latter reports comprise a wide range of products with facts on manufacturing, shipping, and inventories. Another volume of the *American Statistics Index* is the *ASI Abstracts*. This large book summarizes the information of the reports indexed in the *ASI*.

Other Census Bureau publications to research are:

- *Bureau of the Census Catalog and Guide*, which describes all reports and data files issued in recent years;
- *Economic Censuses and Related Statistics*, which covers numerous industries and reports actual monthly sales and economic trends by locality, zip code, and type of merchandise; and
- *County Business Patterns*, which reports research on industries on the local market scene.

These and other Census Bureau publications are available through:

CENDATA
(301) 457-4100

Current publications are kept as references in libraries and at the 47 district offices of the U.S. Department of Commerce and the 12 regional offices of the U.S. Bureau of the Census listed below.

Regional Offices of the U.S. Bureau of the Census

Atlanta, Georgia (404) 730-3833	Dallas, Texas (214) 767-7105	Los Angeles, California (818) 904-6339
Boston, Massachusetts (617) 424-0510	Denver, Colorado (303) 969-7750	New York, New York (212) 264-4730
Charlotte, North Carolina (704) 344-6144	Detroit, Michigan (313) 259-1875	Philadelphia, Pennsylvania (215) 597-8313
Chicago, Illinois (708) 562-1740	Kansas City, Kansas (913) 551-6711	Seattle, Washington (206) 728-5314

Copies of these publications can be purchased from the U.S. Government Printing Office.

Superintendent of Documents
U.S. Government Printing Office
P.O. Box 371954
Pittsburgh, PA 15250-7954
(202) 512-1800

You can access the database edition of *County Business Patterns* at CENDATA, a U.S. Bureau of the Census web site.

CENDATA
http://waffle.nal.usda.gov/agdb/cendata.html

There are also private sector databases you can subscribe to and use for your research.

Ovid Technologies
(800) 955-0906
www.ovid.com

Knowledge Index
(800) 334-2564

Dow-Jones News Retrieval
(800) 522-3567
http://djinteractive.com

NEXIS EXPRESS
(800) 843-6476

You can find the growth rate of the gross national product (GNP) as well as other growth rates in the U.S. Department of Commerce annual publication, *U.S. Industrial Outlook*. It has data on production for the previous year and forecasts for the current year.

Economic Sector

In your industry analysis summary, it is necessary to determine the business economic sector that your industry is in. Several economic sectors exist. The four for business are manufacturing, distribution, retail, and service. Nearly all franchises are in the service sector, but identify for yourself which of these your industry is in. Also determine if your sector is growing and whether growth is slow, moderate, or fast; and if it is not growing, whether it is stagnant or slipping. If you are in two industries, discern and specify this for each.

Industry

In which industry, or industries, is your business? In this context, the term industry refers to all companies selling similar products or services, the support companies that provide their supplies and distribution, and other related companies closely involved in the same products or services.

Total revenue and total units of products or services sold are measures of the size and growth of an industry. For an industry analysis, tabulate the figures for two or three previous years with projections for the current and future years. From this, you can calculate the industry growth rate as a percentage of growth through each of the years given. Then compare these percentages of growth per year with the GNP and its percentage rate of growth over the same years. If an industry's growth rate is higher than the growth rates of the GNP, the industry is expanding. If the growth rates are similar, the industry is stable; and if the growth rates of the industry are lower, the overall growth of the industry is declining.

Industry Description

Now that you have done the necessary research, you can write the next part of your industry analysis — your industry description. For this summary, you will:

- Identify your business economic sector.
- Describe your sector's growth level as slow, moderate, or high.
- Identify your industry, noting its size and rate of growth compared to the gross national product.
- Label your industry's level of maturation as expanding or stable, supported by an actual growth rate in percent.

Industry Trends and Impact Factors

Nearly every industry has trends that cause sales to go up and down. To successfully deal with them, you need to identify them and recognize their impact on your industry and your business.

The most common trends that affect an industry are economic swings and seasonal changes, especially holidays. Other common impact factors are distribution and supply channels, geographic trends and differences, regulatory changes, and technological advancements. If your franchisor has already examined these, you may have data available that can assist you in planning for them. If not, analyze each of these for yourself and decide its effect on your industry.

Is your industry sensitive to economic swings? Often, recessions affect expensive products and services, or big-ticket items, and especially those in the luxury categories. The effects are a downturn in sales. Sales for some industries increase during recessions such as for divorce attorneys, discount stores, and used cars. Some that are virtually unaffected are low-cost items and necessities.

Do seasons and holidays affect your industry? Most retail industries have specific times of the year that are up and down. Real estate finds holiday times of the year worse for sales, while the Christmas season produces highest sales for the mainstream. Does your industry experience better or worse sales in summer, winter, or for back-to-school days? Holidays definitely affect sales for florists.

For candy sales, Valentine's Day, Easter, and Mother's Day are high-volume periods. The wedding industry prepares for June. Sales of outdoor and patio furniture, swimming pools, and boats are stronger in spring and summer than the other half of the year. If seasonal trends influence your industry, adjust your pro forma financial information to account for these.

Do distribution and supply channels affect your industry? Is your industry locally dependent upon one main distributor or supplier for your product or service line? If the answer is yes to either or both, then your local industry may get into trouble if your distributor or supplier does. Your costs may be proportionately dependent on these sources and out of your control. If they shut down, your business may have a serious glitch.

How does your geographic location influence your industry? This can overlap with seasonal effects. For example, if you are in a Sun Belt zone, sunglasses and swim gear are a year-round business. Tourism, mountain gear, marine supplies, and snow ski equipment all enjoy benefits of the correct geographic location.

Can changes in government regulations, whether county, municipal, state, or federal, drastically alter your industry? Regulatory changes have actually founded many industries and caused others to falter. Does your industry depend on insurance benefits or Medicare and Medicaid?

Finally, how do technological advancements affect your industry? The Internet is one of the more advanced recent technological changes. Could your industry someday be wiped out by online sales, or could it be enhanced by them? No one has a crystal ball, but indicators exist that, if read properly, can predict trends and their effects.

Industry Opportunities

After your industry description, write a few paragraphs for your industry analysis, reporting your findings that affect your industry. Be as specific as you can, using statistics where applicable. Like cause and effect, look for opportunities to report on, or forecast with, each finding. If you can use your research to instill the idea that your industry is too well entrenched for competition to break into, then this is a secondary objective here.

After the franchise background and optional industry analysis, you have four areas remaining to complete the franchise overview: the franchise products or services, market segments, customer profile, and reasons for choosing this franchise.

Franchise Products or Services

The purpose of this segment of your franchise overview is to introduce the reviewer to the complete lines of products or services offered through your franchise. If possible, do this with a narrative description. If your lines of products or services are extensive, supplement the description with a table listing your lines of products or services and their prices. This should be a complete mix of all items for sale. Describe the various product or service features that you consider as being unique or superior. Specifically note the proprietary products or services exclusive to the franchise. Also, include any options available.

Knowledge about the competitor's products or services is essential to reviewers of your business plan and assists you in understanding more about your own business and product or service line. If your franchisor has comparisons of your products or services with those of competing franchisors, show the prominent points. Again, this is on the industry level. If your franchisor can give you reasons, specify why your buyers buy your products or services instead of the competitors'. Is it because your franchise has better features, quality, service, prices, or a combination of these? Your franchisor should be able to provide information on how these products or services address user needs; this is important to mention here, as well. Also, describe the methods used in packaging your product or how the services are offered to the customer.

In an appendix to this section or in the exhibits at the end, include any sales brochures published by your franchisor. Mention their significance here, regarding your product or service line, and direct the reviewer's attention to their location within the plan. For this reason, their placement within the exhibits should be in the same order as the text about them. Append any significant technical specifications about the products or services. As a caution, it is recommended that you use all outside printed materials with discretion and only if they support your business plan in telling your story.

Sourcing

If it does not violate the terms of your franchise agreement or the intellectual property of your franchise, explain your sourcing — components and vendors — and the costs of providing your product or service through the franchise. The purpose of this segment is to inform your business plan reviewer of your franchise advantages as well as the controls within your franchise system. Items eight and nine of the disclosure document address these. It is helpful for the reviewer to understand the margins on a per-unit basis, if it is allowable.

Future Products or Services

As a last component of this segment, inform the reviewer of any future products or services to be released by your franchisor, if it is permissible. If not, make a general statement about the ongoing research and development support of your franchisor if it can be quantified by annual amounts of dollars spent, the size of the department, or the qualifications of the research team.

Franchise Services

MBI packages a service to be sold through its franchises. This service is real estate listings, sales, and leasing, and in some cases, property management. For the franchisor, MBI makes no distinctions in providing these services for residential, commercial, industrial, institutional or public properties; however, MBI encourages franchisees to specialize in commercial properties. None of the other real estate franchisors do.

In all transactions, it is MBI's policy to provide this service via MBI agents with a professional, honorable, personable, and attentive attitude. The charge, or commission, for this service is equivalent to the customary standard as used in each geographic area for the type of subject product.

The edge for this service for the customer's benefit is name recognition supported by national advertising, and a deluxe network of referrals through MBI's 965 offices spread throughout the country. A standard nationwide recognizable sign is installed on every property listed for sale or lease at no charge to the customer.

Describe your franchisor's products or services and their prices, emphasizing their special features.

Compare your products or services with those of competing franchisors and describe how yours address user needs.

Describe the packaging and presentation of your products or services.

Explain your sourcing and costs of your products or services.

Describe ongoing research and development and future products or services.

Franchise Market Segments

Many franchisors furnish their franchisees with information on the relationship between market segments and product or service development. Age, income, product or service demand, geography, buying patterns, customer needs, and other demographics typically divide market segments. Include here the most significant information from your franchisor that describes the overall franchise industry. Information on your local franchisee market segments is presented later in the market section, discussed in the next chapter.

Franchise Market Segments

Geography affects the customer demographics, condos and industrial properties sell better in large population centers and in the NE, and West; agricultural properties, in rural areas everywhere.

The business of real estate is in the service sector. As investments, the real estate industry is affected by the national stock market. When the stock market is strong, real estate investments take a back seat; when stocks decline, real estate investments improve. Overall, real estate appreciation is as high as any other investment industry — and therefore, is considered an expanding industry.

Nationally, economic swings affect real estate transactions; however, during economic slumps, listings are on the incline while sales are on the decline. The reverse is true during economic upswings. Nationally, seasonal effects find September as the worst month for the industry; Spring and Summer the best seasons. Seasons and trends in types of properties sold impact local markets significantly.

See Exhibits, Franchise Overview for supporting documentation.

List your business' economic sector and industry, comparing your industry's growth as stable or expanding.

List the general industry market segments for your franchise.

Franchise Market Segments – Nationwide

Sales of	Buyer	Marital Status	Age	Education	Combined Income
Single Family Residential:					
Condominiums	Individuals	55% couples	21–35, 55+	12–16	$30,000–42,000
Homes:					
1,000–1,500 sq. ft.	Individuals	75% couples	21–32	12–14	$30,000–48,000
1,501–2,400 sq. ft.	Individuals	82% families	24–45	14–16	$50,000–70,000
2,401 sq. ft. and over	Individuals	96% families	30–55	16+	$100,000+
Commercial:					
Professional Offices	Small Businesses	N/A	32–50	16–20	$90,000–120,000
Light Retail	Small Businesses	N/A	28–48	14–16	$50,000–75,000
Heavy Retail	Big Businesses	N/A	N/A	N/A	N/A
Industrial Properties	Big Businesses	N/A	N/A	N/A	N/A
Agricultural Properties:					
Ranchettes	Individuals	98% families	30–44	12–16	$75,000–120,000
Large Ranches	Small Businesses	N/A	N/A	N/A	N/A

Franchise Customer Profile

This part of your franchise overview is reserved for the customer profile on the industry level. If your franchise has a typical customer profile, the description of it goes here. For your specific market, you will be doing your own research and making calculations to develop your customer profile in the next chapter of your business plan, where you are entering that data, and not here.

MBI Customer Profile

Our specific franchise profile from the MegaBucks International would be:

Sales of	Customer/ Buyer	Marital Status	Age	Education	Combined Income
Professional Offices	Small Businesses	N/A	32–50	16–20	$90,000–120,000
Light Retail	Small Businesses	N/A	28–48	14–16	$50,000–75,000

On the Big Island of Hawaii, specifically in the North Kona District, the income is above the national average by 7%; the age of the buyer is above the national average by three years, and the education level is higher for offices, lower for light retail, changing our franchise customer profile to:

Sales of	Customer/ Buyer	Marital Status	Age	Education	Combined Income
Professional Offices	Small Businesses	N/A	35–53	17–20	$96,300–128,400
Light Retail	Small Businesses	N/A	31–51	13–14	$53,500–80,250

However, other considerations are taken into account for in our specific market; these are weighed and examined in the next section of this Business Plan, The Market.

Describe the typical customer profile for your franchise.

Reasons for Choosing this Franchise

Finally, list the reasons why you chose this franchise system over others and why you feel it is better for your location or business goals than others are. After you have made the list, trim it to three or four of the most influential factors and enter them here with bulleted points.

Reasons for Choosing MegaBucks

MegaBucks International was selected after reviewing twelve other real estate franchises that are registered in Hawaii. Two were quickly eliminated because they are known to operate on 100% commission; that is, agents pay broker a desk fee. These did not fit our style of business. Three that were nationally acclaimed were already taken, and all three are known more for their residential sales. For our business, MegaBucks International is nationally known, does not operate on a 100% commission basis, specializes in commercial real estate, and did not already have a franchise in our area. All other franchise statistics are comparable; however, after much analysis, the choice became clear and narrowed to one.

After attending MBI's headquarters, we found:

- the corporate staff is very pleasant and helpful, and truly interested in the success of MBI franchisees,
- the national advertising is highly recognizable,
- the regional structure is fine-tuned and efficient in operation,
- the field support services are equally distributed,
- the computer database is massive and user-friendly,
- the franchise system is growing steadily, and
- the entire system is consistent with our way of doing business.

> State three or four reasons why you chose this franchise over its competitors.

Revise Your Franchise Summary

Now that you have completed your franchise overview, revise your franchise summary to emphasize the highlights of your work in the sequence used in the text of this chapter.

Thus far, your business plan has covered your business and your franchise. Now, you are ready to zoom in on your market and examine it closely before deciding on a marketing strategy to capture it. Your market is the subject of the next chapter.

Chapter 6

The Market

Market competition is the only form of organization which can afford a large measure of freedom to the individual.
— FRANK HYNEMAN KNIGHT

You already have your product or service lines through your franchisor, and you already believe in them. But, are they better mousetraps than the competition's? One sure way to build a better mousetrap is to know the mouse.

For any business, it is imperative to know who the customers are and to evaluate whether or not the products or services meet their needs. To identify your customers, you have to address not only who they are, but also what they want. You can only plan a strategy of marketing and sales once you and your franchisor know the answers to those two questions.

To determine their market, nonfranchised businesses often conduct their own investigations to understand their market or pay significant fees for private consultants who specialize in these studies. One of the great advantages of a franchised business is most franchisors have already undertaken much of this research. Even if they haven't fine tuned their understanding of the market for your local outlet, it is not much work to use their findings and translate their worth to your own local scale. Chapter 5 touched lightly on your franchise market, while the segments in the market section encompass a full report on your market in detail, including:

- Exclusive territory
- Market description
- Market size and trends
- Competition description
- Market share

Exclusive Territory

In your opening paragraph on the market, briefly describe the geographic area your franchise serves. If you have an exclusive territory or variation thereof, refer to your franchise agreement and item twelve of the UFOC. These indicate your market area. Describe your territory in terms of boundaries, proximity to support businesses and to businesses with the same customers, traffic flow, and whatever advantages stand out for your particular territory. Insert a map showing your location with boundaries, and key any other points that may be prominent in your description. If your map looks out of place with the body of your business plan, enclose it in the exhibits.

Often your franchisor can estimate a projected number of customers in your territory or your sphere of influence within the franchise system. If that's the case for you, about one-half of the work for this section is already complete, but save this for the paragraphs below.

Territory Map

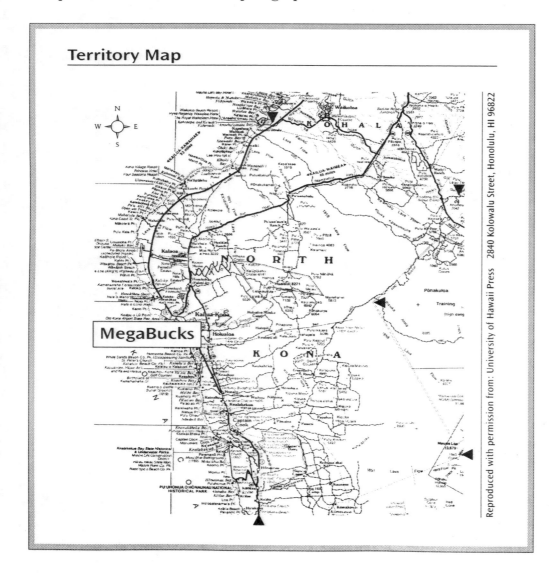

Reproduced with permission from: University of Hawaii Press   2840 Kolowalu Street, Honolulu, HI 96822

Insert a map with important market benchmarks.

Territory

Although MegaBucks International does not grant exclusive territories, MegaBucks Smith and Associates has been assigned a designated area in which no other MBI offices will be set up. This consists of the North Kona district on the West Side of the Big Island. The district encompasses an area of 180 square miles, is bordered on the west by the Pacific Ocean, on the north by Anaeho Omalu (approximately 4 miles south of the town of Waikoloa), east by the irregular shape of the mountain of Mauna Loa, and south by the small town of Kealakekua.

Within this territory there are many commercial business and shopping centers. The five largest in the Kailua-Kona area are: Kaloko Light Industrial Area, Honokohau Harbor, Old Industrial Park, The Crossroads, and Kailua-Kona town. Seventeen smaller centers within Kailua-Kona are: Frame Ten Center, Kopiko Plaza, Lanihau Center, Kona Coast Shopping Center, North Kona Shopping Center, King Kamehameha Mall, Seaside Mall, Akona Kai Mall, Banyan Court, Kona Inn Shopping Center, Kona Market Place, Waterfront Row, Hualalai Center, Territorial Center, Kuakini Tower, Kuakini Plaza, and Kona Trade Center.

Within the Kona Industrial Area there are eight business centers: Kaiwi Square, Gold Coast Business Center, Kaahumanu Plaza, Luhia Centers I–III, Palm Terrace, and Pawai Center.

Our office is located about six miles south of Kailua-Kona on Alii Drive. Another five miles south is the large neighborhood commercial business and shopping center, and the community of, Keauhou. Other small tourist shopping stops exist along the Queen Highway further south to the edge of our southern boundary, Kealekekua — another small business community. Up the mountain, inland, east of Kailua-Kona, is the small mountain coastal town of Holualoa, still within our territory, consisting of arts, crafts, tourist shopping, and other small businesses.

Write an opening paragraph on your market describing the geographic area your franchise serves.

Describe your territory in square miles and its proximity to support businesses and to businesses with the same customers as yours.

Emphasize traffic flows and other specific advantages.

Market Description

After relating your market territory, characterize your market by identifying your customer profile. Use either a few sentences or several paragraphs depending on the amount of effective material you develop.

Most likely your franchisor has already defined your market segments by age, income, product or service demand, geography, buying patterns, customer needs, other demographics, market trends, and overall market size. If this is not the case, obtain what you can from your franchisor paperwork to elaborate on your market and market segments. Your Location Data Report (LDR), if complete, should have some details about your market segments in support of your location.

If your franchise system is new, or small, or if, for whatever reason, your franchisor cannot provide market study results, then research your market for yourself, just as any other business would do. Even if your franchisor can assist with this, it is recommended that you do your own study to compare your discoveries with your franchisor's, as a good precautionary business measure. In this case, continue with your market analysis similar to the methods used for a nonfranchised business plan. You can find nearly everything through most of the same sources given for the industry analysis in Chapter 5.

Market Analysis and Customer Profile

A market analysis helps you understand who your customers are, why they use your products or services, how many customers are in your market, and how you can reach them.

First, to evaluate your market, focus on your market segments by analyzing your customer profiles. Customers, as opposed to consumers, may comprise individual consumers or commercial customers, which are different types of businesses and institutions. Identifying the market means matching up what you sell, at what price, and how you sell it with the customer needs in your targeted market segments. In determining these, several popular types of analyses are used: a customer analysis, consumer demographic analysis, consumer psychographic analysis, and customer geographic analysis.

Customer Analysis

From your franchisor's or your own research, obtain an estimate of the percentages of your total market for each of the customer types: individual consumers and various commercial customers.

If your customers are commercial, are they businesses, governmental agencies, or charitable, medical, educational, or professional associations? What is the size of each? For instance, your franchisor may indicate you can expect to have customers similar to those in the customer analysis below.

Customer Types

Commercial	
Businesses	12%
Institutions	6%
Consumers	82%
Total	100%

If you have commercial customers, you can further detect the markets within them. For example, your customers might be accounting, engineering, and law offices. If you know the types of businesses that comprise a significant percent of your sales — as shown in the commercial business analysis example below — list those businesses by their industries and include this information in the exhibits. Institutions are usually tracked separately

because they are entirely different customers with different buying characteristics such as, government offices, schools, or hospitals. They can also be
included in your marketing plan in the exhibits as commercial institutions.

Commercial: Businesses		Commercial: Institutions	
Accounting offices	4%	Government offices	2%
Engineering offices	5%	Schools	3%
Law offices	3%	Hospitals	1%
Subtotal	12%	Subtotal	6%

Market Description

On the Big Island of Hawaii, specifically in the North Kona District, the
income is above the national average by 7%; the age of the buyer is
above the national average by three years, and the education level is
higher for offices, lower for light retail, changing our franchise customer profile to:

Sales of	Customer/ Buyer	Marital Status	Age	Education	Combined Income
Professional Offices	Small businesses	N/A	35–53	17–20	$96,300–128,400
Light Retail	Small businesses	N/A	31–51	13–14	$53,500–80,250

MegaBucks International has provided a customer analysis of the
buyers for our typical market of sales and leases for light commercial:
retail and medical/business office space.

Customer Analysis

Customer Types

Small Businesses:

Retail	32%
Medical	6%
Business offices	44%
Individual Consumers	18%
Total	100%

Research from the County of Hawaii, Research and Development
Department, results in a very refined list of our potential customer
base for business and medical offices, and light retail space. The next
three tables display this.

Describe your customer profile in as much detail as you have, separating consumers and customers, and use the results and highlights from the analyses that follows.

If applicable, show a customer analysis, with additional breakdowns of commercial analyses, such as business, institutional, and industrial.

Customers – Business Offices

Accountants	9%	Graphic artists	1%		
Appraisers	1%	Home inspection	1%		
Architects	2%	Insurance	7%		
Attorneys	19%	Interior design	2%		
Computer consultants	1%	Investigators	3%		
Contractors	11%	Investments	4%		
Counselors	2%	Modeling agencies	1%		
Employment agencies	6%	Movers	3%		
Engineers	8%	Pest control services	3%		
Escrow and title	4%	Security	1%		
Financing and mortgage	9%	Tax consultants	1%		
		Total	100%		

Customers – Medical Offices

Acupuncture	1%
Clinics	8%
Dentists	18%
Laboratories	17%
Ophthalmologists	3%
Pharmacists	14%
Physicians	32%
Podiatrists	3%
Veterinarians	4%
Total	100%

Customers – Light Retail

Activity centers	1/2%	Florists	3%	Lighting	2%
Art and crafts supplies	1/2%	Frames, picture	1%	Marine	3%
Automobile parts	1%	Furniture	3%	Nurseries-plants	2%
Blinds and draperies	1%	Gift shops	4%	Office supply	1%
Books	2%	Glass shops	2%	Optometry	2%
Candy	1%	Hair cutting & styling	6%	Pet care	2%
Carpet	2%	Hardware	5%	Photography	3%
Chiropractic	1%	Health clubs	3%	Photography equipment	1/2%
Clothing	3%	Home improvements	3%	Restaurants	9%
Convenience stores	3%	Ice cream, frozen	2%	Sports equipment	3%
Copy/mail centers	2%	Importers	3%	Telephones	2%
Dive equipment	1%	Jewelers	4%	Travel agencies	1%
Electronics	4%	Kitchen equipment	1/2%	Video rentals	3%
Equipment rental	2%	Laundry	3%	Total	100%

Consumer Identification

To identify the consumers within your customer base, first check with your franchisor for a consumer profile. If your franchisor has not done one, compile the data yourself (see Chapter 5) and present it using tools called consumer analyses: a consumer demographic analysis and a consumer psychographic analysis.

Consumer Demographic Analysis

Consumer demographics identify your consumers by separating them into percentages according to sex, age group, annual income, marital status, educational level, and residential location. When conducting a demographic study, you may add customized categories to the standard profile study. If your major product is a hot tub, for instance, you may want to know those consumers who already have hot tubs to target them for supplies or upgrades.

To save some legwork, see if your franchisor has already completed a consumer demographic analysis, and if it has, obtain a copy and integrate the results in this sub-segment. As you begin to assemble two or more of these customer profile analyses, you can make calculations from one to the other that give you further determinations. If you want more detail in your customer profile, you can calculate a percentage from the consumer demographics analysis for your customer analysis. For example, if you can show that out of an individual-consumer base of 82 percent that 37.6 percent of your consumers are males, then 30.83 percent of your total customer base are individual male consumers.

37.6% males out of a 82% individual-consumer base equals 30.83% male consumers

(37.6 × .82 = 30.83)

Each of the figures from the demographics can be broken down using a similar calculation to arrive at various consumer category percentages.

Consumer Demographic Analysis

For our consumer demographic analysis and psychographic analysis, MegaBucks International has supplied its findings of the national average for MegaBucks franchisees for commercial sales in light retail and offices.

Consumer Demographic Analysis

Our Buyers			Income:	Under $40,000	2.4%
Sex:	Male	64.6%		$40,000–$59,999	17.9%
	Female	36.4%		$60,000–$79,999	36.6%
Age:	18–24	2.7%		Over $80,000	43.1%
	25–34	16.9%	Marital status:	Married	52.7%
	35–44	48.8%		Single	47.3%
	45–54	21.7%	Education:	Under 12 yrs.	4.2%
	55+	9.9%		12–14 yrs.	15.1%
				15–16 yrs.	42.3%
				More than 16 yrs.	38.4%

Display a consumer demographic analysis.

Consumer Psychographic Analysis

A less objective study of the characteristics of your consumers is a consumer psychographic analysis. This study attempts to define psychological reasons why your consumers purchase your products or services and helps you learn a little about consumer lifestyles. Can you identify the psychological factors that influence purchases by Dr. Wizard, Ms. Gadget, Miss Glamour, or Mr. Macho? Are your consumers impulse buyers or deliberate buyers? Are they price conscious or brand conscious? Are they conservative or liberal? These are very helpful to know when planning your marketing strategy. Objective characteristics to look for are included in the Consumer Psychographic Analysis. If the results indicate significant affects on your market, make a pie chart to show your psychographic segments.

If your customers include commercial businesses in addition to consumers, assemble a customer psychographic analysis. Are your business customers free-spending or frugal; are they innovative or slow to change; are they technologically oriented; do they have strong management or strong employee input; and are they business or community leaders or slow to make decisions? These characteristics are merely examples. You can customize a list of characteristics geared to your products and services.

Consumer Psychographic Analysis

	Light Retail Yes	Light Retail No	Professional Offices Yes	Professional Offices No
Behavioral				
Impulse buyer	√	—	—	√
Deliberate buyer	√	—	√	—
Socially responsible	√	—	√	—
Hedonistic	√	—	—	√
Cultural				
Conservative	—	√	√	—
Liberal	√	—	—	√
Environmentally aware	√	—	√	—
Brand conscious	—	√	√	—
Self-image				
Trend setter	√	—	—	√
Family oriented	√	—	√	—
Homemaker	—	√	√	—
Technologically adept	—	√	√	—

Show a consumer psychographic analysis.

Customer Geographic Analysis

A customer geographic analysis starts with a description of the area or areas you intend to serve and identifies the density of your customers in that area. This survey may be readily available from your franchisor or obtainable through the same methods discussed in Chapter 5. If you have an exclusive territory as part of your agreement, then most of your customers reside in that area. If your territory is very large, you may want to locate where your customers come from within the various sectors of territory. A certain percentage of people, more than likely, also come from outside your area.

When you have completed the above research and analyzed it, use the results and highlights to finish your market description. Add any tables, charts, and graphs similar to the one displayed here to support the findings in identifying your market and customer profile. Completing the study is not an exact science. Naturally the more accurate the facts are, the more accurate the complete analysis is, but because most of your information is approximate, quantifying your market is usually a subjective, rather than objective, process.

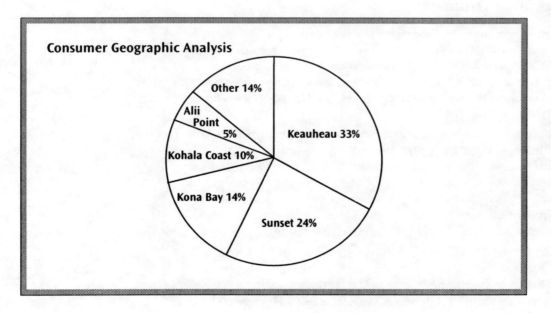

Graph a customer geographic analysis.

Market Size and Trends

For your third market segment, write a brief description of your market size and trends. Has the research above answered the question: what is the size of your market in terms of customers and consumers?

By using calculations for the percentages of the market and by doing a little investigation of the population census at your local county or municipal planning departments, you can determine the market size and growth rate for your specific territory.

Ask your franchisor for its analysis of the market trends. Does your franchisor's research and development department tune in to consumer changes by age groups, buying habits, disposable income, and leisure interests? Is one age group of the market going to be increasing purchases or is one educational level going to limit an increase of purchases of your products or services? These are only projections, but usually a large franchisor already has opinions on market trends.

After you have completed this review, separate the conclusions drawn from the calculations about your market size and market trends. As to your consumers, list the overall population of your area and the percentages of the population that match your consumer and customer profiles. Make comparisons of population, anticipated numbers of customers, and overall area in square miles of your territory. Express any trends in your market you or your franchisor can forecast. Can you make any conclusions about opportunities in the market now and for the future? Also, if you can make accurate growth projections of the market size, include them here.

Market Size and Trends

Using the marketing materials above with the population figures of our territory, we can formulate some projections of our market size. The population of the North Kona district is constantly changing because of a continuous transient migration, incoming and outgoing from a second-home base and the heavy tourist traffic. The County uses a figure of 70,000 as a year-around average.

From the County, we were given statistics for our district to adjust customer profile as provided by the franchisor. While age and education figure into the customer profile, our Regional Director at MegaBucks International has advised to concentrate on the combined income factor as a first priority. The franchisor has statistics to show that most of the potential customers with the correct combined income fall into the correct mix of age and education (see Exhibits, The Market).

For light retail, the bulk of our potential customers will have a combined income of at least $53,500, which narrows the population to 32.8% in the North Kona district (per county statistics, see Exhibits, The Market), or a potential customer base of 22,960. However, the Kohala Coast customers are not figured into this population base. The Kohala Coast, while only a small population of 22,000, has a much higher combined income. Using our $53,500 basis, the pro-rata potential customer base is as high as 100%, or 22,000.

If we add the percentages from the consumer geographic analysis excluding the Kohala Coast, we get 90% of our customer base coming from the North Kona district, so our customer base of 22,960 at this point represents 90% of our total (if the Kohala Coast can support the balance 10% — 2,551 — based on their combined income). Since it has

continued

Describe your market size and trends as concisely as possible.

Market Size and Trends (continued)

already been established that the Kohala Coast could supply as much as 22,000 customers based on income, the ten percent figure coming from that area as predicted by the geographic analysis is very plausible: 2,551 out of the 22,000.

Therefore, the total market basis for light retail, by combined income, would be: from the North Kona district, 22,960 (90%); and from the Kohala Coast, 2,551 (10%), equaling 25,511 potential customers.

This number should now be adjusted for age and education. Again, MBI has discovered a very high correlation between combined income, correct age group, and level of education: a computed 95%. Even though this is supported (see Exhibits, The Market), our style of business is conservative and we have lowered the factor to 90% for this business plan. Our final number for the market share for light retail is 22,959.

For professional offices, we can go through the same calculations: for Kona, the percentage of combined income of people with at least $96,300 a year, is dramatically lower, 8.2% or 5,740. This represents 90% of the market. For the Kohala Coast, the combined income percentage is still quite high, 88%, or 19,360. Since we will have only 10% of the total from Kohala Coast, that region will supply 638 customers for its 10% of our total. The total is 6,378 for professional offices for combined income. MBI gives us a correlation of 93% to account for age and income differences, so again if we use a more conservative adjustment of 89%, the total market share for professional offices is 5,676.

At this point, we can fine-tune both of these numbers for other findings. For instance, if we use our customer analyses, we can calculate the size of the market to target for a specific user, e.g., dentists, 18% for professional offices. The calculation reveals a market size of 1,021 to target our territory for a possible dentist user.

If we use our consumer demographic, supplied by the franchisor, we can calculate the number of males, 64.6%, of each of these figures: 14,831 males for retail space, 3,667 males for professional offices although these particular stand-alone numbers may not be very useful. However, they can be combined with other consumer demographics to build a specific mailing list depending on our particular need.

While our weather is fairly stable compared to other climates, we still have seasonal changes. From early October, when the international triathlon takes place, until Easter, we have our heaviest season of transients. The 70,000 average grows significantly and usually peaks in December. We are the "south," for people flying south for the winter.

As to economic swings, we are subject to them as has been reported for the franchisor, and on par with the industry. However, we have two factors in our favor in our geographic location. When vacationers come to the islands, they begin immediately thinking of how they can do

continued

State the overall population of your area and the percentages that match your consumer and customer profiles.

Describe the projected market trends. Draw conclusions about your opportunities in the market now and in the future.

Market Size and Trends (continued)

business here in order to relocate, and being in a holiday mood, they tend to forget their troubles at home and look to a brighter future. During economic slumps on the mainland, sales in Hawaii have persisted in both residential and commercial during the winter season when vacationers visit and second-home homeowners return (see Exhibits, The Market, MLS statistics). The second factor has to do with the heavy investors that live on this island. When the stock market declines, the investors tend to move their money into real estate. All of our experienced employees in real estate have seen this time and again.

Another geographic effect that impacts our market, is the ocean world we live in here. There are many marine businesses and marine-related and support businesses. This fact needs to be considered when planning marketing strategy. It even affects the way people dress and their needs surrounding this culture must be addressed in planning promotions and targeting specialized market needs.

Competition Description

It is necessary to find as much accurate data as possible about the competition — for your business' marketing program, your business plan, and your investment offering or financing request. If your franchisor provides an LDR, much of this information is available to you — typically, there is a section that covers comparable businesses within your retail trade zone, whether they are franchises, chain outlets, or independents. In addition, the LDR coverage of the competition usually includes image, the strength and quality, years in operation, pricing, hours of operation, and facility conditions and facility cleanliness. For this segment in your market section, write a summary and list all of the competitors within your territory.

Competition

According to MLS, there are fourteen real estate offices in our territory which is designated Zone 7 by the Hawaii County Board of Realtors, Inc. Alphabetically, these are: Ala Hali Realty, Inc., Black and Jones Realty, Centurian Baker, Ltd., Charles Smith Realty, Greater Homes Conway, Johnson Real Estate, Ka'alu'u Beach Realty, Kailua-Kona Realty, Kealekekua Realty, Koa Woods Brokers, Mary Poppins Real Estate, Orchid Island Realty, Prudence Fees Enterprises, and White-Sands Properties.

Identify your competitors.

Main Competitors

Whether or not your franchisor furnishes this material for your business plan, you need to answer four questions concerning your main competitors.

- Who are the major competitors?
- What are the keys to their success?
- What are their strengths and weaknesses?
- How do you compare with them?

While you may be limited in making customized adjustments to your business by your franchisor's business format, it is still a good idea to know why the competition does as well as it does. In a new paragraph of the competition segment, list your main competitors and include their keys to success: price, product or service features, quality, customer service, convenience, training, distribution, or reputation.

If your franchisor cannot give you local specifics on the competition, it is up to you to compile the research. Check the Yellow Pages and then make a detailed visual observation with maps. A complete estimate of all competitors' shares of the business helps in the calculations. Describe their businesses in terms of comparable factors with yours.

Although this procedure is subjective, you can use a competitor analysis, a handy tool, to help you and the reviewer to understand how you compare with the competition. Fill it out using points similar to a grading system. Values are one to four, with four being the highest appraisal.

Compute the calculations and develop your own analysis of the outcome in your summary on main competitors. If the competitors are franchises, compare some of the published franchise data about their franchisors with yours, particularly comparing growth of outlets over the previous three years. What are the corporate strengths of competing franchises in your area? Compare field support services, numbers of corporate employees, growth rates, and numbers of total franchise outlets. This information is readily available in source books.

If the competitors' ads reveal less competitive prices, particularly poor promotional attempts or inferior professionalism, then append them as exhibits to support the comparisons for the reviewers to study.

Main Competitors

Within our territory we have three major competitors: two franchised agencies and one independent. The independent, Johnson Real Estate, is the strongest, having its own development company and a large real estate staff. The real estate division is supported by in-house development projects when other real estate is slow; however, this has been advantageous for other Realtors in two ways:

continued

List your main competitors and their keys to success as you know them.

Main Competitors (continued)

1. Although the company's own development projects are never offered for listing, they are usually placed on MLS and are, hence, available for outside sales participation increasing the inventory for other Realtors alike.

2. Oftentimes, the real estate staff is so busy working their in-house inventory that they do not have the time to work other MLS listings.

While Johnson Real Estate has a very strong office, in a good location and in a professional setting, their reputation as having a lack of integrity in honoring their deals with other brokers has caused them to be ostracized somewhat. Title and escrow companies and lenders do not like to work with them.

The second strongest competitor, Centurian Baker, is a franchised outlet of Centurian National, and specializes in residential sales with much less activity in commercial. They are very successful in the residential market helped by national name recognition and they have all the advantages of a strong franchise system. Centurian National has a much less organized franchise system than MegaBucks International. Centurian does not provide any local database support, nor is it comparable in field support services. The franchisor has no field inspections and is not easily accessible for management assistance.

Much of the same can be said for the third competitor, Greater Homes Conway and Associates, which is a franchised outlet of Greater Homes of America, another nationally franchised real estate organization. However, this particular franchise, our competitor, seems to be mismanaged as the broker is usually on the mainland, and they have a reputation of constant turnover of sales agents, especially new ones that have just completed their sales training. Greater Homes of America is on decline. Their numbers of franchised outlets have diminished every year for the last three years.

MegaBucks Smith and Associates is a much smaller office at the start of business than all three, but of the three, our location and ambiance will be on par with Johnson (our location could be arguably better) and is much better than the other two franchised Realtors.

Summarize the highlights of your findings about your competitors.

Competitor Analysis

Item	MegaBucks Smith & Associates	Johnson Real Estate	Centurian Baker	Greater Homes Conway
Commercial strength	B	A	C	C
Years in operation	1	7	11	12
Product knowledge	A	A	B	C
User friendliness	A	B	B	B
Customer service	A	B	B	C
Location	A	A	C	B
Convenience	A	B	B	C
Ambiance	A	A	B	B
Image	A*	D	B	B
Physical condition	A	A	B	B
Cleanliness	A	A	B	C
Hours of operation	A	A	B	B
Marketing	A	A	B	C
Total points**	48	49	45	42
Average points	3.69	3.77	3.46	3.23

 * Image based on composite image of experienced employees that have been in the area.
** Using system of A=4, B=3, C=2, D=1.

Display a competitor analysis.

Market Share

Your marketing objective in the business summary is an estimate for increasing your market share. For that summary, you used discoveries from a market share analysis to understand your market. Include the market share analysis that supports the findings, as in the MegaBucks example below. Refer to your business summary and the example in Chapter 4 to review how this market share analysis is developed.

Market Share

We will capture 29.0% of the commercial market our first year. This is not only a goal, but a realistic expectation based on our market share analysis. Achieving this, we will have reached a gross revenue of $14,500,000 which is consistent with our financial forecasts and with the total sales revenue released by MLS for commercial and business transactions of just under $50,000,000 for Zone 7, our territory. The graph for next year shows an 8% increase in sales for MegaBucks, and we anticipate our closest competitor to stagnate, and our two franchised competitors to actually decline, in commercial and business sales and leases, created by our impact in the industry.

Describe your market share summarizing the market share analysis, the market share distribution, and a forecast of market share for next year.

Market Share Analysis

Business	Strength	Franchise Factor	One of Four Competitors		Market Share (numerator)
MegaBucks Smith	3	1.2*	0.25	=	0.9
Johnson Real Estate	4	1.0	0.25	=	1.0
Centurian Baker	2	1.2*	0.25	=	0.6
Greater Homes Conway	2	1.2*	0.25	=	0.6
Total Market Share (denominator):					3.1

Our market share: .9 / 3.1 = 29%

* As a rule-of-thumb, a franchised business has 20% more of the market than a nonfranchised business; this is an assigned factor of 1.2.

Display a market share analysis.

Another subjective tool for determining market share is a market share distribution. This is an accurate tool for measuring existing businesses on past performance when you know the numbers; however, this is rarely the case for a new franchise. Typically, you can only estimate these numbers from business and trade publications and other sources as explained in Chapter 5.

For a start-up business, the numbers are forecasts, and as such, the market share distribution is no more accurate than the market share analysis. Nevertheless, try your hand at these estimates to see how your franchise compares to others in your market.

Market Share Distribution

	MegaBucks Smith & Associates	Johnson Real Estate	Centurian Baker	Greater Homes Conway
Sales: commercial and business	$14,500,000	$16,100,000	$9,700,000	$9,700,000
Percent of total $	29%	32.2%	19.4%	19.4%

Display a market share distribution.

When you have completed both the market share analysis and the market share distribution, write a final description of your market segment under a heading, Market Share, summarizing the results and emphasizing the important elements of your analyses. If you anticipate increasing your market share because of certain advantages that you have over the competition, give the reasons in support of this. You may want to develop additional visuals that project your expectations and depict your gains in the market share. Graphs can best illustrate these projections.

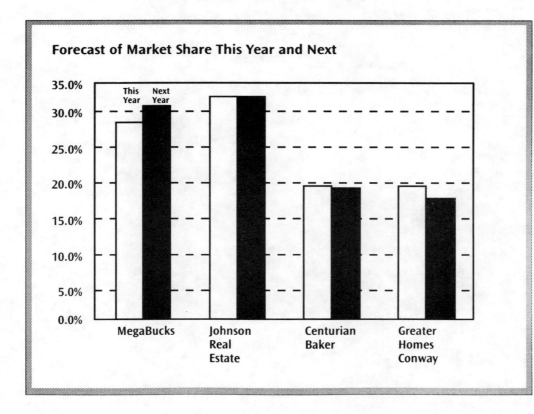

Forecast of Market Share This Year and Next

Graph your market share for this year and a forecast for next year.

Now That You Know Your Market

Once you have completed the study of your market and learned who your customers are and why they buy your products or services, the next job is to reach them. This is where marketing comes in, the subject of the next section in your business plan and of the next chapter.

Chapter 7

The Marketing Plan

The business that considers itself immune to the necessity for advertising sooner or later finds itself immune to business.
— DERBY BROWN

After you have finished researching your market and the competition, it is time to develop your marketing plan. While the market section identifies your customers and their needs, the marketing plan section focuses on how you plan to meet those needs — your strategies for creating customer prospects, or leads, and your programs for generating sales. The marketing plan describes both your marketing strategy and your sales program.

The following topics are included in any good marketing plan section. This chapter will explain each segment for you.

- A marketing summary
- A franchisor marketing plan
- A franchisee marketing plan
- A marketing budget and advertising plan
- The sales force and forecast

An important activity of marketing is the continual monitoring of customer needs and demand for your products or service. While a sales program concentrates on the salability of products or services, a good marketing plan determines the level of customer demand for them and actively monitors customers' changing needs. With this information, you can coordinate your business' strengths and weaknesses with the demand to maximize your ability for meeting your customers' needs. By doing so, you can deliver your products or service more effectively than your competitors.

For the most part, a strong franchisor does its own market surveys and marketing analyses before signing you on and starting your outlet. These surveys and analyses have already identified the major customers for your products or services and the best ways for getting them to buy. Merging the franchisor's marketing plan with yours is not difficult.

In most franchise systems, the franchisee pays a co-op advertising royalty to the franchisor. For this, the franchisor accepts most of the responsibilities and provides most of the finances associated with your marketing plan. For example, the franchisor has the greater responsibility to:

- make customers aware of the franchise products or services,
- convey the franchise's message to customers about the products or services, and
- reinforce that message.

Most franchisees have a lesser responsibility for marketing these concepts, but your responsibility for acquiring actual sales increases to 100 percent. As the franchisee, you convey the message about your company and location and make the sales. Your franchisor generally assists you with these responsibilities by supplementing the marketing techniques you implement to complete your overall marketing plan. In fact, your franchisor usually exercises great control over your marketing and advertising for the sake of consistency within the entire franchise system.

Marketing Summary

This is another of those summaries that, while placed as the opening of this section, should really be written last to summarize the analyses and to heighten the reviewer's interest in your marketing strategy. Be sure it covers the key elements of your marketing plan.

- Highlights of your franchisor's marketing plan
- Media and promotions used to reach the customer
- Your message to customers about your products or services
- Key elements of your franchisee marketing strategy
- Your marketing promotions
- Your marketing budget or advertising plan
- Your sales force and its special training

Marketing Summary

It is the marketing plan of MegaBucks International to blitz all national advertising media to instill name recognition and develop a national awareness of their specialized services. With several distinctive advantages over its competitor, MBI specializes in commercial real estate, a comprehensive national database, and an incomparable relocation network. As a result, it is our marketing plan to develop local customer awareness of our convenient location and professional staff. We will use direct mail, local television, radio, regional magazines, the local newspaper, Yellow Pages, signs, and special events to implement this plan and show our listings. Besides a pre-opening, grand opening, and holiday parties, we have one big annual gala, the MegaBucks auction. This marketing strategy for the first year will cost $22,000 — a reasonable figure since we have an in-house Marketing Director.

Our sales force is the motor behind the drive of our operation. We have a General Sales Manager/Operations Manager, a Commercial Sales Manager and three assistant Sales Managers — each with their own specialization. Sales meetings are conducted weekly with special monthly and quarterly programs, to redefine objectives and present incentives. Approximately half of the weekly meetings are specifically designated as sales training meetings.

Summarize the highlights of your franchisor's marketing plan and your franchisee marketing strategy.

Franchisor Marketing Plan

This next segment describes your franchisor's marketing plan. In it, discuss how your franchisor deals with the four major factors for conveying the message about your products or services and their benefits to your customers. These factors, called the four Ps of the market mix, are product, price, place, and promotion. If your franchisor's master marketing plan does not cover all of the four Ps, your plan must address those omitted.

Product

If your franchise is nationally known, exposure of your products or services is largely your franchisor's responsibility. However, for a lesser-known franchise or for your local marketing, you can include information in your marketing programs and advertising that portrays your products or services and sends the message of how they benefit your customers.

Price

In addition to a listing of the sales prices of all your products or services and the benefits of the prices for your customers, you may want to examine other price considerations for inclusion in your marketing materials. How are the prices determined? How do they compare to the competition? What is your franchisor's pricing policies regarding discounts, new product items, and special pricing schedules for promotional programs? How do your franchisor's prices yield savings to the customer?

Place

For your marketing strategy, show any market research that supports your geographic market for your products and services. This involves studies of local consumer habits, local competitor demographics, and population figures — possibly already done by your franchisor. Note how your location is convenient for the customer in terms of having ease of access, egress, parking, a drive-through window, or other advantages.

Promotion

In addition to your franchisor's marketing, your promotions must make the consuming public aware of the benefits of your products or services. Even more important for you as the franchisee, you must make them aware of the benefits of your company and your location. When describing your franchisor's marketing plan, request your franchisor to supply any marketing findings that address the five Fs of customer wants. These are commonly taught in marketing classes to categorize the customers' needs for:

- Function. The needs of customers that are met as a result of their using your products or service.
- Finances. The price advantage, or savings, for the customer who buys your product or service over alternative choices.
- Freedom. The benefit of convenience your products or services yield to the customer, affording a savings of time and effort.
- Feelings. The enhanced self-image or pleasure your product or service provides the customer.
- Future. The benefit of future savings of time, effort, money, or some other benefit produced by buying your product or service now.

Franchisor Marketing Plan

It is the marketing plan of MegaBucks International to use all national media — national television, network radio, national magazines, professional real estate journals, and special large-scale syndicated public events — to advertise and strengthen the development of its name recognition. MBI coordinates and implements its marketing plan and advertising aggressively with great style. Since all franchises pay a 2% advertising royalty and because any unused portion must

Describe your franchisor's marketing plan.

continued

Franchisor Marketing Plan (continued)

be returned to the franchisees, this fund is purposely planned and exactingly spent in its entirety for the benefit of the franchise system.

Franchised real estate offices in general provide special benefits to their customers that independent agencies can not. Typically they provide:

- better national warranty programs,
- national name recognition, and
- national advertising.

MegaBucks International offers all of these and more:

- specialization in commercial real estate,
- standardization in sales and escrow procedures,
- unmatched research via a comprehensive national company-owned database, and
- an incomparable relocation service.

These are provided in nearly a thousand offices spread throughout the United States (except for the extreme Northeast). Of the services listed, the relocation service is one that needs further explanation.

Simply put, a relocation service is a network system between franchised outlets wherein one office in one location will cooperatively work with another office in an entirely different location to affect a real estate transaction to occur at either location. If a couple is living in New York and is to move to San Francisco, a purchase in San Francisco can be arranged through the New York office in advance; or, if the same couple moves to San Francisco first, they can still work a sale on their New York property with assistance through the San Francisco office. MegaBucks International provides this complete relocation service for commercial offices and retail outlets, as well.

When customers lease or purchase through an MBI office, they are assured of quality and friendly service backed by an ethics code of the highest honor. In every transaction, agents are trained to make our clients aware of the full range of MBI services, the future benefits of using the database research, the relocation service, and most of all, that MBI will still be around, conveniently available and just as professional, when that client is ready to make his or her next transaction.

> Emphasize how it conveys the message to and benefits for customers.

Franchisee Marketing Plan

After describing your franchisor's marketing plan, you are ready to focus on your own marketing strategy. State how your marketing plan meets customer needs. List the marketing programs that you expect to use — drawn from those described in this chapter and from your own resources.

If you plan to use several mediums, show them in chart format with time schedules. Also note your objectives and the milestones you expect to achieve from each medium. In your descriptions, be specific and make your strategy clear to the reviewer. The following material will assist you in writing this segment.

Your Franchisee Marketing Strategy

To develop your marketing strategy, you have three questions to answer.

1. How much of the total marketing plan does your franchisor do?
2. How much of the total marketing plan do you need to do?
3. How much money is available in the budget to implement your marketing strategy?

These three questions are weighed against each other to get the maximum results from your marketing plan. The first one, your franchisor's marketing, is something your franchisor can easily answer.

Answer the third question next because it will provide the information necessary to develop your responses to the second question. The amount of money available in your budget is not limitless and can be exactly determined while developing your marketing plan.

As mentioned in Chapter 2, Variable Costs, it is common among most franchisors to collect two percent of gross sales for the central, or co-op, advertising fund. As suggested, contact your franchisor and other franchise owners to get an idea of what they spend, or check with your accountant to get an average of what similar businesses spend for local advertising.

In the example Franchise Business Forecast in Chapter 2, two percent is used for co-op advertising and two percent for local advertising — a total budget expense of four percent. For many businesses the need may be higher or lower. MegaBucks Smith and Associates, for example, separates their marketing expense from their advertising expense, resulting in budgeted amounts quite different from many franchises.

Also in the Franchise Business Forecast in Chapter 2, both the co-op advertising and the local advertising — shown as the last two entries under variable costs — are an exact percentage of gross sales every month. For your business, this may or may not be a valid example. Many businesses have a seasonal impact, as does MegaBucks. It may be more accurate for your marketing plan to use ten percent of gross sales for some months, six percent for others, and 14 percent for others, with the total of all months averaging to the annual target of ten percent. This is often adjusted by quarter rather than by month, but monthly adjustments are common due to special holidays and seasonal events with a monthly influence.

Once you know your budget, your marketing plan can reflect where you expect to spend the funds. Then you can also see how much you need to do to implement your marketing plan — the answer to the second question.

Begin with an examination of the marketing portion of your overall marketing plan. How much do you need to contribute in making your customers aware of your products or services? It may be very little, if your franchisor has major marketing campaigns. How much of the message do you need to convey to your customers about your products or services? Is your main requirement merely to send the message about your company and your location? How much of that message do you need to reinforce? Does most of the budget need to be used to acquire actual sales?

Once you have answered these questions, you will know how much of the total marketing plan you will need to develop. Then you can finish your marketing plan, filling in the four Ps and the five Fs you need to emphasize to your customers for your specific company and location.

As you complete your marketing plan strategy, keep in mind your customer profiles while considering the marketing programs and media to choose. Here are the most commonly used — some may apply to you and others may not.

- Advertising gifts, such as caps, notebooks, and calendars
- Billboards and signs
- Broadcast media advertising, such as television and radio
- Brochures and flyers
- Cultural and special events programs
- Direct mail
- Free product samples
- Internet web sites
- Point-of-purchase displays
- Print media advertising, including newspapers, magazines, business and trade publications, and the Yellow Pages
- Public speaking
- Rental display cases
- Sales programs and promotional sales
- Trade shows

Even if all of the above apply to your products or services, the target market, the message, and the budget are the three considerations that dictate the priorities of your choices.

Because media advertising represents a large portion of most franchisee's marketing plans, it is only prudent to take a closer look at this. For effective exposure through media advertising, your ads must fit the customer profile, must cover several types of media to reach the market, and must repeat themselves. At one time, marketing consultants advised that it took three ads before the consumer noticed a product or company; today, this estimate has increased from five to nine exposures to assure customer recognition.

Planning an ad to fit your customer profile is a matter of using your market analysis to match up your target markets with a media source that reaches them most effectively. Therefore, you will want to survey which media serves your customer profile best and, in some cases, at which times. For example, if your consumer demographics reveal your target market is primarily male, age 35 to 44, you might find it desirable to advertise your particular product or service on local television during baseball or football games. Your research can give you other examples, such as, while more men than women read newspapers, women read newspaper ads more often than men. More stay-at-home parents listen to FM radio stations in late morning hours, while more white-collar businesspeople listen to news stations during morning commute hours.

Television and Radio

It should come as no surprise that television and radio are the most costly media. National television and radio ads are reserved for promoting or sustaining name recognition for the franchise system. These are not used for targeting specific or local markets. Held in reserve for your franchisor, here is the place for the two percent central or co-op advertising fund.

Local television and radio are another matter. While still expensive, these local media can be very strong advertising forums for franchisee businesses. Ask local cable TV and radio stations for their demographics. Use guaranteed time slots matched to the demographics for the correct times for your business. These are a little more expensive than the volume advertising plans that sell a quantity of spots per month in the best-time-available-slots plan. By using guaranteed time slots, you get much better exposure to your consumer demographics and, consequently, a more efficient return in the end.

Magazines

Similar to national television and radio, national magazines serve better for franchisor ads in promoting the franchise name and your products or services in general; however, regional magazines are a medium to consider. Reader demographics are available from most magazines, so you can match those with your buyers to find which publications best suit your market. Magazines are expensive compared to newspapers, but they offer much better print reproduction and much longer relative exposure life.

A disadvantage for most monthly magazines is the long lead time needed to place an ad before it actually appears in print. For weekly magazines, this is typically much shorter.

If you are considering regional magazines in your marketing plan, weigh the demographics of your consumers with those of special interest magazines as well as with those of general interest magazines. You may find a publication that stands out exceptionally well as being read by a large market segment of your consumers.

Business and Trade Publications

There are, also, several national publications with regional editions, such as *The Wall Street Journal.* Depending on your customer base, business and trade publications can be excellent places to advertise for commercial customers, both businesses and institutions. Magazine advertising is more expensive than newspapers; however, national and regional publications also have relatively longer exposure lives. If the journals are of newspaper-type paper quality, there is no reproduction advantage; on the other hand, if they use slick paper with a quality finish, ads can have photographic reproduction as stunning as that which is found in regular magazines. These are considerations to weigh. Again, research the demographics of these publications and match them to your commercial, business, and institutional customers.

Newspapers

The main advantage of newspaper advertising is the ability to reach specific targeted markets with minimum lead time. The disadvantages are short-exposure life and poorer quality reproduction, usually black and white only, although more color is available today than in the past. Newspaper advertising can be expensive in some communities where one paper dominates circulation.

Direct Mail

Depending on the nature of your products or services, some business and trade publications can supply mailing lists of prospective consumers in your territory. These can be especially effective for acquiring new customers through direct mail promotions. If your business has a system for recording addresses of previous customers, direct mail is a viable medium for attracting repeat and referral business. Remember that direct mail works better the more personalized it is; the more it resembles form letters or junk mail, the more likely it is to be discarded.

Yellow Pages

The Yellow Pages of your local telephone book can be the best source of local advertising for the cost, exposure life, and effectiveness, depending on your type of business. One or more copies of the Yellow Pages reach every home and office that has a telephone, and stays there a full year. If your franchisor doesn't have readily available ad designs, solicit the help of a good ad designer, use bold or thick borders and color ink if these touches are not in conflict with your franchise's advertising restrictions and design criteria. Purchase as large an ad as you can afford if your product, service, and business are ones that stand any chance of customers resorting to the Yellow Pages to find your products or service or your location.

Cultural and Special Events

Popular once again among cultural and special events are the short ads run at your local movie theater. Here again always consider your customer demographics. If your consumers are mainly middle-aged and conservative, you do not want to run a local video ad with "The Rocky Horror Picture

Show." On the other hand, the true story, "Sarah Winchester, Lady of Mystery," might be a safe bet.

Besides movies, watch for any special event that may have an audience that fits your customer demographics profile. Look for music, drama, and sporting events at the high school, junior college, college, university, and the semipro and professional levels. You may have access to municipal events, rodeos, concerts in the park, ice shows, operas, ballets, plays, circuses, special events at the zoo, trade shows, races, and automobile and boat shows. When these reach your consumer, the ads have a strong promotional effect that suggests your business is in the know or in the swing of things.

Billboards and Signs

If billboards are effective for your type of business and can reach the targeted market, they can be very effective. Many realtors, especially franchised realtors, say that all types of signs are their number one advertising media, far outpacing newspapers and publications.

Nearly every business needs and uses a business sign for identification of its location for local traffic. Also, if your business has commercial vehicles, a very effective use of signage is a business sign or decal on the sides or rear of a vehicle or both. One vehicle can provide a great deal of exposure while driving around town during a typical day as a delivery, courier, or shuttle vehicle.

The Internet

Because most franchisors have a web site or home page on the Internet that directs viewers to local franchisee locations, it is most likely that you do not need to have your own specific advertising spot in this medium. However, give it some thought when formulating your marketing plan. Your particular business may benefit from one, especially if you have products purchased by mail order.

Franchisee Marketing Plan

Because MegaBucks International supports us with national advertising, which delivers the name recognition and defines our services, it is our role to deliver our message to the customer: that we are locally present, centrally located with convenient access and parking, and have a capable, friendly staff. To do this, we have planned a "pre-opening" for people in industry-related businesses and leaders in the local community. This is to be followed by a large public grand opening. Besides the usual direct-mail invitations, we have budgeted spots on local cable television and radio, ads in two regional magazines and the local newspaper, and additional special purpose flyers to be distributed in local businesses and some by direct-mailing.

For our product — real estate leases, listings, and sales — our advertising mainstays are newspaper, signs, and the Multiple Listing Service (MLS). These are scheduled throughout the year with heavier emphasis placed on those months corresponding to our peak season of real estate on the Big Island — October through April. Similarly, we are going to support these same months with local television and radio spots, repeating the message that we are here and showing a leader listing or two in each ad.

While we have an in-house professional Marketing Director, we still plan to use the services of an advertising agency to kick off our marketing campaign, and a graphic design consultant for the printed materials, magazine, newspaper, and Yellow Pages' ads. Television, radio, and magazine ads are selected both by our in-house Marketing Director and by the advertising agency to best match our customer profile — for television and radio, by channel or station and time slots.

Our message through these media is that if we represent you as our client, we will take care of everything, from negotiating, through coordinating your lender, escrow and title company services, and hand delivering all the paperwork affiliated with the transaction, to closing the deal. Our slogan will be "we take care of everything, all you have to do is sign."

Besides membership in the MLS, we are members of the National Board of Realtors and Hawaii County Board of Realtors.

In addition to regularly planned sales promotions (see Sales Force), we will have an annual Christmas party, a Fourth of July party, and an annual promotional auction in October. While these auctions are local, they are national MegaBucks' sponsored functions, with donated prizes from local businesses, to be sold with MegaBucks coupons that are then matched with real cash by MegaBucks International, to be distributed to designated charities. Held all over the country in October, the auctions draw national and local attention alike. For another direct-mail function, our comprehensive MegaBucks' database will be used for relocation service, leads, repeat and referral customers. We send out holiday, birthday, and "anniversary of sale" cards to every client and, for those to whom it applies, every perspective client.

Describe the areas needed to supplement your franchisor's plan: the message to your customers.

Describe the marketing programs with objectives that you plan to implement. List the milestones you expect to achieve.

Marketing Budget and Advertising Plan

For the next segment, compile a special budget that schedules and allocates the costs of your marketing programs and your media choices for a calendar year. This is called a marketing plan budget, or marketing budget, and covers costs for all marketing programs including special sales programs, promotional sales, brochures, advertising gifts, free samples, trade shows, and advertising media. If, in addition to a marketing budget, a separate media advertising budget is presented in a marketing plan, it is called an advertising plan. Notice the monthly (seasonal) adjustments in the MegaBucks example.

In many cases, although your franchisor controls the central advertising fund, the franchisor may still advise you as to how and where to spend your local advertising to get the most impact. If this is the case, take your franchisor's lead and avoid trying to reinvent the wheel. If your franchisor is not involved in your local marketing, then the decisions are yours about how and where to spend the budget. In the MegaBucks advertising plan, $10,028 is used for the advertising portion of their marketing plan.

Prepare a yearly marketing budget that allocates marketing programs and advertising media expenditures. Also provide an advertising plan.

Marketing Budget

Months	Ad Agencies	Graphic Design	Printed Materials	Advertising Plan	Direct Mail	Signs	Member-ships	Enter-tainment		
January	$1,000	$ 500	$ 250	$ 1,618	$ 600	$ 200	$ 500	$ 220		
February	0	0	0	1,618	300	200	80	220		
March	0	0	0	1,318	300	200	80	220		
April	0	0	250	518	120	200	80	100		
May	0	0	0	110	120	200	80	100		
June	0	0	0	110	120	200	80	100		
July	0	0	250	410	120	200	80	100		
August	0	0	0	110	120	200	80	100		
September	0	300	0	218	300	200	80	100		
October	0	0	250	1,498	300	200	80	220		
November	0	0	0	1,198	300	200	80	220		
December	0	200	0	1,302	600	200	80	220		
Totals	$1,000	$1,000	$1,000	$10,028	$3,300	$2,400	$1,380	$1,920	=	$22,028

Advertising Plan

Media	Local Television[1]	Local Radio[2]	Regional Magazines	News-paper[3]	Yellow Pages[4]	Special Events
January	$ 480	$ 218	$120	$ 500	$ 0	$ 300
February	480	218	120	500	300	0
March	480	218	120	500	0	0
April	0	108	0	110	0	300
May	0	0	0	110	0	0
June	0	0	0	110	0	0
July	0	0	0	110	0	300
August	0	0	0	110	0	0
September	0	108	0	110	0	0
October	480	218	0	500	0	300
November	480	218	0	500	0	0
December	480	322	0	500	0	0
Totals	$2,880	$1,628	$360	$3,660	$300	$1,200 = $10,028

Schedules: 1. Daytime cable network.
2. Guaranteed designated spots.
3. Weekends only.
4. A portion of Yellow Pages advertising is paid by MegaBucks International.

Sales Force and Forecast

In this segment of your marketing plan, if your franchise requires a sales force, detail a sales strategy with sales promotion campaigns. If costs include compensation for bonuses, special catering, or party and entertainment costs, indicate these. For major programs, provide a description with a schedule and objectives. This should also indicate if these are special discount sales or promotional campaigns. Other promotional sales are price-leaders, such as products or services with very little markup intended to lure new customers, limited low-priced offers, or special free gifts with purchases to boost low sales periods.

Describe the organization of your sales staff and designate a manager or director and detail his or her responsibilities. Also describe the staff's compensation. If sales are by commission, indicate the structure with overrides for managers if applicable. As part of the organization, indicate the training, motivational techniques, and sales meeting frequency. Explain your policy for following up leads and for repeat and referral customers — internal forms for tracking these can be included in the business plan exhibits.

To go along with the description of your sales promotions, create a model sales forecast explaining assumptions and emphasizing important points. Both monthly and annual forecast charts should accompany these programs.

Sales Force and Forecast

Our sales force consists of a General Sales Manager, Steve Swan, who also doubles as Operations Director since the function of our operations is providing a service of sales, leases, and listings. He is assisted by our Marketing Director, Mark McKinsey. Directly under Steve, is our Commercial Sales Manager, Barry O'Brien; the Relocation Director, Paulette Sia; and three Assistant Sales Managers, Marcia Clay, Judy George, and David Wong (also our leasing specialist). The Marketing Director is salaried, while the Sales Manager/Operations Director receives a base salary and overrides on commissions from sales of his staff. The rest are on straight commission — assistant managers have a 65/35 split.

Describe your sales organization showing roles, responsibilities and compensations.

Our sales strategy is to provide the best service possible, selling the customer on the MegaBucks franchise, our specific company and our agents, under the philosophy that the current sale is not as important as future repeat and referral transactions that can come from a happy client.

Write your policy for following up leads, repeat, and referral customers.

Sales meetings are once a week and consist of two types on an ongoing basis: sales training meetings and sales contests. Regardless of the specific subject of a meeting, one of the common objectives is to review the sales forecast and the current progress made. During meetings, agents' successes are updated on a board, and awards are given for the "salesman of the month". Each month, the Sales Manager incorporates a special promotion with incentives to stimulate sales, listings, and leases in one of these general sales meetings. We have four quarterly events for special sales promotions outlining new, special objectives for the quarter, and offering an incentive to the top producer. These functions are either catered, or free breakfast or lunch events.

Write a sales strategy with sales promotional campaigns.

Describe training and motivational techniques and frequency of sales meetings.

Weekly incentives are small-ticket items, such as a free tank of gas and a car wash, free portable "open house" signs, free postage for a volume mailing, or gift certificates for items such as dry cleaning, professional copies, or a restaurant lunch for two. Monthly incentives include small bonuses, dinners for four for fine dining, one night at a local resort, and other things in this genre. Quarterly incentives include free trips and large-ticket items.

Provide a schedule with special objectives for major programs.

Sales training consists of listening to motivational tapes, review of agents' methods of following up leads, repeat and referral customers, and accessing information from our office database as well as those of MLS and MegaBucks International. Top sales staff

continued

Sales Force and Forecast (continued)

share their experience with junior members, and all sales people are encouraged to enlighten others with newfound knowledge on techniques, problem solving, and strategy. Sales meetings, whether training or contests, are the places to reinforce company policies and MegaBucks' philosophy of an excellent relocation service and sales via professional, honorable, personable, and attentive attitudes.

Display a sales forecast.

Sales Forecast

Month	Units Leases	Lease w/o Residuals	Units Listings	Listing Net Income	Units Sales	Sales Net Income	Total Sales	Costs of Sales	Gross Profit
January	5	1,700	3	30,000	3	42,000	73,700	54,649	19,051
February	5	1,600	3	30,000	3	42,000	73,600	54,574	19,026
March	5	1,500	3	30,000	3	42,000	73,500	54,500	19,000
April	5	1,400	2	20,000	2	28,000	49,400	36,630	12,770
May	5	1,300	2	20,000	2	28,000	49,300	36,556	12,744
June	5	1,200	2	20,000	2	28,000	49,200	36,482	12,718
July	5	1,100	3	30,000	3	42,000	73,100	54,204	18,896
August	5	1,000	3	30,000	3	42,000	73,000	54,130	18,871
September	5	900	4	40,000	4	56,000	96,900	71,851	25,049
October	5	800	5	50,000	5	70,000	120,800	89,573	31,227
November	5	700	6	60,000	6	84,000	144,700	107,295	37,405
December	5	600	6	60,000	6	84,000	144,600	107,221	37,379
Subtotals	60	13,800	42	420,000	42	588,000	1,021,800	757,665	264,135

Revise Your Marketing Summary

Finally, remember to return to your marketing summary and write or rewrite your draft to discuss and highlight all the data and essential information you have discovered.

Having read about your business, your franchise, your market, and your marketing plan, the reviewers will want to know whether you are capable of executing your marketing plan. Their attention is next focused on your management qualifications and your organizational structure, which is covered in Chapter 8.

Management Qualifications

Management by objectives works if you know the objectives.
— PETER DRUCKER

The purpose of this section of the business plan is to instill confidence in the reviewer that your business is well-founded and rock solid with an experienced, capable, and hard-working management staff leading the way. Three areas need to be addressed: your operations framework or organizational structure, the experience of the individuals of your management team, and your franchisor's management structure and experience.

Your management qualifications section should include each of the following subsections.

- A management summary
- Your organizational structure
- Your management team
- A personnel plan
- The franchisor's management experience, key statistics, and field support services

Management Summary

As with most of the previous sections, the management qualifications section begins with a summary. Once again, write this paragraph after the balance of this section is completed, so you can present the analysis of your findings and emphasize the important features.

Management Summary

Our president and CEO is Denver Smith, R, CCIM, a multiple-award-winning salesman and previous general sales manager with over twenty-five years in real estate. Under him are three managers: Office, Marketing, and General Sales. Under the General Sales Manager/ Operations Director are the Relocation Director and Commercial Sales Manager. These are assisted by three assistant managers with separate departmental functions: commercial leasing, office sales and retail sales. Four of our managers have been number one in sales and listings in other offices before coming here with thirty-three years of combined experience as "top producers." The overall real estate experience of the entire staff is 140+ years. As to education, our Marketing Manager holds an MBA in marketing in addition to his real estate success, and six of eight of our other managers have a minimum of a bachelor's degree in college. Their specific qualifications and responsibilities are further detailed in this section.

Our personnel plan shows ten employees at this time: four salaried, one with salary-base plus commissions' overrides, and five — on straight commission. We intend to increase our employees to eighteen before the end of the first year adding seven more salespeople, and an escrow coordinator.

As part of our management team, we are reviewed regularly by our very capable MBI Regional Director and field representatives, and meet with Region on a monthly basis. MBI's assurance of our quality management is controlled through MBI's data processing, field efficiency inspections, quarterly audits, monthly reports, quarterly reviews, ongoing training — via conferences, seminars, and newsletters — and through corporate incentives, such as contests and awards.

Summarize your organizational structure, management team, personnel plan, and the supporting management components of your franchisor.

Organizational Structure

A description of your organizational structure follows your management summary. This is a complete picture of the employees in your business. To go along with the text, provide a complete a personnel list, in ranking order, with positions and job descriptions. If you have not hired all your employees, list the positions and job descriptions noting they will be hired after you obtain funding. Also add the names of other owners and shareholders.

Organizational Structure

At start of business, the organization of MegaBucks Smith and Associates consists of the following structure: At the top is our president and CEO, Denver Smith. Directly under him are: our Office Manager, Lisa Soma; our Marketing Manager, Mark McKinsey; and our General Sales Manager/Operations Director, Steve Swan. In the office, we also have a secretary/receptionist, Deborah Smith. Immediately under Steve is our Relocation Director, Paulette Sia, and the Commercial Sales Manager, Barry O'Brien. Barry is responsible for three assistant managers: Office Sales, Marcia Clay; Retail Sales, Judy George; and Commercial Leasing, David Wong.

By the end of the year, we expect to be operating at full strength, with seven more sales agents and an escrow coordinator. Within the second year, we expect to promote our Office Manager to Controller and add another bookkeeper.

List of Startup Employees

Name	Title
Denver Smith	President/CEO/Sole Proprietor
Lisa Soma	Office Manager
Deborah Smith	Secretary/Receptionist
Mark McKinsey	Marketing Manager
Steven Swan	General Sales Manager/Operations Director
Paulette Sia	Relocation Director
Barry O'Brien	Commercial Sales Manager
Marcia Clay	Office Sales
Judy George	Retail Sales
David Wong	Commercial Leasing

> Describe your organizational structure with names and titles or functions.

> Also provide an organizational chart.

In addition to the personnel list, create a diagram, called an organizational chart, that depicts your management personnel, your consultants, and employees by function to show your operation at peak performance. This chart displays employees' vertical and lateral relationships to one another. Even if you have assembled only part of your team at the time of your writing, fill in those you expect to have when up and going.

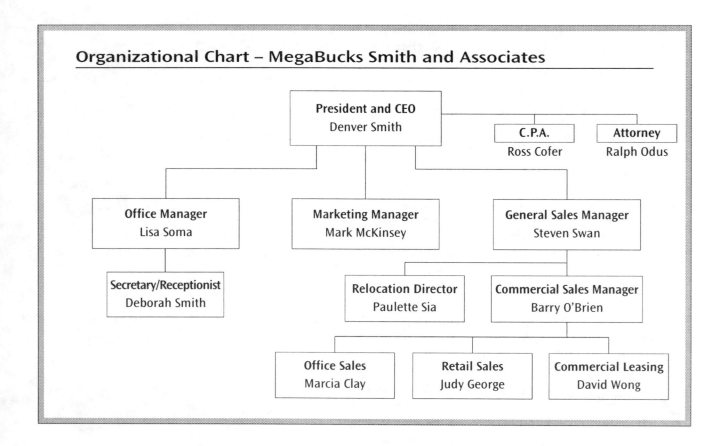

Management Team

To show investors you have assembled a solid management team, you can present information about the two basic sources of personnel you have at your disposal. The first source is your own business staff, that of your outlet. If it is only you, you are limited to discussing your own qualifications, although you can make the most of it by deftly marketing your education, experience, traits, talent, and capabilities to your best advantage. If this is the case, then it is appropriate to include your full personal résumé in this section rather than in the exhibits. A detailed format for a personal résumé, which is different than a traditional résumé to obtain employment, is discussed in Chapter 11.

If your business is large enough to include other management staff, all the better. When you present these team members in their designated roles and market their qualifications, you show more confidently that you have a strong and diverse management team. If your management team is very small, then add your business consultant team — your independent certified public accountant and attorney — however, accurately depict them as consultants, not employees.

The second source is established, successful, and ready to help you get your business off to a good start, as soon as you sign your franchise agreement. In effect, the franchise organization is part of your management team. As an 'assistant manager,' it is available to consult and advise you — to lend it's assistance and expertise at your beck and call. However, since this team is not under your direct control and, in many ways, is not as important to the plan's reviewer as are you and your management staff, it's information is inserted after your first team.

The director, or manager, roles which most financiers and business plan reviewers expect to see are the chief executive officer (CEO), chief financial officer (CFO), director of operations, and the director of sales and marketing. Depending on your franchise, other key personnel can be added or substituted. One pivotal manager in many franchises is the production manager. Other franchises have specialty positions such as an escrow coordinator or relocation director.

Management Team

Manager	Name
President, Chief Executive Officer	Denver Smith
Marketing Manager	Mark McKinsey
General Sales Manager/Operations Director	Steven Swan
Commercial Sales Manager	Barry O'Brien
Office Manager	Lisa Soma

While complete résumés for all five of these key managers are included in the exhibits (see Exhibits, "Management Qualifications"), summary résumés are included here for the reviewer's cursory perusal.

President/CEO

Denver Smith has over ten years experience as a licensed real estate broker with twenty-five years of experience in the industry. He is the winner of the coveted MegaBucks *Numero Uno* award, for the state of Hawaii, eighteen times in twenty-three years and has successfully reached sales averaging $9,000,000 annually for the last three years. Mr. Smith has a bachelor's degree in business from the University of Missouri and has successfully completed his CCIM and other post graduate courses from the University of the Pacific and the University of California. He is married, with two children, and just recently moved to Kailua-Kona to start our MegaBucks franchise.

continued (on page 107)

Identify your own management staff: include yourself and your managers.

Provide a brief summary of the qualifications of each member of your management staff.

Provide key personnel full business-plan résumés in the Exhibits.

In addition to listing these officers and describing their roles, it is much more interesting and convincing to the reviewer if you provide summary résumés to establish their roles in your business. A summary résumé is only one or two paragraphs, as in the MegaBucks examples. Full résumés should be included in the exhibit section as discussed in Chapter 11.

Chief Financial Officer

For this position, CFO, defer to your franchisor. What person at the franchise level is chief financial officer or who will be overseeing your records and can be listed as the CFO of your business? List this person by full name and consult the UFOC, item two for his or her qualifications, education, and background. If a full résumé is available in the UFOC, use it in an edited or summarized version. If it is not, get responses by telephone and construct the résumé similar to yours but briefer. After the name, give the title as "Chief Financial Officer for [your franchise name]," to clearly indicate that this person is at the franchisor level. An advantage of franchising is that you can list this person — with his or her strong credentials — as a member of your team.

If you have an in-house accountant, another option is to list this person with his or her qualifications as your CFO. If you have an internal bookkeeper, you can list this person as controller or office manager in addition to your franchisor's CFO; and indicate that all financial inquiries should be directed to your controller for an expedient response. If you are going to list a controller, use a summary résumé of only one paragraph, or two at the most, instead of a full résumé as in the example.

Director of Operations

For director of operations, you have several choices. You may:

- Have one in your own outlet,
- Give yourself this title in addition to CEO,
- Assign the title to an existing manager or employee without fully assigning all the duties associated with the position, or
- Borrow again from your franchisor's repertoire of directors.

In any event, it is better to have one than not. Include a business plan résumé or a summary résumé, or both, depending upon the importance of the position to your operation. If you opt for your franchisor's director of operations, refer to item two of the UFOC and, again, make it clear that this person is an employee of the franchisor.

Sales and Marketing Director

For your sales and marketing director, it is best to identify a person from your own business, either an employee or you. If you elect to list one from your franchisor, do not use the franchisor's sales and marketing director who is responsible for selling franchises; select the director who is in charge of sales and marketing of the products or services. If it is not clear who this person is among your franchisor's directors and managers, use the director of the advertising fund or the person responsible for marketing research to help promote sales for the products or services for the franchisees. If this person is not listed in item two of the UFOC, find out who he or she is and get the necessary background to put together a summary résumé in your business plan. If you assign a franchisor member, make it clear this person is the franchise director or manager.

Anytime you use corporate employees, do not just photocopy their résumés from the UFOC or other franchisor materials. Instead, reprint them in the same style and format as your résumé, or as summary résumés, so that they fit seamlessly into your business plan. The understanding you are trying to convey is that they are a part of your team. You chose the franchisor, so in effect you chose them; you want to make this clear to the reviewer.

Management Team (continued)

Marketing Manager

Mark McKinsey holds an MBA in marketing from California State University at Stanislaus and has fourteen years experience in real estate sales and marketing. For the last three years, Mark has been the top producer in commercial units sold in the California-Nevada region for Delta Commercial Real Estate in San Francisco. Besides marketing, Mark serves several secondary functions, one is that of "sales closer." He is one of our two best "closers." He is married and has two children; the McKinseys just recently moved to Kailua-Kona.

General Sales Manager/Operations Director

Steven Swan comes to us from our independent competitor, Johnson Real Estate, where he was also their top producer for the last five out of six years in commercial real estate. Since the franchise system is new to Steve, he accompanied Denver Smith to Kansas City and attended the two-week training course for new franchisees at MBI. Steve is married, has four children, and has lived in Kailua-Kona for eleven years. He has a bachelor's degree in education.

Commercial Sales Manager

Barry O'Brien comes to us from another competitor, Greater Homes Conway, where he was top producer for the last five years in all sales, with many commercial transactions. Barry is also very experienced in leasing and will have no problem supervising our assistant manager in charge of leasing. Barry holds a bachelor's degree in business from the University of Hawaii. He has lived in Kailua-Kona all his life of thirty-one years. Barry is married and has three children.

Office Manager

Lisa Soma comes to us with Mark McKinsey from Delta Commercial Real Estate in the downtown San Francisco office, where she has been office manager for the last sixteen years. Lisa has a bachelor's in business accounting and has taken numerous continuing classes and advanced computer courses. She is married; her husband is a physician who has relocated with her to "paradise."

Provide summary descriptions of your management staff: include yourself, your managers.

Provide key personnel résumés in the Exhibits.

Responsibilities and Duties

President: is overall in charge of administration, income and expense, marketing, sales and closings, and making a profit. The president directly supervises the Office Manager, the Marketing Manager, and the General Sales Manager/Operations Director. He is still indirectly in charge of, and has the final say in, all matters of recruiting, hiring, and training. As the Broker-in-Charge, the president must supervise and sign every transaction.

Marketing Manager: serves several functions in our organization. First, in his primary role, he is in charge of marketing: overall supervision and coordination of the marketing plan, the marketing budget and advertising plan. He is directly responsible for placing all ads and implementing all promotions comparing media types and times with our customer profile, and monitoring costs. With the general sales manager, the Marketing Manager takes the lead in designing all incentive programs. In his secondary role, our Marketing Manager is also financing and closing officer. As to financing, he assists agents and clients in finding financing needed to close a transaction, but as one of two closing officers, he assists agents in soliciting signatures from clients to "close" the sale.

General Sales Manager/Operations Director: directly supervises the Commercial Sales Manager and the Relocation Director. He is also the primary manager directly responsible for conducting sales meetings and training. One of his major functions is recruiting and hiring new sales agents — our big goal is to find seven new ones this year. Indirectly he is responsible for all sales and the supervision of all agents and their transactions. As top Sales Manager he coordinates with the Marketing Manager in brainstorming and implementing incentive programs. While he is allowed to sell directly, he is the number one closing officer, and oversees the closing of sales for all agents along with the Marketing Manager. As Operations Director, he is in charge of all operations of sales, listings, and leases — our products.

Commercial Sales Manager: is in charge of commercial sales on a lower echelon from the General Sales Manager. The Commercial Sales Manager is directly responsible for the sales performances of three agents in charge of departmental sales: office sales, retail sales, and leasing. He is also the alternate for conducting sales meetings and fulfills this role about one-third of the time. While he also sells directly, he oversees the agents' transactions and checks their paperwork for contract accuracy. Although he is not in charge of recruiting, hiring and training, his consideration in such matters is highly regarded.

Office Manager: is in charge of all accounting reports and all accounting activities: makes payroll, pays MBI Regional, keeps the general ledger, and so forth. As the company grows, this position will be divided into Controller/Office Manager in charge of supervision of in-house

continued

Responsibilities and Duties (continued)

bookkeeper(s). One of this manager's secondary functions is to monitor the computer software and assist the Relocation Director in database updating and reporting, and train agents in computer use and accessing information. This is an important function for the success of our operation — the agents' ability to input and access data to follow-up on clients, new leads, and repeat and referral prospects.

Besides résumés of each of the principals in your business, include a personal financial statement for each of the would-be guarantors of loans. Also, include the two most recent years' income tax returns of your principals and guarantors. These documents can be appended here but are better located in the exhibits at the end of your business plan.

Business Consultants

Finally, following your management team, add summary résumés of your business attorney and business accountant. Cover their educational and significant occupational experience. If it is appropriate and they agree to it, obtain their permission to list them as members of the board of directors of your company.

Personnel Plan

Now that you have introduced all of your staff, by way of the organizational structure, and your management team, write a short paragraph about the number of your employees specifying numbers of both part- and full-time employees at the beginning of operations and the numbers you project to have when you reach peak operational performance. Along with this information include your personnel plan, which is basically a chart of the departments by employee, function, and salary, as in the MegaBucks example. For salaries, use gross amounts including benefits.

Personnel Plan

At start of business, we have ten full-time employees. By the end of the year we anticipate having eighteen as can be seen on the Personnel Plan detailed below.

continued

Describe the number of part- and full-time employees at opening and the projected increase at peak operation.

Personnel Plan (continued)

MegaBucks $mith and Associates

Personnel Plan

	First Year	Second Year
Administration:		
President (CEO)	$ 24,000[1]	$ 80,000
Office Manager	30,000	
Office Manager/Controller (CFO)		48,000
Secretary/Receptionist	24,000	26,400
Sales and Marketing:		
Marketing Manager	$ 50,000	Commission
General Sales Manager/Operations Director[2]	12,000	14,400
Commercial Sales	Commission	Commission
Salesperson	Commission	Commission
Salesperson	Commission	Commission
Salesperson	Commission	Commission
Salesperson		Commission
Salesperson		Commission
Salesperson		Commission
Salesperson		Commission
Salesperson		Commission
Salesperson		Commission
Other:		
Escrow Coordinator		Overrides
Lease Coordinator		Overrides
Relocation Director	Commission	Commission
Total Personnel	10	18
Total Payroll	$140,000	$168,800
Payroll Burden	$ 22,400	$ 27,008

1. Base draw, receives special commissions plus profit of the company.
2. Operations Director receives Base Salary plus Overrides on Commissions.

Show a table of your personnel plan with roles and salaries for the first and second years.

Franchisor Management Experience

In a franchise business plan, an integral part of your management qualifications is this segment on franchisor experience. It separates the franchise business plan from the standard format of a nonfranchised business more than any other section. While there is much detail needed for this portion on your franchisor, fortunately nearly everything is readily available to you through the UFOC and the nonprotected resources your franchisor has supplied to you. Because all franchises have somewhat different materials, it is generally much easier to glean all of the specifics that can't be found in the disclosure document from a published source book on franchises, such as *Bond's Franchise Guide* or *The Franchise Redbook* due to be published by The Oasis Press in the fall of 1999.

The purpose of the franchisor information is similar to the segment on your management team's experience information. It should portray a stable corporate structure to convince the reviewer your franchisor management is strong and sound.

Management Team of Your Franchisor

For your franchisor's management team, return to the UFOC, item two. List the positions and names of the directors and officers you have not used for your own team. In addition, include three or four of the most pertinent résumés in the exhibits section — reformatted to match the others in your business plan.

Franchisor's Basic Information

The basic information, or salient data, of a franchisor, as part of its corporate structure, provides the answers to who it is, where it's located, a succinct description of the nature of its business, and how it can be reached. The information should include the following:

- Correct corporate name
- Address
- Very brief description of its product or service
- Telephone number
- Toll-free telephone number
- Fax number
- Internet or website address
- E-mail address

Franchisor Management Experience

The management team of MegaBucks International that is directly in our franchise chain of command is:

President and Chief Executive Officer – Donald R. Frump

Vice President and Director of Operations – L. Scott Creedy

Vice President and Director of Franchises – Lawrence P. Marshall

Chief Financial Officer – Tracy C. Godfrey

Vice President of Western Division – Fielding W. Winslow

Regional Director, Region Nine – George R. Collins

(For résumés of the above, see Exhibits, Management Qualifications.)

Franchisor Headquarters:

MegaBucks International, Inc.
1234 Walnut Street
Kansas City, Missouri 64110-2356

Franchisor of Real Estate Offices

(816) 622-3400
(800) MEGABUCKS
FAX: (816) 622-3401
Internet: http://www.MegaBucks.com
email: MegaBucks@aol.com

List four to six directors and officers that were not included in your management team.

Franchisor Key Statistics

Statistical data that can be used to compare one franchisor to another and can be presented in a table is helpful to a reviewer in assessing your franchise's strengths. Franchisor key statistics are easily-listed standard abbreviations used to make quick comparisons among franchisors in the same business or industry and are usually comprised of one word or two- or three-character abbreviations.

You want to present the statistics of your franchise to show a favorable picture as compared to others in your business, especially those that have a presence in your area. These statistics are readily available in most source books and will be especially easy to extract from *The Franchise Redbook*.

Chart the franchisor key statistics for both your franchise and your franchise's prominent competitors. You may want to show all the data or, for the best effect, only specific portions. If your franchise is in an industry with several other competitive franchises, such as pizza or fast food, just list the facts for three or four of your strongest franchise competitors. If your franchise is in an industry with only two or three other franchisors, your choices are clear.

Franchisor Key Statistics

	MegaBucks International	Centurian National	Greater Homes of America
Number of corporate employees	114	320	97
Start-up cost	$35–70K	$50–100K	$18–110K
Total investment	$100–150K	$25–100K	$18–110K
Franchise fee	$25K	$15–25K	Varies
Royalty	5%	6%	3–6%
Advertising royalty	2%*	2%	1%
Experience required	Y	Y	N
In business since	1964	1955	1976
Franchised since	1967	1958	1978
Number of franchised units:			
Last year	842	1,844	410
Two years ago	784	1,803	530
Three years ago	683	1,781	598
Number of company-owned units:			
Last year	123	0	0
Two years ago	101	0	3
Three years ago	176	0	5
Total units for the past three years:			
Last year	965	1,844	410
Two years ago	885	1,803	533
Three years ago	859	1,781	603
Projected new units	63	50	100
Concentration by regions	W,C,SW,NW	W,C	W,SE,NE
Registration (number of states)	48	50	50
Type of sites recommended	FB,SF,SC,OC,RM	FB,SF,SC	FB,O,SF,SC
Size of site required	1,200–3,000	2,000–3,000	2,000
Length of training time	8 Days HQ, 2 Days Reg.	40+ Hrs. HQ	4 Days HQ
Suggested for franchisees:			
Number of full-time employees	5–8	7–10	4
Number of part-time employees	0	2	0

Display a table of Franchisor Key Statistics.

Type of sites abbreviations:

FB – Free-standing Building

SF – Store Front

SC – Strip Center

OC – Office Complex

RM – Regional Mall

O – Other

* 2% Advertising: 1% national, 1% local.

Field Support Services

Some of the most important benefits franchisors provide for their franchisees are field support services. These services are intended to provide controls that increase the chance for success for both you and your franchisor. The most significant are:

Data Processing (DP)	Store or Grand Opening (O)
Central Purchasing (CP)	Inventory Control (IC)
Evaluation of Operations (EO)	Franchisor Conferences (FC)
On-site Training (ST)	Telephone Hotline (H)

List the services your franchisor provides and give a short description of the service. Accentuate those support services you regard as special safeguards for assuring the success of your franchise business. The increased chances of success provided by strong field support services can mitigate many concerns of a reviewer who must reconcile the risk factors of your business. Special training and the number and function of the field representatives are essential services the reviewer should know about also — at least, to the extent your franchise program allows.

Assuming you have landed your franchisor, you are probably already aware of these and thoroughly understand them, especially if you have already undergone training. If you are not familiar with them, investigate the field support services in detail with your franchisor to complete this information and to thoroughly understand your business-format franchise. Also, check your franchisor's Internet web page, and briefly describe it as part of the field support service.

Finally, compare the field support services your franchisor provides with those of the competitors you have mentioned before. Emphasize the differences that give your franchise an edge.

Field Support Services

MegaBucks International provides a full gamut of field support:

- **DP, Data Processing.** Upon the closing of every transaction, a CA (Commission Approval) request is forwarded to MBI Regional. This form is very extensive and tracks the type of advertising used, customer/consumer profile (whether repeat or referral), transaction accounting, and much more that we are not allowed to disclose without revealing "intellectual" material.

- **CP, Central Purchasing.** MBI provides, through a selection of approved vendors, the availability, volume pricing, and controlled

continued

List the field support services that your franchisor provides with a short explanation of each. Include special training, and field representative support.

Field Support Services (continued)

quality of many products: business cards, stationery, envelopes, labels, flyer-formats, apparel, signs, and much more. The franchisees retain the ability to shop the approved vendors for the best service and price. The best feature of MBI's central purchasing is the voluminous offerings of continuing training, educational courses, and motivational seminars that are coordinated by MBI and available on an ongoing basis almost everywhere in the country, especially frequent in the heaviest regions of concentrated outlets.

- **EO, Evaluation of Operations.** Our Regional Manager, assisted by field representatives, executes efficiency inspections. In addition, MBI provides extensive monthly evaluation reports, and quarterly audits accompanied by oral and written evaluation reports. These corporate people are available via the hotline to answer questions at all times.

- **ST, On-site Training.** Training is available for startups during the first month of business. For other ongoing training, see Central Purchasing above.

- **O, Grand Opening.** Our Regional Manager or one of his or her assistant field representatives is present on site for startup businesses.

- **FC, Franchise Conferences.** Regional conferences are scheduled monthly (not required) and one annual national conference is held in every region (required).

- **H, Telephone Hotline.** A 24-hour toll free number is available. If the monitoring operator cannot answer a question, a message is passed along to the appropriate MBI representative who will reply within one hour, usually immediately.

In addition to these, MBI publishes a monthly newsletter with management advice, training information, and general business tips.

Comparing the above field support services with our local franchised competitors:

Centurian National provides: Data Processing, extent not known; Evaluation of Operations, similar to ours but exclusively monitored by only one assigned field representative; no Site Training; Grand Opening assistance; Franchise Conferences, monthly regional (required), and two national, one on the east coast and one on the west coast (one required); and a toll-free Telephone Hotline.

Greater Homes of America provides: Evaluation of Operations, quarterly only; On-site Training, two days at startup on an as-needed basis; Grand Opening, as needed; Franchise Conferences, four district and one national; and a toll-free Telephone Hotline.

Compare your franchisor's field support services with those provided by competing franchisors in your territory.

Revise Your Management Summary

When you finish this section, remember to return to your management summary to make sure it covers the highlights discovered throughout this material. Next, you are ready for the heart of the business plan — the pro forma financial information.

Chapter 9

Financial Pro Formas

... the dreams of the future [are] better than the history of the past.
— PATRICK HENRY

From a reviewer's perspective, this section of your business plan is the most critical for assessing just how much dollars and sense your business makes. As a start-up franchisee, the financial material you include in this section deals only with predictions and projections of your expectations for the future of the business you are preparing to launch. In accounting, the Latin term *pro forma* identifies a financial projection presenting forecast, rather than current or past, data.

Even though these financials are forecasts, logical and real assumptions determine the numbers. These pro formas are comprised of several documents that are presented in the following three segments:

- Pro forma income statements
- Pro forma statement of cash flows
- Proforma balance sheets

Before you can develop the pro formas, however, you must identify the important assumptions you will use as the basis of your projections and create an assumptions chart and a break-even analysis to support the hypotheses of your pro formas. You worked on these in Chapter 2 in order to produce your One-year Franchise Business Forecast.

This section, like others, begins with a summary for the reviewer. The segments of this section for a start-up franchisee are:

- Financial summary
- Important assumptions
- Break-even analysis
- Pro forma income statement for one year and three or five years

- Pro forma statement of cash flows
- Pro forma balance sheets for one year and three or five years
- Business Ratios (as conclusions drawn from the financial pro formas)

For an ongoing business, of course, this forecast is based on past performance, previous and existing financial information, business trends, and expectations from the accounting results. Therefore, you need to include current and historical financial statements in this section. These generally consist of four additional documents:

- A summary income statement showing year-end figures for three or five years, or as much as you have;
- A current income statement;
- A current statement of cash flows; and
- A current balance sheet.

You introduce these documents immediately after the financial summary, prior to your assumptions.

Financial Summary

The first segment of the financial section of your business plan should begin with a brief summary of your financial plan. Just a few paragraphs will suffice and should briefly cover the following findings:

- Your key assumptions;
- Your break-even point;
- How well you expect to do overall in the first year;
- How fast you expect to grow, after you reach peak performance;
- What the peak performance is in terms of:
  — Revenue earned (sales),
  — Cost of revenue earned (cost of goods sold),
  — Operating expenses, and
  — Income (profit); and
- How well you expect to do, predicted for three or five years.

As with the other summaries, you can more effectively point out the highlights if you compile all your research and analyze it first, then write your summary.

Financial Summary

In the financial forecasts presented here, the single greatest key to reaching our projections relies upon our success in obtaining our market share of 29% in the North Kona district. Once accomplished, break-even will occur the seventh month of business and we will hit our target of $1,021,800 in net revenue earned by the end of the year. Since our staff has been planned top heavy for the first year to develop our company, it is no surprise that our profit will be minimal. Our main management objective is to add eight more sales personnel by year-end. This will create a large jump in sales, variable costs, and profit, which, at that time, the numbers become very viable as can be seen by the business ratios (see Return on Assets and Return on Equity). Peak performance will be in the third year when our staff is operating at full strength and the operating loan has been retired.

For our first year: gross sales – $14,597,143; net sales – $1,031,800; cost-of-sales – $757,665; operating expense – $227,175; and operating income – only $36,960; but everyone is fed and our machine is in action. Years two through five establish the results. For year five: our net sales climb to $1,893,682; cost-of-sales – $1,404,165; operating expense – $277,430; and operating income – $212,087. Throughout the next five years, the projections show that we can accomplish all of this with a reasonably sound cash flow and well-balanced Balance Sheets. The last segment on ratios supports this.

Summarize your financial plan, with key assumptions, break-even point, and a forecast for the first and three or five years.

Project sales, cost of goods sold, operating expense, and profit.

Important Assumptions

While assembling your financial forecasts in Chapter 2, you or your accountant made basic assumptions to estimate the predicted revenue and the fixed and variable costs for planning your One-year Franchise Business Forecast. These forecasts are always considered assumptions for predicted financial outcomes and do not necessarily become known factors until your business is up and running.

For this section on the financial pro formas, you need to re-develop your earlier financial material for more accuracy and to further expand it to include three or five year projections. This means revisiting your assumptions using information based on the research that you have discovered concerning your market. The assumptions that affect revenue might be the number of monthly sales or the percent of increase in monthly sales throughout the year. The assumptions that affect expenses could be the amount and interest rate of financing dictating the amount of the loan payment, certain costs that affect the cost of goods, the rent payment, the number of employees, the amount of payroll expense, and others.

One of the most important assumptions to show is your expected market share and to translate it into sales, in an attempt to fine tune your monthly revenue earned for the first year. Typical franchisee assumptions begin with average sales units and average gross sales dollars per month. Your study of the market should have revealed yearly increases which will help you develop your longer range, three or five year forecast of revenue earned. If you are making assumptions about seasonal impacts or trends and how they affect your monthly or yearly figures, these should be included for the reviewer, as well.

The table below gives a few of the generic assumptions to consider. Some of these may not apply to your franchise, while you may need to include others. You can see from the MegaBucks Smith and Associates example how specialized they can get.

Assumptions

	Year 1	Year 2	Year 3	Year 4	Year 5
Average unit sale					
Average monthly sales					
Fixed costs					
Variable costs (as percent of revenue)					
Market share					
Average unit cost					
Interest rate (short-term debt)					
Interest rate (long-term debt)					
Inventory turnover					
Payment days					
Collection days					
Expenses in cash (as a percentage)					
Sales on credit					
Personnel burden (as a percentage)					
Tax rate, as a percentage					

As you develop your financial pro formas, be sure to identify and write down the assumptions you are using. When you have finished, be sure all of the key assumptions you've used match your forecasts and are reflected in your list of assumptions.

Present your assumptions in this segment of your franchise business plan as a table introduced by an explanation of all the assumptions critical to your forecasts and those not easily portrayed in the table.

Important Assumptions

For the financial pro formas, we have made certain assumptions in our calculations, such that:

- We reach our share of 29% of the market in the North Kona district,
- Average sales units are 2,000 square feet,
- Average listing units are 2,000 square feet,
- Average leases are 1,000 square feet,
- Commercial commissions gross 7% on double-ended transactions,
- The majority of sales agents remain on a 65/35 split,
- The seasonal impact begins in October and lasts through most of March,
- Our requested operating loan is paid off in two years,
- Legal expense remains minimal (MegaBucks International provides most legal assistance as a franchisee service),
- Accounting expense drops dramatically when another bookkeeper is hired in the second year, and
- Seven new qualified sales agents and an escrow coordinator are recruited by the end of this year.

Introduce assumptions with a narrative explaining the most important ones to your forecasts.

Five-year Assumptions

	Year 1	Year 2	Year 3	Year 4	Year 5
Fixed costs	$227,175	$260,337	$265,889	$271,567	$277,430
Variable costs	74.15%	74.15%	74.15%	74.15%	74.15%
Average Gross Commission					
Listings: 2,000 sq. ft. at 2.5%	$10,000	$10,000	$10,500	$10,500	$11,000
Sales: 2,000 sq. ft. at 3.5%	$14,000	$14,000	$14,700	$14,700	$15,400
Average escrow	60 days	60 days	60 days	60 days	60 days
Personnel Burden	16%	16%	16%	16%	16%
G.E. Tax Rate	4%	4%	4%	4%	4%

Use a table to detail each assumption, for every year of your forecast.

Break-even Analysis

After the assumptions, return to the work you completed in Chapter 2 for your break-even analysis. For your business plan, use a similar format but combine the shortfall and profit columns into a single column called Profit (Loss). If, for financing purposes, you want to display your working capital requirement, you can add another column, cumulative loss, and a footnote to highlight your calculation as in the MegaBucks example.

In lieu of a break-even schedule or in support of it, many business software programs can create a break-even chart displaying a line graph of profit versus sales, with profit going from negative to positive as sales increase. This shows the amount of sales in terms of dollars that have to occur for negative profit (loss) to become positive (gain). The break-even point is where the sales line crosses the profit line at zero. If you have access to this, it is one of the better charts to place in your business plan.

Write a brief statement explaining the break-even point, stating how many sales in terms of dollars and units have to be generated until the business's profit becomes positive and at what point in time. Follow this narrative with a schedule similar to the one in the MegaBucks example.

Break-even Analysis

We will reach break-even in the seventh month after opening when net sales hit $1,000,000+. Our first six months losses will have totaled $20,599 at that point. For the break-even analysis, we have assumed annual gross real estate sales of $14,597,143 with 7% commissions to the house, a net revenue of $1,021,800; fixed costs to average $18,931 per month and variable costs to equal 74.15% of Revenue.

Key break-even assumptions:

- That our sales begin two months before opening with our first closings to occur the first month,
- That sales fluctuate with the seasonal effect of the Kona market, increasing the last five months as the season improves, and
- That the impact of our sales force is synchronized with our market share.

Provide a narrative break-even analysis explaining the sales needed to reach the point when the business begins to make a profit.

MegaBucks $mith and Associates

Break-even Schedule – First Year of Business

Month	Revenue Forecast	Fixed Costs	Variable Costs	Profit (Loss)	Cumulative (Loss)
January	$ 73,700	$ 22,165	$ 54,649	$ (3,114)	$ (3,114)
February	73,600	19,596	54,574	(570)	(3,681)
March	73,500	19,297	54,500	(297)	(3,981)
April	49,400	18,788	36,630	(6,018)	(9,999)
May	49,300	18,031	36,556	(5,287)	(15,286)
June	49,200	18,032	36,482	(5,314)	(20,599)
July	73,100	18,443	54,204	454	
August	73,000	17,794	54,130	1,077	
September	96,900	18,143	71,851	6,906	
October	120,800	19,354	89,573	11,873	
November	144,700	18,465	107,295	18,940	
December	144,600	19,070	107,221	18,309	
	$1,021,800	$225,783	$757,665	$38,353	

Support your analysis with a break-even schedule.

Our working capital requirement is $20,599; with a 50% cushion, this comes to $30,898.

Pro Forma Income Statements

The next three segments of your franchise business plan are the pro forma financial statements, which depict the projections for your operations over a specified planning period. These statements and pertinent support materials are vital to your plan, so be sure they are as accurate as possible.

The franchise business forecast you did to determine your capital investment needs in Chapter 2 combines two projections: income and cumulative cash flow. Most reviewers want these separated — a standard accounting practice — into two documents: a pro forma income statement and a pro forma statement of cash flow. From the pro forma income statement reviewers can see if you are making a profit, and from the pro forma statement of cash flow, they can see if your company has enough cash to pay the bills. The first of the three pro forma segments is the income statements.

One-year Pro Forma Income Statement

A pro forma income statement is similar to a business forecast but without the cash flow totals. It is also called a pro forma profit and loss statement or a pro forma income and expense statement. Operating income, also called net income or income before taxes, is usually the bottom line. In a paragraph placed either before or following your detailed month by month pro forma income statement, summarize your projected annual revenue earned and justify it with your market share or with your franchisor and other franchises' figures, or both. You can point out any other annual projection that is a significant concern for your business, as well.

First-year Pro Forma Income Statement Summary

The gross revenue in our Pro Forma Income Statement for the first year totals $14,597,143. This is commensurate with the projections provided by MegaBucks International and three MegaBucks franchisees in their first year of business (earnings are adjusted for Hawaii):

Average First-year Sales Projections

From MegaBucks International	$14,600,000
From MegaBucks Chase	$12,620,012
From MegaBucks Burbank	$15,990,758
From MegaBucks Alameda	$14,090,886
Average First-year Sales	$14,325,414

Also, this is in agreement with our market share ("The Market"), showing $14,500,000 for this same number in our area.

Present a summary.

Include a month-to-month Pro Forma Income Statement for the first year of business.

Also show a long-range Pro Forma Income Statement, year-to-year for three or five years.

MegaBucks Smith and Associates
First-year Pro Forma Income Statement

Month	Jan.	Feb.	March	April	May	June	July	Aug.	Sept.	Oct.	Nov.	Dec.
Gross Sales	1,052,857	1,051,429	1,050,000	705,714	704,286	702,857	1,044,286	1,042,857	1,384,286	1,725,714	2,067,143	2,065,714
Revenue Earned (Commissions)	73,700	73,600	73,500	49,400	49,300	49,200	73,100	73,000	96,900	120,800	144,700	144,600
Cost of Revenue Earned												
General excise tax	1,032	1,030	1,029	692	690	689	1,023	1,022	1,357	1,691	2,026	2,024
Supplies	553	552	551	371	370	369	548	548	727	906	1,085	1,085
Commission	47,905	47,840	47,775	32,110	32,045	31,980	47,515	47,450	62,985	78,520	94,055	93,990
Royalties	3,685	3,680	3,675	2,470	2,465	2,460	3,655	3,650	4,845	6,040	7,235	7,230
Co-op advertising	737	736	735	494	493	492	731	730	969	1,208	1,447	1,446
Local advertising	737	736	735	494	493	492	731	730	969	1,208	1,447	1,446
Total Cost of Revenue Earned	54,649	54,574	54,500	36,630	36,556	36,482	54,204	54,130	71,851	89,573	107,295	107,221
Gross Profit	19,051	19,026	19,000	12,770	12,744	12,718	18,896	18,871	25,049	31,227	37,405	37,379
Operating Expense												
Lease or rent	2,200	2,200	2,200	2,200	2,200	2,200	2,200	2,200	2,200	2,200	2,200	2,200
Property tax and insurance	150	150	150	150	150	150	150	150	150	150	150	150
Maintenance	50	50	50	50	50	50	50	50	50	50	50	50
Utilities	300	300	300	300	300	300	300	300	300	300	300	300
Payroll	11,667	11,667	11,667	11,667	11,667	11,667	11,667	11,667	11,667	11,667	11,667	11,667
Employee benefits	1,867	1,867	1,867	1,867	1,867	1,867	1,867	1,867	1,867	1,867	1,867	1,867
Telephone	400	400	400	400	400	400	400	400	400	400	400	400
Janitorial	160	160	160	160	160	160	160	160	160	160	160	160
Other insurance	500	500	500	500	500	500	500	500	500	500	500	500
Legal	100	0	0	100	0	0	100	0	0	100	0	0
Accounting	320	320	320	320	320	320	320	320	320	320	320	320
Marketing and entertainment	4,151	1,682	1,383	774	117	118	429	(120)	229	1,340	551	1,156
Internet	50	50	50	50	50	50	50	50	50	50	50	50
Miscellaneous	250	250	250	250	250	250	250	250	250	250	250	250
Total Operating Expense	22,165	19,596	19,297	18,788	18,031	18,032	18,443	17,794	18,143	19,354	18,465	19,070
Operating Income	(3,114)	(570)	(297)	(6,018)	(5,287)	(5,314)	454	1,077	6,906	11,873	18,940	18,309

Five-year Pro Forma Income Statement

Nearly all business plans include a three or five-year pro forma income statement, with totals given for each year. Your market growth research for the market study in Chapter 6 should give you an idea of your percentage of increases for this forecast. If you need additional help with this, a good software program is *Profit Mentor*™ available through Management Advisory Services.

Management Advisory Services
Moss Adams, Inc.
1001 4th Avenue, 27th Floor
Seattle, WA 98154-1199
(206) 442-2600
FAX (206) 233-9214

Supporting Evidence

In addition to your pro forma income statements, add any supporting evidence you have for your projections — such as those derived for your business forecast in Chapter 2 — for your operating income: revenue earned, variable costs, and fixed costs. For instance, if your franchisor provided sales projections and earnings figures and if you obtained others directly from other franchisees, construct a tabulated average as in the MegaBucks example summary above. Reviewers accept this as more realistic than a forecast from only one source, such as your franchisor.

If your CPA assists in compiling figures for the projections of sales and earnings, add the CPA's signed documentation here in the financial section or in the exhibits. Be sure to add all of your CPA's supporting assumptions to your important assumptions segment.

Sometimes a probability forecast is also used; however, the reliability of this type of projection is questionable and only as good as the person making the percentaged adjustments. Without support for the percentages, and there rarely is any, reviewers may feel you have compiled the sales data on such loose calculations that they could lose confidence in your other projections.

MegaBucks $mith and Associates

Five-year Pro Forma Income Statement

	Year				
	1	2	3	4	5
Revenue Earned	1,021,800	1,328,340	1,594,008	1,753,409	1,893,682
Cost of Revenue Earned					
General excise tax	14,305	18,597	22,316	24,548	26,512
Supplies	7,664	9,963	11,955	13,151	14,203
Commission	664,170	863,421	1,036,105	1,139,716	1,230,893
Royalties	51,090	66,417	79,700	87,670	94,684
Co-op advertising	10,218	13,283	15,940	17,534	18,937
Local advertising	10,218	13,283	15,940	17,534	18,937
Total Cost of Revenue Earned	757,665	984,964	1,181,957	1,300,153	1,404,165
Gross Profit	264,135	343,376	412,051	453,256	489,517
Operating Expense					
Lease or rent	26,400	26,400	26,400	26,400	26,400
Property tax and insurance	1,800	1,800	1,800	1,800	1,800
Maintenance	600	624	649	675	702
Utilities	3,600	3,708	3,819	3,934	4,052
Payroll	140,004	168,800	172,176	175,620	179,132
Employee benefits	22,401	27,008	27,548	28,099	28,661
Telephone	4,800	5,760	5,933	6,111	6,294
Janitorial	1,920	1,958	1,998	2,038	2,078
Other insurance	6,000	6,120	6,242	6,367	6,495
Legal	400	1,000	1,100	1,200	1,300
Accounting	3,840	800	824	849	874
Marketing and entertainment	11,810	12,519	13,270	14,066	14,910
Internet	600	600	630	630	650
Miscellaneous	3,000	3,240	3,499	3,779	4,081
Total Operating Expense	227,175	260,337	265,889	271,567	277,430
Operating Income	36,961	83,038	146,163	181,689	212,087

Pro Forma Statement of Cash Flow

This segment of the pro forma financial information is a pro forma statement of cash flow. When the operating cash flow on the pro forma statement of cash flows is separated from the business forecast, the format is simplified and much shorter. A cash flow projection for operations is merely a forecast of the cash receipts and disbursements.

The purpose of the cash flow statement is to demonstrate your actual cash position in any given month. The calculation for cash-and-carry businesses is merely the running total of the monthly profit or loss. Shown below is a portion (months four through ten) of a typical pro forma cash flow for a cash-and-carry business that only has an operating cash flow — from the One-year Franchise Business Forecast in Chapter 2.

Operating Cash Flow Pro Forma Sample

Month:	4	5	6	7	8	9	10
Operating Income	(1,454)	(619)	190	980	2,058	3,132	4,215
Cash Flow (cumulative)	(9,383)	(10,002)	(9,812)	(8,832)	(6,774)	(3,642)	573

It is typical for all new businesses to have a negative cash flow for the first few months of business. In the sample above, cash flow is negative every month until the tenth month when the business has $573 in positive cash flow available. A cash flow analysis, which involves cash needs including loan repayment, allows for two important conclusions to be drawn.

- The worst case cash scenario, in the sample above, is that during the fifth month of the business you need $10,002 working capital to handle the negative cash requirements.

- A loan repayment window occurs as the cash flow turns positive in the tenth month. If lender funds are used, the eleventh month is the earliest a payment can be made, unless you increase the working-capital requirement to allow the cash flow to handle an earlier payment.

Another essential consideration for you to make regarding cash flow of your business is when you extend credit to customers — a time lapse exists from the sale to the collection of funds. When you separate revenue into cash sales and accounts receivable, you can get a truer picture of cash flow if you calculate cash receipts less disbursements, instead of revenue less expenditures.

A comprehensive statement examines cash flows from operating, investing, and financing activities, with financing cash flow further divided into debt and equity. The total cash flow is called the comprehensive cash flow or net cash flow, and the statement is called a statement of cash flows. Your accountant or franchisor field support may use this format, as seen in the MegaBucks example, or a version of it for your formal statements.

MegaBucks $mith and Associates
Pro Forma Statement of Cash Flows

Month	Jan.	Feb.	March	April	May	June	July	Aug.	Sept.	Oct.	Nov.	Dec.
Cash provided by operations cash received from sales	73,700	73,600	73,500	49,400	49,300	49,200	73,100	73,000	96,900	120,800	144,700	144,600
Cash paid for costs of goods sold	(54,649)	(54,574)	(54,500)	(36,630)	(36,556)	(36,482)	(54,204)	(54,130)	(71,851)	(89,573)	(107,295)	(107,221)
Operating expenses	(22,165)	(19,596)	(19,297)	(18,788)	(18,031)	(18,032)	(18,443)	(17,794)	(18,143)	(19,354)	(18,465)	(19,070)
Net cash provided by (used in) operations	(3,114)	(570)	(297)	(6,018)	(5,287)	(5,314)	453	1,076	6,906	11,873	18,940	18,309
Net cash provided by (used in) investments	0	0	0	0	0	0	0	0	0	0	0	0
Net cash provided by (used in) financing	0	0	0	0	0	0	0	0	0	0	0	0
Total increase (decrease) in cash	(3,114)	(570)	(297)	(6,018)	(5,287)	(5,314)	453	1,076	6,906	11,873	18,940	18,309
Cash beginning of period	(3,114)	(3,684)	(3,981)	(9,999)	(15,286)	(20,600)	(20,147)	(19,071)	(12,165)	(292)	18,648	36,957

Display a month to month Pro Forma Statement of Cash Flow for the first year of business.

Pro Forma Balance Sheet

The pro forma balance sheet is an estimate of future assets and liabilities predicting equity, or net worth, at a given point in time. The assets of the business are cash, real estate, franchise fee, vehicles, equipment, furniture, fixtures, signage, inventory, and supplies, as well as accounts and notes receivable. Accounts receivable are amounts you are owed by customers and notes receivable are any loans owed to you secured by promissory notes or by other security. For many of these items two values exist: a fair market value and a cost basis value. For your balance sheet, use the cost basis value, which is the actual purchase cost to you.

The liabilities of the business include accounts payable (anything owed by invoice that is not on a note), unpaid salaries and employee benefits, and notes payable (debts on loans and notes), interest expense, lease payments, and taxes payable. For a pro forma balance sheet, omit unpaid salaries and employee benefits because you are building in a projection that covers paying them.

On a balance sheet, assets are listed first, broken down and separated into current assets, fixed assets, and other assets, customarily in that order. After assets, and balanced to them, are the liabilities and equity. For a start-up company, a pro forma balance sheet is prepared with numbers that correspond to a point in time just before opening the business. Include in your financial plan a pro forma balance sheet for your first year with quarterly projections and a pro forma balance sheet for three or five years showing year-end forecasts for each year.

Start of Business Pro Forma Balance Sheet

Assets   Date _____

Current Assets:

    Cash, on hand and in banks   _____

    Accounts receivable   _____

    Interest receivable   _____

    Inventory   _____

    Supplies   _____

    Prepaid expense   _____

    Other   _____

    Total current assets   _____

Fixed Assets:

    Real estate   _____

    Vehicles and equipment   _____

    Furniture, fixtures, and signage   _____

    Total fixed assets   _____

Other Assets:

    Franchise fee   _____

    Other   _____

    Total other assets   _____

Total Assets   _____

Liabilities and Equity

Current Liabilities:

    Accounts payable   _____

    Current maturity long-term debt   _____

    Accrued taxes   _____

    Royalties payable   _____

    Co-op advertising payable   _____

    Other   _____

    Total current liabilities   _____

Long-term Liabilities:

    Long-term debt   _____

    Other   _____

    Total long-term liabilities   _____

Total Liabilities   _____

Total Equity (Net Worth)   _____

Total Liabilities and Equity   _____

> Include a Pro Forma Balance Sheet dated to correspond to the opening of business. For an existing business, use the current date.

MegaBucks $mith and Associates
First-year Pro Forma Balance Sheet

	1st Quarter	2nd Quarter	3rd Quarter	4th Quarter
Assets				
Current Assets:				
Cash (on hand and in banks)	10,000	30,000	50,000	75,000
Accounts receivable	0	10,000	25,000	40,000
Quick Assets	10,000	40,000	75,000	115,000
Interest receivable	0	100	700	2,000
Supplies	400	400	400	400
Prepaid expense	2,000	2,000	2,000	2,000
Other	0	0	500	1,000
Total Current Assets	12,400	42,500	78,600	120,400
Fixed Assets:				
Office real estate	400,000	400,000	400,000	400,000
Other real estate	0	0	0	0
Vehicles and equipment	10,500	10,500	10,500	10,500
Furniture, fixtures and signage	20,000	20,000	20,000	20,000
Computer system	5,000	5,000	5,000	5,000
Telephone system	12,000	12,000	12,000	12,000
Total Fixed Assets	447,500	447,500	447,500	447,500
Other Assets:				
Franchise fee	25,000	25,000	25,000	25,000
Other	0	0	0	0
Total Other Assets	25,000	25,000	25,000	25,000
Total Assets	484,900	515,000	551,100	592,900
Liabilities and Equity				
Current Liabilities:				
Accounts payable	2,000	4,000	6,000	8,000
Current maturity long-term debt	0	0	0	0
Accrued taxes	450	900	1,350	1,800
Royalties payable	3,675	2,460	4,845	7,230
Co-op advertising payable	1,470	984	1,938	2,892
General excise tax	1,029	689	1,357	2,024
Other	200	0	220	360
Total Current Liabilities	8,824	9,033	15,710	22,306
Long-term Liabilities:				
Long-term debt	300,000	300,000	300,000	300,000
Operating loan	60,000	60,000	60,000	60,000
Other	0	0	0	0
Total Long-term Liabilities	360,000	360,000	360,000	360,000
Total Liabilities	368,824	369,033	375,710	382,306
Total Equity (Net Worth)	116,076	145,967	175,390	210,594
Total Liabilities and Equity	484,900	515,000	551,100	592,900

MegaBucks $mith and Associates
Five-year Pro Forma Balance Sheet

	1st Year	2nd Year	3rd Year	4th Year	5th Year
Assets					
Current Assets:					
Cash (on hand and in banks)	74,000	96,000	43,000	112,000	120,000
Accounts receivable	40,000	50,000	64,800	70,000	75,000
Quick Assets	114,000	146,000	107,800	182,000	195,000
Interest receivable	2,000	3,000	3,240	3,500	3,750
Supplies	400	630	800	896	983
Prepaid expense	2,000	2,000	0	0	0
Other	1,000	1,400	1,500	1,550	1,600
Total Current Assets	119,400	153,030	113,340	187,946	201,333
Fixed Assets:					
Office real estate	400,000	416,000	432,640	449,946	467,943
Other real estate	0	0	40,000	41,600	43,264
Vehicles and equipment	10,500	17,500	17,500	15,000	22,500
Furniture, fixtures and signage	20,000	36,000	38,000	40,000	42,000
Computer system	5,000	4,600	4,232	5,893	5,422
Telephone system	12,000	11,040	10,156	9,344	8,597
Total Fixed Assets	447,500	485,140	542,528	561,783	589,726
Other Assets:					
Franchise fee	25,000	25,000	25,000	25,000	25,000
Other	0	0	0	0	0
Total Other Assets	25,000	25,000	25,000	25,000	25,000
Total Assets	591,900	663,170	680,868	774,729	816,059
Liabilities and Equity					
Current Liabilities:					
Accounts payable	8,000	11,000	11,880	12,830	13,856
Current maturity long-term debt	0	0	0	0	0
Accrued taxes	1,800	1,800	1,800	1,800	1,800
Royalties payable	7,230	5,534	6,642	7,306	7,890
Co-op advertising payable	2,892	2,213	2,657	2,922	3,156
General excise tax	2,024	1,550	1,860	2,045	2,210
Other	360	375	392	410	430
Total Current Liabilities	22,306	22,472	25,231	27,313	29,342
Long-term Liabilities:					
Long-term debt	300,000	297,000	294,030	291,090	288,178
Operating loan	60,000	59,600	0	0	0
Other	0	0	0	0	0
Total Long-term Liabilities	360,000	356,600	294,030	291,090	288,178
Total Liabilities	382,306	379,072	319,261	318,403	317,520
Total Equity (Net Worth)	209,594	284,098	361,607	456,326	498,539
Total Liabilities and Equity	591,900	663,170	680,868	774,729	816,059

Business Ratios

Once your pro forma financial statements are complete, many interesting assessments can be done. Known as business or accounting ratios, these assessments compare specific figures in the statement of income and the balance sheet to arrive at a useful ratio — usually expressed as a decimal or percentage. While business ratios are valuable tools for financiers and lenders in measuring a business' solvency, liquidity, efficiency, and profitability, they are also valuable to you as management aids for determining the health of various aspects of your business. Because a start-up business typically has poor ratios the first year, reviewers tend to put more emphasis on capital requirements, the break-even point, and the calculation of business ratios on projections for future years. For ongoing businesses, ratios are analyzed on past, current, and pro forma financial statements.

If you choose to report your results of some of the important business ratios, either list them at the bottom of the statement of income or prepare a separate chart, as in the MegaBucks example.

While literally hundreds of accounting ratios exist, only the more popular ones are covered here. In these ratios, debt is equal to total liabilities; short-term debt is current liabilities; and quick cash is equal to cash plus marketable securities and accounts receivable. The ratios are grouped together in several categories.

Business Ratios

MegaBucks $mith and Associates
77-6452 Alii Drive
Kailua-Kona, Hawaii

Ten Important Business Ratios

	Year 1	Year 2	Year 3	Year 4	Year 5
Quick Ratio	5.11	6.50	4.27	6.66	6.65
Current Ratio	5.35	6.81	4.49	6.88	6.86
Debt to Equity	1.82	1.33	0.88	0.70	0.64
Collection Days	14.29	13.74	14.84	14.57	14.46
Sales to Assets	1.73	2.00	2.34	2.26	2.32
Working Capital	$97,094	$130,558	$88,109	$160,633	$171,991
Accounts Receivable Turnover	25.55	26.57	24.60	25.05	25.25
Accounts Payable Turnover	127.73	120.76	134.18	136.66	136.67
Return on Assets	6.24%	12.52%	21.47%	23.45%	25.99%
Return on Equity	17.63%	29.23%	40.42%	39.82%	42.54%

Include the most enhancing ratios at the bottom of your Pro Forma Income Statement or prepare a separate table and place it after your financial statements.

If you have access to computer software, you can easily graph these ratios and include them with the ratios in your business plan. Graphed ratios for the MegaBucks example business plan are shown. Some examples of the more popular graphs also accompany a few of the ratio explanations that follow.

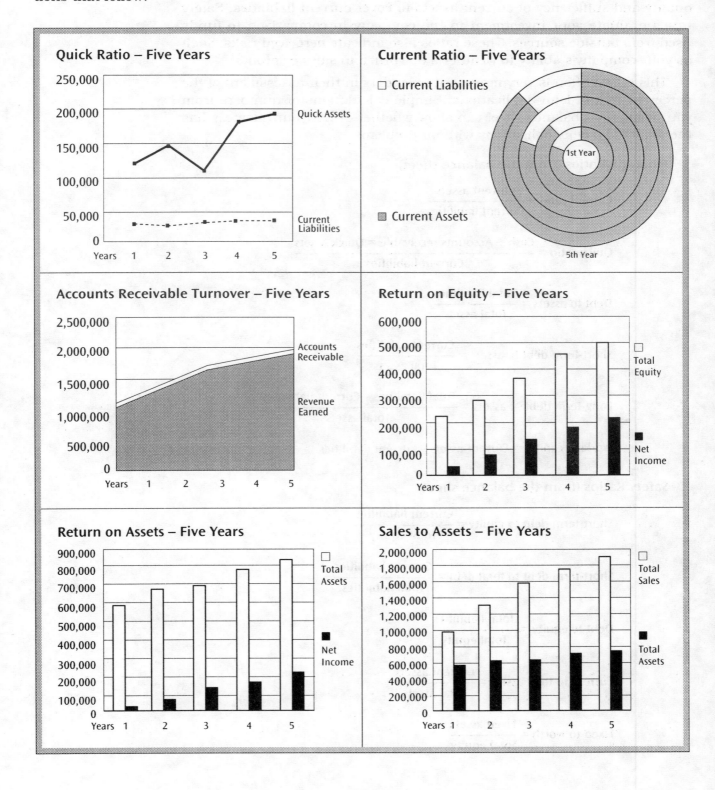

Solvency Ratios

Solvency ratios provide a measure of your company's overall financial ability to pay its debts. Liquidity ratios examine your company's overall financial position and its ability to pay short-term debt. They also evaluate the quality and sufficiency of current assets to cover current liabilities. Safety ratios evaluate your investment in the company in comparison to funds used from outside sources. These ratios also indicate perceived risks, such as your company's ability to weather a downturn in sales or profits.

This information is very important to lenders in their assessment of the perceived risk of loan applications. Simple calculations of numbers from your company's balance sheet can show whether or not your business has the ability to pay its obligations without problems.

Liquidity Ratios (from the balance sheet)

$$\text{Current ratio} = \frac{\text{Current assets}}{\text{Current liabilities}}$$

$$\text{Quick ratio} = \frac{\text{Cash} + \text{Accounts receivable} = \text{Quick assets}}{\text{Current liabilities}}$$

$$\text{Debt to assets} = \frac{\text{Total liabilities}}{\text{Total assets}}$$

$$\text{Short-term debt to assets} = \frac{\text{Current liabilities}}{\text{Total assets}}$$

$$\text{Long-term debt to assets} = \frac{\text{Total liabilities} - \text{Current liabilities}}{\text{Total assets}}$$

$$\text{Working capital} = \text{Current assets} - \text{Current liabilities}$$

Safety Ratios (from the balance sheet)

$$\text{Short-term debt to equity} = \frac{\text{Current liabilities}}{\text{Total equity}}$$

$$\text{Short-term debt to total debt} = \frac{\text{Current liabilities}}{\text{Total liabilities}}$$

$$\text{Debt to equity} = \frac{\text{Total liabilities}}{\text{Total equity}}$$

$$\text{Current to total assets} = \frac{\text{Current assets}}{\text{Total assets}}$$

$$\text{Fixed to worth} = \frac{\text{Fixed assets}}{\text{Total equity}}$$

Safety Ratios (from the income statement)

Net quick assets = Quick assets – Current liabilities

$$\frac{EBIT}{Interest} = \frac{Net\ income}{Interest\ expense}$$

$$EBIT\ to\ interest = \frac{\left(\dfrac{Gross\ profit}{Revenue\ earned}\right) - Operating\ expenses}{Interest\ expense}$$

To give you a better idea of what these ratios do for a franchise start up, the quick ratio, the current ratio, the debt-to-equity ratio, and the EBIT-to-interest ratio are explained in more detail later in this chapter. These four ratios are some of the more popular to include in a franchise business plan.

Efficiency Ratios

These ratios provide the information necessary to compare your company's operating performance with other companies and with the average for your industry. Levels of acceptability vary among different industries, but, generally, retail stores should have higher turnover ratios.

Activity Ratios (from the income statement and the balance sheet)

$$Collection = \frac{Accounts\ receivable}{Revenue\ earned} \times 365$$

$$Sales\ to\ receivables = \frac{Revenue\ earned}{Accounts\ receivable}$$

Operating Ratios (from the income statement and the balance sheet)

$$Accounts\ payable\ to\ sales = \frac{Accounts\ payable}{Revenue\ earned}$$

$$Accounts\ receivable\ turnover = \frac{Revenue\ earned}{Accounts\ receivable}$$

$$Accounts\ payable\ turnover = \frac{Cost\ of\ revenue\ earned}{Accounts\ payable}$$

$$Receivables\ to\ payables = \frac{Accounts\ receivable}{Accounts\ payable}$$

$$Cost\ of\ revenue\ to\ payables = \frac{Cost\ of\ revenue\ earned}{Accounts\ payable}$$

$$Sales\ to\ assets = \frac{Revenue\ earned}{Total\ assets}$$

Operating Ratios (from the income statement and the balance sheet) (continued)

$$\text{Sales to net working capital} = \frac{\text{Revenue earned}}{\text{Current assets} - \text{Current liabilities}}$$

$$\text{Inventory turnover} = \frac{\text{Cost of revenue earned}}{\text{Inventory}}$$

Later, several of these efficiency ratios are discussed more fully to help you better understand their uses and calculations. Be sure to take the time to get a clear understanding of how they work. Your accountant can assist you, also, in this process.

Profitability Ratios

These ratios can be used to examine the profit level made by your company and to determine if your company yields profits comparable to alternative investments. They also can be used to assess your business' value as an investment and to compare your business' success with the rest of the industry in terms of profit in such areas as gross margin, net profit margin, and return on assets.

The return on assets ratio and the return on equity ratio are explained in more detail later. Those discussions can help you visualize how these ratios use numbers from the income statement and balance sheet to provide valuable management information.

(from the income statement)

$$\text{Return on sales or Pretax profit margin} = \frac{\text{Net income}}{\text{Revenue earned}}$$

$$\text{Gross profit margin} = \frac{\text{Gross profit}}{\text{Revenue earned}}$$

(from the income statement and the balance sheet)

$$\text{Return on assets} = \frac{\text{Net income}}{\text{Total assets}}$$

$$\text{Return on equity} = \frac{\text{Net income}}{\text{Total equity}}$$

$$\text{Sales to equity} = \frac{\text{Revenue earned}}{\text{Total equity}}$$

Most-used Business Ratios

It is unnecessary for you to calculate all of the above ratios. They are presented here for you to choose from if you want to use any in your business plan or in case a lender requests a particular one. It should be pointed out that the ratios listed here have other names; the ones given seem to be the most universal.

Your franchisor may have comparative ratios that you can use to measure yourself against other franchises in the system and, perhaps, your competitors. In addition, several organizations such as Robert Morse Associates (RMA) or Dun & Bradstreet furnish comparative data evaluating how your business stacks up with others with respect to most of these ratios. These consulting organizations assign your business one or more SIC (standard industrial classification) numbers, depending on your specialties. Besides your particular SIC number, the consultants also narrow down the field by matching your business to those with similar earnings. They can provide comparisons of your standard ratios with ratios of businesses in the same categories of your SIC and your range of earnings. Many people go to the trouble to get the RMA (Robert Morse Associates) ratios and make the comparisons within their business plan, but it is not necessary because banks and lenders have their own access to RMA ratios.

For the nonfranchised business, it is more of a management tool to acquire these RMA or Dun & Bradstreet ratios to track itself with peers as a measure of control. For franchised businesses, your franchisor supplies much of this management support.

To help you understand how to use these ratios, 13 of the more popular business ratios are explained below.

Quick Ratio

A liquidity ratio, the quick ratio equals quick assets divided by current liabilities. Quick assets are those things that can be converted to cash quickly and are equivalent to cash, such as cash, accounts receivable, and marketable securities. A low ratio means you could have difficulty in meeting your current credit responsibilities. A high ratio indicates you could have excess in cash, securities, or both, or it suggests you could have poor collection of your accounts receivable. A ratio of 1.40 demonstrates that, for every $1.00 you have of current liabilities, you have $1.40 in cash, securities, or accounts receivable to pay off those obligations.

Current Ratio

Another liquidity ratio, the current ratio equals current assets divided by current liabilities. Both of these numbers are readily available totals in the balance sheet. Current assets are defined as those assets that can be converted to cash within one year. Likewise, current liabilities are those obligations that must be paid within one year. A low ratio signifies the company may have problems in meeting its short-term obligations as they become due. A high ratio may represent an excessive investment in current assets or a low utilization of short-term credit. A ratio of 2.75 means that for every

$1.00 of current liabilities, you have $2.75 in current assets to meet them. When the current ratio is below 1.00, working capital is negative; conversely, when the current ratio is above 1.00, working capital is positive. Working capital is current assets minus current liabilities.

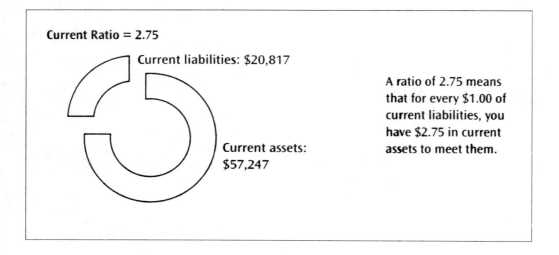

Current Ratio = 2.75

Current liabilities: $20,817

Current assets: $57,247

A ratio of 2.75 means that for every $1.00 of current liabilities, you have $2.75 in current assets to meet them.

Debt-to-Equity Ratio

A safety ratio, the debt-to-equity ratio equals total liabilities divided by total equity. This is a measure of the business' financial commitment. A low ratio is better than a high ratio, but a low ratio can imply the company may be underutilizing its leveraging ability. A high ratio signals that the business is more risky than average. A ratio of 1.40 reveals that for every $1.00 you have invested in the business, creditors have $1.40 invested in it with you. This is regarded as one of the more important safety ratios to be read as a measure of the business' ability to weather a slow period in sales and profits.

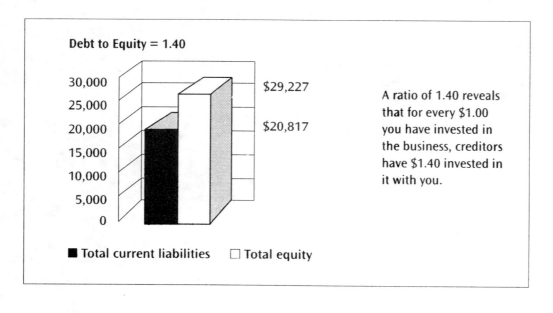

Debt to Equity = 1.40

$29,227

$20,817

■ Total current liabilities   □ Total equity

A ratio of 1.40 reveals that for every $1.00 you have invested in the business, creditors have $1.40 invested in it with you.

Gross Profit Ratio

Also called the gross profit margin, this profitability ratio is expressed as a percentage. It show what percentage of each dollar is left after paying all costs of goods or direct expenses. The gross profit ratio is used to examine the effectiveness of your pricing policies and the efficiency in providing your products or services. For example, a 39 percent gross profit margin means that for every $1.00 of sales generated, a gross profit of $0.39 is earned.

EBIT-to-Interest Ratio

EBIT is an acronym for "earnings before interest and taxes." It is another safety ratio that you can use if you have any interest expense — from your income statement. Determining the ratio is a three-step calculation. First, you need to figure the gross profit ratio. Then you figure the EBIT which is the gross profit ratio minus the operating expense. To get the EBIT-to-interest ratio, divide the EBIT amount by your total interest expense.

$$\text{Step 1. Gross profit ratio} = \frac{\text{Gross profit}}{\text{Revenue earned}}$$

$$\text{Step 2. EBIT} = \text{Gross profit ratio} - \text{Operating expense}$$

$$\text{Step 3. EBIT to interest} = \frac{\text{EBIT}}{\text{Interest expense}}$$

Lenders often review a loan applicant's financial statement for this ratio as a measure of your business' ability to generate sufficient profit to pay interest payments.

Average Collection Ratio

For cash-and-carry businesses this is an irrelevant statistic. For others, it is an efficiency ratio. Average collection, sometimes called collection days or, simply, collection, equals accounts receivable divided by revenue earned, and the results multiplied by 365 — Dun & Bradstreet uses 360. The result is the estimated average number of days for collecting the payment of bills. This assumes the accounts receivable ending balance used is typical for the period used.

Sales-to-Assets Ratio

An operating ratio, the sales-to-assets ratio is equal to revenue earned divided by total assets. A low ratio can suggest you are investing too much in assets compared to your level of sales. A high ratio could indicate you might not be spending enough, suggesting you may need to upgrade equipment or other assets. A ratio of 9.64 indicates that for every $1.00 invested in assets, you have $9.64 in sales.

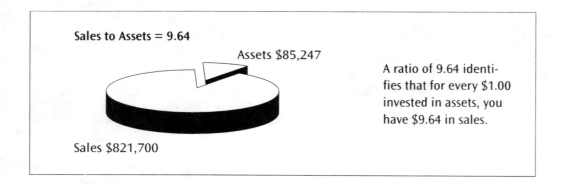

Sales to Assets = 9.64

Assets $85,247

A ratio of 9.64 identifies that for every $1.00 invested in assets, you have $9.64 in sales.

Sales $821,700

Working Capital Ratio

Called an operating ratio and sometimes a liquidity ratio, this is really a mathematical difference rather than a ratio. Working capital equals current assets less current liabilities. This is similar to the current ratio, but it is a measure in terms of dollars and is the requirement to pay short-term obligations. A low figure can indicate you have difficulty making payroll or payments to suppliers. When the current ratio is below 1.00, working capital is negative; in the same way, when the current ratio is above 1.00, working capital is positive.

Inventory Turnover Ratio

Another operating ratio, inventory turnover equals cost of revenue earned (from the income statement) divided by inventory (from the balance sheet). The ratio points out the number of times you turn over inventory in a year. A low number may imply over-stocking, could suggest a surplus of out-of-date inventory, or could represent a planned surplus. A high number may reveal a shortage of needed inventory or a more successful marketing effort than anticipated.

When 365 is divided by this ratio, the result is the inventory turnover in days. For instance, if your inventory ratio is 21.38, then 365 days divided by the ratio (21.38) equals 17 days, or an inventory turnover of 17 days.

$$\text{Inventory turnover days: } \frac{365}{21.38} = 17 \text{ days}$$

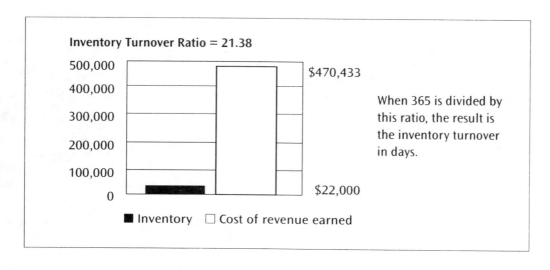

Inventory Turnover Ratio = 21.38

$470,433

When 365 is divided by this ratio, the result is the inventory turnover in days.

$22,000

■ Inventory   □ Cost of revenue earned

Accounts Receivable Turnover Ratio

Accounts receivable turnover is an operating ratio that is equal to revenue earned divided by accounts receivable. This is a measure of the number of times accounts receivable were collected during the period. Again, this assumes the ending balance you use for accounts receivable is typical for the time period you use.

Accounts Payable Turnover Ratio

This is another operating ratio, sometimes referred to as an activity ratio. Accounts payable turnover equals cost of revenue earned divided by accounts payable. This yields the number of times accounts payable were paid off during the period, assuming the ending balance for accounts payable is typical for the period used.

Return on Assets Ratio

Return on assets, a profitability ratio also known as an operating ratio, equals net income divided by total assets and is expressed as a percentage. It is an indicator of the efficiency of your assets in generating a return. If your return on assets is 35 percent, it means your business produced a return of $0.35 for every $1.00 used for assets.

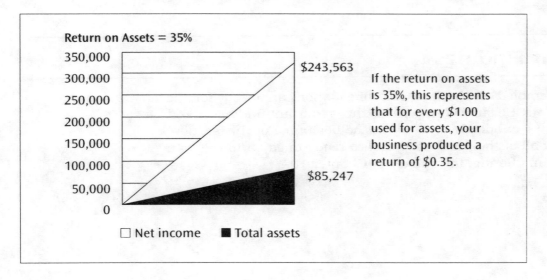

Return on Equity Ratio

Another profitability ratio, return on equity equals net income divided by total equity and is expressed as a percentage. Because total equity is your investment in the business, this ratio is a measure of the return your business is generating on your investment in the company. If the return on equity is 12 percent, this signifies that for every $1.00 you invest in the business, the business produces a return of $0.12, or 12 percent. As a management tool, owners watch this ratio closely. However, you cannot simply compare this to a return on other investments because, in addition to the return, your business is paying the bills and developing other hidden equities, such as an increasing business value and possibly real estate equity.

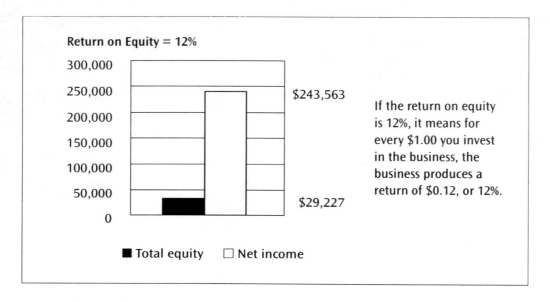

For additional information on the use of these and other analytical tools, you may want to get The Oasis Press' publication *Business Owner's Guide to Accounting and Bookkeeping* by José Placencia, Bruce Welge, and Don Oliver.

Compile Your Findings

After you have assembled all the financial information, analyze it for the most important points. Be sure to emphasize the significant findings about your business in your financial summary at the beginning of this section. Now that you know all of the numbers, you are ready to go on to the loan request or investment offering, the subject of Chapter 10.

Loan Request or Investment Offering

A banker is a person who is willing to make a loan if you present sufficient evidence to show you don't need it.
— HERBERT V. PROCHNOW

This last section of the body of your business plan is your financial request. It expands the financial objective introduced in your abstract and your business summary and describes the amount and type of financial assistance that you are trying to obtain. The title of this section of your business plan can vary, depending on the type of financial assistance you are seeking and the type of fund raising the reviewer represents.

Typically, as a franchisee, your primary sources of raising capital are through commercial lenders. If this is your aim, title this portion of your business plan, Loan Request. If you are anticipating cashing in on one of the no-money-down aspects of generating start-up capital, use the title, Investment Offering. This targets the type of investor arrangements you are going after, including capital from a limited or general partner or from an investor or member in a limited liability company.

Other sources, such as private placement offerings of stock with accredited or sophisticated investors and many venture capital groups, are usually beyond the scope of most franchisees; however, because they are possible sources for some, these and other options for financing are described in Part III.

To help you structure your request or offering, it is important to understand the types of vesting (ownership) that may affect your choice between seeking loan funds or investor capital. The final decision of vesting depends on the type of financing resources you desire and can obtain. For example, if you get a conventional loan, you have no need of partners so you could consider sole ownership. Then, there are several types of sole ownership. If you want more liability protection, you might select a regular corporation; if you want less tax impacts, you might choose an S corporation. On the other hand, if you want to and are in a position to obtain funds from investors, you may need to select a partnership. Then, your partners may have some influence on the type of partnership vesting — a limited or general partnership or an LLC.

In any event, it is necessary for you to understand the types of vesting, so you, and possibly your financing entity, can select the type of ownership that best suits your financial arrangement. The following are the most frequently used types of vesting for small businesses.

Types of Vesting or Ownership

While it may seem insignificant at first, it is sound planning to discuss the various types of business ownership with your accountant and attorney. If you and your spouse are going to own 100 percent of the business, you could elect to form a corporation — either a regular or a subchapter S corporation — or a limited liability company. You could also retain the ownership as a sole proprietorship. If you are going to share ownership with others in addition to your spouse, you could set up a general partnership, a limited partnership, a corporation, or a limited liability company.

For the purposes here, the main differences lie in the areas of responsibility, liability, control, and tax consequences. For example, the partners of a general partnership share proportionally in profits and losses, commensurate with their ownership percentages. All partners are equally responsible for debts and are, typically, equally involved in decisions of management. In a limited partnership, however, one partner is the general partner of the partnership and has all the responsibility, while the limited partners have an investor status — no direct involvement in the management and liable only for their investments.

Corporation

A regular corporation, sometimes referred to as a C corporation, is often formed as an association of several individuals. Nevertheless, one person can form and own a corporation, which is considered by law as one legal entity similar to one person. Corporations are state regulated.

A corporation affords advantages of personal protection by limiting liability from passing through to the owner of individual obligations. A corporation can have the authority to transact business, to buy and sell property, to enter contracts, and to exercise any other power granted within its charter. Ownership interest can be transferred, meaning sold. While the corporate veil gives some limited protection, you pay taxes first on profits for the corporation and again at the personal level on any personal dividends or salaries. In addition, if your business has the protection of a corporation, most franchisors and lenders require personal guarantees.

Subchapter S Corporation

An S corporation provides protection similar to a regular corporation, but all profits and losses pass through to the individuals who are the shareholders. This cuts out one step in taxation, as taxes are assessed the same as for a sole proprietorship. This ownership is similar to a general partnership; however, in an S corporation, loss deductions cannot exceed the amount invested by a shareholder. This type of ownership is restricted to a maximum of 50 stockholders, but it is common for one or two individuals to form one. There are some restrictions as to what types of businesses can qualify for S corporation ownership.

General Partnership

A general partnership is a voluntary association of two or more parties to own and manage a business. Sometimes one of the partners may be a corporation rather than an individual. The partners have ownership interests as per agreed-upon percentages, sharing profits or losses according to their percentages of ownership. They also have percentages of control and liability equal to their ownership interests, with a written agreement as the governing document. Partnerships are much like a marriage; they work well as long as the relationship between the partners is sound, but jealousies and differences of opinion can creep into a partnership and ruin the entire business. For that reason, a clause regarding buying and selling the business should be written into the agreement from the beginning.

Limited Partnership

A limited partnership is comprised of a general partner and one or more limited partners. The general partner operates the business and is legally responsible for it and its indebtedness with unlimited liability. The limited partners, also called limiteds, are investors and are liable only to the extent of their investments, but are not participants in the management of the partnership. In this arrangement, you would be the general partner; the investors are limiteds buying agreed-upon percentages of the business and infusing the capital you need. All profits are divided as per the agreement, and earnings are taxed personally.

Limited Liability Company

This most recently developed type of ownership is a new hybrid form of corporation and partnership with the best aspects of both. The limited liability company (LLC) can allow the tax benefits associated with a partnership business while veiling its owners with the limited liability protection of a corporation. It is an unincorporated business but formed under procedures established by state law and controlled by a written agreement.

An LLC is taxed as a partnership for federal income tax purposes, yet the owners are not personally responsible for the debts, obligations, or other liabilities of the business entity. The members manager the business, but the control of day-to-day operations can be broad or limited to one manager, you, by the terms of the agreement. All states and the District of Columbia have passed legislation permitting LLCs. Although many states allow a one-owner LLC, check with your attorney because some gray areas still exist between state laws and the Internal Revenue Service on this issue.

Another vesting entity called a limited liability partnership (LLP) is very similar to an LLC. Professional groups such as doctors, dentists, lawyers, and accountants frequently elect this form of ownership when they have two or more working partners who wish to limit their liability from the malpractice of the other partners.

Sole Proprietorship

By far the most common type of ownership for small businesses, the sole proprietorship is the easiest to set up and the easiest to understand. No special regulations exist; you, as the owner, simply own all the stock and keep all the profit, with earnings taxed personally. The biggest disadvantage is you are personally responsible and liable for every business decision. In the event of death or retirement, there is no business continuation.

Loan Request and Investor Offering

Now that you have reviewed the types of vesting, your choice may be clearer as to whether you are going to be writing this proposal as a loan request or as an investment offering. To cover all the bases, you may wish to write both versions and submit the appropriate plan to debt and equity financiers.

Loan Request

If you are doing this section as a loan request, begin with a narrative summary explaining the request. Briefly state your exact needs and append it with a schedule of how the loan proceeds are to be used, breaking down the items and corresponding dollar amounts.

When you write your summary request, it is important to keep in mind that every money source will want to know the answers to the following five essential questions.

- How much money do you need?
- What do you plan to use it for?
- How can the money improve your business?
- How are you going to pay it back?
- If your plan for the above doesn't work, what's the backup plan?

Answer these questions in your summary, even if the answers are repeated in an appended schedule and elsewhere in your business plan.

In a typical franchisee loan request, all costs are added to obtain the total funds needed, then your cash investment is subtracted to arrive at the requested loan amount. Remember to increase your working capital by 50 percent. After the presentation of your financial calculations, include the terms you are requesting and the types of collateral you are proposing. Types of collateral are discussed in Chapter 13 under Debt Financing.

Loan Request

This business plan has shown that MegaBucks International publishes a range of $100,000 to $150,000 for total initial investment. A quick check with the franchisor discloses that these "total initial investments" usually include rented or leased facilities.

Our total of the hard and soft costs is $214,750, or about $64,750 higher than the maximum initial investment as shown by MegaBucks International because we have elected to purchase our facility rather than rent or lease. Our exact needs are $60,600 as can be seen from the detail on the appended loan request. To date, we have $154,150 cash invested.

Our president and owner, Denver Smith, owns a 9,645 square foot commercial lot, free and clear, on Henry Street worth $14.00 per square foot. It is his wish to secure the operating loan, if necessary, with this collateral.

The exact use of the $60,600 shown on our request details $15,000 toward the balance of the down payment for the facility, $12,000 for the telephone system, $3,600 for three unpurchased desk set-ups and $30,000 for our cash flow during the first six months of operation. This is commensurate with our working capital requirement as shown in the Financial Pro Formas section of this business plan. The number we are requesting has the recommended 50% safety margin, as the exact amount of cash needed to reach the break-even point is $20,599.

With this new operating loan in place, we can finalize the escrow of our purchase, and begin operations immediately. Although we have forty-five days left to close, the seller will accept an early closing if the opportunity arises.

In addition, we are requesting interest-only payments for the first six months during startup (until break-even), at which time we would like to trigger the principal and interest payments and fix the interest rate at 3% over the then-current short-term Treasury bills.

As a backup plan, Mr. Smith is willing privately to take out a 50% land loan on the lot without going through MegaBucks Smith and Associates; however, he is more acceptable to, and would first rather, borrow the funds through the entity for which they're intended.

Summarize the loan request stating your exact needs.

Answer the five essential questions.

State your backup plan.

Include a schedule of how the loan proceeds are to be used.

MegaBucks $mith and Associates

Loan Request

Hard Costs:	Paid	Needed
Facility (balance of down payment) (See Exhibits, Loan Request, for contract and receipt of deposit)	$ 85,000	$15,000
Equipment		
Computer equipment	5,000	
Telephone		12,000
Furniture (balance, see Exhibits, Inventory):		
7 desk set-ups	8,400	
3 desk set-ups		3,600
Fixtures (all improvements complete):		
Office partitions	14,000	
Carpet	8,000	
Painting	2,000	
Decorator items	—	
Signage	5,200	
Vehicles	Leased	
Total of Hard Costs	**$127,600**	**$30,600**
Soft Costs:		
Inventory	$ N/A	
Supplies	800	
Franchise fee	25,000	
Miscellaneous deposits needed	750	
Preopening costs (in working capital)	—	
Working capital		$30,000
Total of Soft Costs	**$26,550**	**$30,000**

Total Funds to Open	$214,750
Less My Cash Investment	154,150
Requested Loan Amount	$ 60,600

Terms Requested

1. Length of loan: 10 years, amortized over 20.
2. Interest rate: 3 % over short-term Treasury Bills.
3. Loan fee: 1 Point.
4. First six months interest-only payments until break-even and profit.
5. Waiver of prepayment penalty for early loan payoff.

Collateral available: Denver Smith has equity in a commercial lot which is free and clear (no debt, no encumbrances), valued at $135,000, which can be used as security for this operating loan.

Be sure to recheck the numbers on your loan request. It is essential they be consistent with the pro forma financial data in the rest of your business plan. Although you may have specific ideas as to the terms you want, investigate your lender's programs and attempt to coordinate your request with a program the lender already offers.

Investment Offering

This section may also serve as an offering to investors for limited partners, general partners, or members of an LLC. As you would do for a loan request, preface this with a narrative summary detailing your financial needs and the structure for the investors' involvement. This descriptive summary should also answer the five essential questions which every money source is looking for, as explained above.

Again, generate an appended schedule listing your financial needs and describing how the proceeds are to be used — similar to the loan request. Instead of discussing loan terms, however, include your proposed offering — the involvement you propose for the partners or investors:

- The type of ownership entity,
- The terms of payback for the investors' funds, and
- The return-on-investment to the investors.

You might also mention possible terms of a buy-out of your investors' interest at a certain point, as in the example on the next page.

Besides your narrative description and its attached list, it is not enough to assume all of the materials are assembled to complete an investment offering. What is covered here is a simple proposal, similar to a letter of intent. Once your investor shows strong interest, you will need to provide additional information, such as risks, which depend on the securities and disclosure requirements in your state, and a complete agreement that encompasses the legal issues, which vary from state to state. Your attorney can assist you with these.

Because states have different laws involving investment offerings and because some franchisors have certain restrictions regarding nonworking partners or investors, it is a good idea to have your attorney and your franchisor review your final business plan draft. In particular, have your attorney review your business plan as an investment offering before you present it to prospective investors.

Investment Offering

This business plan has shown that MegaBucks International publishes a range of $100,000 to $150,000 for total initial investment. A quick check with the franchisor discloses that these "total initial investments" usually include rented or leased facilities.

Our total of the hard and soft costs is $214,750, or about $64,750 higher than the maximum initial investment as shown by MegaBucks International because we have elected to purchase our facility rather than rent or lease. Our exact needs are $60,600 as can be seen from the detail on the appended investment offering. To date, we have $154,150 cash invested of our own funds.

Our president and owner, Denver Smith, is looking for a partner to invest the outside capital needed of $60,600 in exchange for 25% ownership. The funds are needed to open business.

The exact use of the $60,600 shown on our request details $15,000 toward the balance of the down payment for the facility, $12,000 for the telephone system, $3,600 for three unpurchased desk set-ups and $30,000 for our cash flow during the first six months of operation. This is commensurate with our working capital requirement as shown in the Financial Pro Formas section of this business plan. The number we are requesting has the recommended 50% safety margin as the exact amount of cash needed to reach the break-even point is $20,599.

With the type of ownership as a limited partnership, the investor, as a limited partner, cannot expect to receive any return until the seventh month after opening (until after break-even). From our pro formas, at the end of the fifth year of distributions, the investor will have received $164,985, a 272% return on investment — 54.4% annualized return, while still owning 25% of the business. If at that time, the limited partner elects to sell his or her share of the business, Mr. Smith will purchase it at fair market value. Our agreement will also include a stipulation that Mr. Smith is given the right of first refusal to purchase the investor's share if and when the investor wishes to sell at any time after two years. If the partners have difficulty in coming to an agreement of the ownership value at the time of sale, the value of the business can be determined via an appraisal using the standard rules of arbitration.

As a backup plan, Mr. Smith owns a 9,645 square-foot commercial lot, free and clear, on Henry Street worth $14.00 per square foot. If the business does not generate a minimum of 25% return on investment by the end of the 18th month of business for the limited partner, Mr. Smith will finance the Henry Street property with a 50% land loan and use the funds to buy out the limited partner for the face amount of the investment plus 8% annualized interest, at the option and sole discretion of the limited partner.

The exact details and terms are specified in the Agreement of Formation of the limited partnership.

Sidebar notes (right margin):

Summarize your financial needs and create the structure for the investor's involvement.

Answer the five essential questions.

Cover the type of ownership, the investor's role, the terms of payback, and the return-on-investment.

State your backup plan.

Include a schedule of how the funds are to be used.

MegaBucks $mith and Associates

Investment Offering

Hard Costs:

	Paid	Needed
Facility (balance of down payment) (See Exhibits, Loan Request, for contract and receipt of deposit)	$ 85,000	$15,000
Equipment		
Computer equipment	5,000	
Telephone		12,000
Furniture (balance, see Exhibits, Inventory):		
7 desk set-ups	8,400	
3 desk set-ups		3,600
Fixtures (all improvements complete):		
Office partitions	14,000	
Carpet	8,000	
Painting	2,000	
Decorator items	—	
Signage	5,200	
Vehicles	Leased	
Total of Hard Costs	**$127,600**	**$30,600**
Soft Costs:		
Inventory	$ N/A	
Supplies	800	
Franchise fee	25,000	
Miscellaneous deposits needed	750	
Preopening costs	(In working capital)	
Working capital		$30,000
Total of Soft Costs	**$26,550**	**$30,000**

Total Funds to Open	$214,750
Less My Cash Investment	154,150
Investment Requirement	$ 60,600

Investor Offering Proposal: A Hawaii limited partnership

Investor's Capital	$60,600
Ownership of Investor	25%

After break-even (the sixth month of business), the investor, as a limited partner, will receive 25% of the net income starting the seventh month of business and thereafter. From our projections, at the end of the fifth year of distributions, the limited partner will have received 54.4% annual return on investment and still own 25% of the business. If, at that time, the limited partner wishes to sell his or her partnership interest, the general partner will buy the limited partner's share of ownership at fair market value. For other terms and conditions, see Agreement of Formation of the limited partnership of MegaBucks Smith and Associates in the Exhibits.

Revise Your Request or Offering

Finally, review your completed loan request or investment offering for clarity and accuracy. The next section of your business plan is the final one, the business plan exhibits, and the subject of the next chapter.

Chapter 11

Business Plan Exhibits

There is no advancement to him who stands trembling because he cannot see the end from the beginning.
— E. J. KLEMME

While most of the relevant supporting information and schedules should be included in their respective sections, many documents are either too cumbersome there or have no particular place in the body of your business plan. Support documentation of this type, still needed for the reviewer, is grouped together as exhibits at the end of the business plan.

It is important to limit the size of this section. The days of the 100-page business plan are gone. The rule of thumb now is that the group of exhibits should be no longer than the main body of the business plan.

If you elect to use the long-form personal résumé — rather than the shorter summary form introduced in Chapter 8 — for the principals and managers of your franchise business, it is best to locate them in the exhibits section. Inserting them in the management qualifications section tends to disrupt the flow of the reading, due to the length of these documents. In light of this, the discussion of the full personal résumé is presented here as a part of the exhibits section.

The other important factor in preparing your exhibits is to make them easy for the reviewer to find. This chapter discusses these elements of the exhibits section:

- Table of contents
- Exhibits
- Management team résumés

Table of Contents of Exhibits

The exhibits start with a table of contents identifying a complete list of the materials included, referencing them with tabbed indexes or by page number. On the contents page should be the title, "Contents of Exhibits," "Exhibits," or "Business Plan Exhibits." Use the same format as the one you used for your business plan table of contents.

Contents of Exhibits

Franchisor Overview

1. Industry Statistics from MBI
2. Market Segments from MBI as compiled from the U.S. Bureau of the Census
3. Market Share, local Multiple Listing Service (MLS) statistics

The Market

4. Market Size and Trends: from MBI
5. Population and Income, Hawaii County statistics
6. Demographics, correlation of age, education, income: from MBI
7. MLS statistics

Management Qualifications

8. Résumés, MegaBucks Smith and Associates:
   - Denver Smith
   - Mark McKinsey
   - Steven Swan
   - Barry O'Brien
   - Lisa Soma
9. Organizational Chart, Officers and Directors: MBI
10. Résumés, MegaBucks International
    - Donald R. Frump
    - L. Scott Creedy
    - Lawrence P. Marshall
    - Tracy C. Godfrey
    - Fielding Winslow
    - George R. Collins

Financial Pro Forma

11. Personal Financial Statements: Denver Smith
    - Statement of Income
    - Balance Sheet
12. Personal Income Tax Returns: last two years

continued

Contents of Exhibits (continued)

Loan Request

13. Purchase Agreement and Deposit Receipt

14. Inventory: furniture, equipment, and signage

Other MegaBucks International materials

15. Company Profile

16. Year-end Public Report

17. Location Data Report

Other legal documents

18. MegaBucks Smith and Associates license to do business in Kona

19. Resolution to Borrow $60,000

20. Certificate of Good Standing

Other facility documents

21. Photographs: site, elevation, and interior

22. Site plan and floor plan

Insurance

23. Letter from Jones and King Insurance explaining all coverages

Business references

24. Lender references

25. Partnership references

26. Letters of Intent to purchase from seven clients (under separate cover, Addendum to Business Plan)

   • Uniform Franchise Offering Circular

   • MBI Franchise Agreement

   • Articles of Incorporation

   • Preliminary Title Report

Exhibits

Although the exhibits suggested below relate to many businesses, you are the best person to judge those exhibits most important to support your business plan and those necessary to customize your plan for the reviewer you are targeting. To control the size of your plan, it is best to present only those items that support your text; therefore, use your best discretion in considering the many suggestions in this chapter.

After reviewing these topics, if you feel your business plan may be too large because of voluminous or awkward-sized documents, a solution is to take out the least supportive and inconvenient items but list them on an Addendum Directory page. This page then goes into your business plan exhibits with a note that these additional items are available under separate cover. Then package these secondary items together in a separate binder with the title "Addendum to the Business Plan." with its own table of contents. Keep it on file for anyone who requests it.

For your primary exhibits, include only material covered within the main body of your business plan. Do not introduce new material in the exhibits. If you have new material that is significant, it is best to rewrite the appropriate section; but if time does not permit, separate the new material as a separate addendum to your business plan under a different cover.

Following is a comprehensive list of suggested materials that are included in various business plans. Identify those that are essential for yours.

Business Plan Support Documents

☐ Research findings on your industry, market, and competitors that is too cumbersome to enclose in its appropriate sections of your business plan.

☐ Résumés, personal financial statements, credit reports, and personal tax returns.

☐ A list of all equipment, fixtures, furniture, and signage with corresponding costs.

☐ An inventory of supplies with corresponding costs.

Franchisor Materials

☐ Any excerpts from the franchisor UFOC that are appropriate and permitted by your franchisor.

☐ Franchisor marketing materials, especially sales brochures and flyers.

☐ Technological reports, descriptions, and drawings of your products or services.

Legal Documents

☐ A copy of your franchise agreement.

☐ A copy of your business license.

☐ A copy of any fictitious business name statements.

☐ If your business is a corporation, a copy of the certificate of incorporation, articles of corporation, and your state Status of Good Standing Certificate.

☐ If your business is a general partnership, a limited partnership, or limited liability company, a copy of the statement of partnership or agreement of formation.

Facility Documentation

☐ If you lease your facility, a copy of the lease or a summary that gives all the major data. Include address; whether your facility is free-standing, in a regional mall, or at a strip center; the square footage; monthly rent; cost per square foot; term of lease; amount of deposit; and any specified increases.

☐ If you are buying your facility, a preliminary title report and a copy of your contract or signed escrow instructions.

☐ If you have already purchased your facility, a copy of the deed, escrow closing statement, or some evidence of purchase.

☐ A copy of a real estate appraisal of your facility, if available. Lenders now must obtain their own directly since federal regulations have tightened, but there is no harm in presenting one if available, especially if the numbers are strong and the appraisal is necessary to your business plan.

☐ Photographs of your facility.

☐ A layout or floor plan of your facility and the site layout, especially showing parking and the locations for entering and exiting.

Insurance Coverage

Provide a list of your business insurance — verified by your franchisor's requirements. Here is the typical coverage needed.

☐ Worker's compensation insurance, generally required by state law, to cover employee losses due to job-related injuries.

☐ Liability insurance, which covers your liability if anyone is injured at your location as well as damage to customers' property.

☐ Life insurance on you, as owner, and on any other principals.

☐ Fire, burglary, and business-interruption insurance, the latter of which provides you an income, typically up to a specific amount for a specific time, if your business is stopped due to fire or other circumstances beyond your control.

☐ Inventory insurance, if the nature of your business dictates the need.

☐ Product liability insurance, to protect against customer lawsuits for injury caused by items sold.

Business References

☐ Trade references, giving the company name, trade relationship, name of contact person, address, and telephone number.

☐ Lender references, with the same detail as above.

☐ Previous or current partner and business references.

☐ Endorsements from sources or customers.

☐ Purchase agreements, or letters of intent, from existing or future customers.

☐ Photographs of your operation, if open for business.

Remember that you can include anything else you may deem necessary as supporting documents for the text of your business plan.

Management Team Résumés

The format of a résumé for a business plan is somewhat different from the traditional résumé to obtain employment. While several good résumé formats exist, a suggested one that is well-accepted gives categories or topics using descriptions or lists introduced by bullet points, whichever is more appropriate for each category.

Use the latest personal computer software programs with desktop publishing techniques such as borders, boxes, various type sizes and styles, bold face, and shadow lines for emphasis or clarity. It is all right to use a college-level vocabulary, but avoid long or flowery words in favor of simpler ones when their meaning is clear. Use objective rather than subjective adjectives when possible, and always avoid first person. Keep the length to no more than two pages; only the principals' and one special manager's résumés are this length. Otherwise, limit those you include to one page.

Name and Title

If you already have your business letterhead, use it for the first page of this résumé. If not, use your desktop publishing software to develop a letterhead in a professional format, listing the name of your company, address, telephone number(s), and fax number. You can also include your Internet and e-mail addresses. This first page is similar to a cover page or introductory page for the other résumé pages to follow. If you add the résumés of other key managers, it is recommended to use plain stationery without the letterhead. Begin with your name and your title: owner, chief executive officer, or president. Two or more titles are permissible.

Profile

Under your name and title, introduce your profile with a sidehead or crosshead. The description in the profile should be only about three or four sentences — clauses are acceptable — and identify your pertinent history to this point, such as in the example for Denver Smith.

Qualifications Summary

The next résumé category, the qualifications summary, is the one area in which you can embellish your skills and qualifications. While this can be in paragraph form, bulleted lists are considered quicker and easier to read, as in the example. The more objective your information is, the more believable your qualifications are — for instance, the first statement listed in the example is something that can easily be validated, if need be.

Education

Except for specialized classes or training that might be directly related to business or the technology of your business, omit your high school years, but list your undergraduate and graduate education, if any, to the highest grade level completed.

In addition to formal education, list all professional and post-school business-related courses, technical schools, seminars, training programs, computer classes, and other employee training classes or certifications that reflect your educational background, skills, and accomplishments. Arrange the list so your most recent education is listed first and then work your way back chronologically. Give the name of any college or university or private program sponsor, the city and state, followed by the degree or specific classes in your field, and the year the degrees were issued or the subjects studied. See the example.

If your educational background is limited, it is acceptable to reach a little into your high school curricula, especially if you had some specialty courses that are pertinent, such as business law or salesmanship. Even applicable apprenticeships are sometimes listed. One company owner, who was quite embarrassed that he had never graduated from high school, left education off his résumé entirely. His educational experience wasn't missed with all of his business accomplishments filling the page. Another creative entrepreneur with the same problem boldly typed "On-the-Job Training: 1974 to Present" and then listed every project and, across from each, a one-word description of what she had learned. The result was quite impressive.

Experience

The next category, experience, is the one most often reviewed in earnest. This part of the résumé is only slightly different from that of job-seeker résumés. Experience, in this case, refers to employment or occupational experience; nevertheless, if you have military experience and feel your training or past duties enhance your ability to orchestrate your current business, then include that background in this category of your résumé. Again, list your experience in reverse chronological order. Put dates in the justified left column under *Experience* and list the jobs to the right. One popular format gives the name of the company you worked for or owned, your title underneath on the second line, and a short job description under that.

The lines thus far described are indented to match the indents of all the information above. If any special projects or awards are influential, create a line space and indent these to a second indent under each job entry, as in the example shown for Denver Smith.

The first job to describe is your current franchise position as chief executive officer and owner of your present new business. For a job résumé, you may have been taught to list every job you've held, from the present back to school. However, for your business plan résumé, it is only important to mention the positions that are appropriate support to your present business. Emphasize those most relevant to your current position as franchise owner. If you feel it is essential to fill in the complete chronology, then be very brief in describing those jobs unrelated to your business plan.

The strongest picture of your past is when you can show that your recent jobs bear an influence on where you are today. This sends a signal to the reviewer you are on a forward trend increasing in momentum to this point, with experience that has brought you to being the CEO of your present franchise.

References

For a franchise business plan, it is acceptable simply to state that references are available upon request. If you choose to list references, however, mention only those that are professionally relevant or that may be strong character testimonies. List no more than three with name, title, business, and telephone number. While these should be people who can verify your honesty, they should also be persons who have knowledge of the major areas of your background and abilities. In other words, it is better to have professional references than personal ones.

MegaBucks $mith and Associates
77-6452 Alii Drive
Kallua-Kona, Hawaii 96740
(808) 555-1234 – FAX (808) 555-1111

Denver Smith – Owner, Chief Executive Officer

Profile:

Over ten years as a licensed real estate broker in sales and leasing in all markets: residential — custom homes, subdivisions, and multi-family; commercial — shopping centers, banks, restaurants; professional — office, medical and dental; and industrial parks. For the last three years, specialized in gross sales of real estate development, involved in rezoning and soliciting major homebuilders.

Qualifications Summary:

- Has successfully reached sales averaging $9,000,000 per year for the last three years.
- Is an excellent organizer, combining creativity with tenacity and strong verbal, written, and presentation skills.
- Has expertise in the latest computer software and such specialized programs as Microsoft Project and CADD.

Education:

- University of California, San Francisco, California
  - — Continuing education courses in real estate – 1994
  - — Continuing education courses in architecture – 1992
- University of the Pacific, Stockton, California
  - — Post-graduate courses in business – 1991
- University of Missouri, Columbia, Missouri
  - — Bachelor of Business Administration – 1990

Certificates and Licenses:

Hawaii Real Estate Broker, CCIM

Experience:

1998–present: MegaBucks Smith and Associates
Owner, CEO, President
Responsible for recruiting, training, operations, advertising, sales, and administration.
Sales: $14,000,000 first year

1990–1998: Century 21 Lacerte and Associates
Sales Agent: Commission sales, commercial real estate
Awards:
- Received C21 Award for Best Regional Sales – 1997
- Salesperson of the Year – 1997

For your résumés, use a business letterhead for the first page with updated information to include facsimile number, Internet and e-mail addresses.

The Final Touches

Before you make copies of your business plan for distribution, have your figures checked by an accountant or bookkeeper and the text proofread by an editor or proofreader. Then make the corrections, reprint the pages, and check that your changes were done accurately.

An accurate, easy-to-read, and well-organized text conveys professionalism and credibility. Too often, the important step of checking the accuracy of the entire business plan is avoided or forgotten and, despite all your work, a few typos, missing words, poor sentence construction, or inaccurate figures can spoil an otherwise good presentation. Until you do these things, your business plan is not really a finished product.

Your Franchise Business Plan Is Complete

When you have completed your business plan, you are ready to begin the critical process of shopping for your financing; finding partners, investors, lenders, or some combination of these; and making personal presentations of your business plan. Part III deals with these issues and suggests some possible resources to contact.

Part III

Your Financing Resources

Chapter 12

Sources for Equity Financing

If one advances confidently in the direction of his dreams, and endeavors to live the life which he has imagined, he will meet with a success unexpected in common hours.
— HENRY DAVID THOREAU

Having completed your business plan, you are now ready to submit it. But who should you send it to for the best results?

The answer to this really starts with the amount of cash or liquid assets, if any, you have available to invest into your new franchise venture. In Chapter 2, you discovered the amount of capital you will need for your investment requirement. Focusing on that, you have several options.

If your own capital base is insufficient, or if your choice is not to use your personal funds, it is possible to get into business with no money down in several ways. One is selecting a franchisor that provides 100 percent financing; other options involve using other people's money.

When using other people's money, however, you give up some ownership by taking in one or more partners or selling stock to acquire the start-up funds. If your business plan is well-written and feasible, this should not be too difficult. People in a nonfranchised business have to convince prospective partners or investors that they have the skills and capability of running the business. This is very difficult to do, however, unless they already have experience. In a franchised business, the task is much easier if you direct the attention of your would-be partners or investors to the franchise-training program and the history of the franchisor's other successful franchisees and ongoing support. Moreover, in the franchise system, many of these other successful franchisees are readily available for the reviewers to contact in undergoing their own decision process. For your part, the basic skill needed, besides integrity, is the ability to sell the reviewers on the merits of your franchise through your business plan. This — coupled with the national statistics of the success rate for franchising in general and those of your franchise in particular — is one realistic approach for a successful outcome in starting a franchise with no money down. Still others exist as well.

Equity Financing

Equity financing is a method of raising capital by selling a portion of your business to investors. For many hard costs, such as real estate or fixtures, it is not difficult to raise funds through conventional lenders. For these, you can frequently obtain a real estate loan or set up an equipment lease. However, for soft costs, such as marketing, personnel salaries, and operations overhead, debt financing is difficult and sometimes impossible to find. If you need to raise capital, but you do not have the collateral or current ability to meet debt-service payments for a traditional loan, you may have to consider equity financing as a means and to give up some ownership. The two major sources of equity financing are venture capitalists and individual investors.

Venture Capital

Venture capital financing is a specialty area of finance that is characteristically high-risk — created for high-risk businesses that can yield high returns to offset the risks. The businesses funded are usually less desirable to conventional lenders for various reasons, one being the newness of a company, such as an unproved company or a start-up company.

A professional venture capitalist is trained in this area of finance to manage a pool of venture funds for a group, or syndicate, of passive investors who invest in growing companies. These higher-risk investors expect greater rewards. Although venture capitalists are typically slow to get in — usually three to six months for funding approval — they are quick to get out. In addition, while there is normally no collateral requirement, the group sometimes requires an option to seize your business if you fail to make the pay-off agreement.

As franchising became recognized as a legitimate method of business expansion, the 1980s saw an increasing number of venture capital groups making commitments to promising franchisees. This trend took a downturn with the recessional period of the early 1990s. A significant turning-point year in this period was 1994 when venture capitalists still invested $60 million in seed capital for start-up companies. Seed capital, as opposed to start-up capital, is an investment in the developmental stage of an idea. Start-up capital takes a new business into full operation. The amount of venture capital for start-up investments currently remains much higher than that raised for seed capital.

Although you give up some ownership for both venture capital groups and individual investors, venture capital ownership is normally temporary, designed for you to repurchase the shares at some point in time at a guaranteed prearranged price. For example, suppose you are planning to start a franchise with a total investment need of $400,000. A venture capitalist group decides to finance your business in return for 45 percent of your corporate stock. You agree to repurchase those shares for $500,000 in five years. During that time, you distribute profits in the form of dividends, paying 45 percent to your venture partners. At the end of the five years, you have paid $300,000 in dividends to them and you repurchase the stock for $500,000 as agreed. They have doubled their original investment, but you now own 100 percent of your business.

Venture capital sources include major corporations with cash surpluses, insurance companies, management consulting groups, and information pools. For a membership directory of venture capital firms, you can contact the National Venture Capital Association.

National Venture Capital Association
1655 North Fort Myer Drive, #700
Arlington, VA 22209
(703) 351-5267

In addition, there are organizations that link investors and those needing seed capital. One example is:

Venture Capital OnLine
423 10th Street
Wilmette, IL 60091
(847) 256-0403
e-mail: bvp@vcapital.com

Another resource is to register with a service for seeking venture capital; many exist on the internet. One of these, a subsidiary of *American Venture Magazine*, is:

American Venture Capital Exchange
Internet: http://www.avce.com

Another source that is updated twice daily on the internet is:

Venture Capital Resource Library
20912 Coventry Lane
Lake Forest, CA 92630
(949) 583-2741
Internet: http://www.vfinance.com
e-mail: aaron@vfinance.com

While venture capitalists are a major source for equity financing, they regularly deal only in large dollar amounts and are therefore a limited resource for smaller businesses. Besides the small amounts funded for start-up capital, other less desirable businesses they fund are businesses that are already highly leveraged.

A typical venture capital arrangement forces these companies into giving up further equity by issuing warrants. Warrants are issued to venture capital investors giving them the right to purchase additional stock in the future, generally by a stipulated date, at a preset price. Some franchise agreements have restrictions making it difficult, and in some cases impossible, to allow investments by venture capitalists. Unless you are getting into franchising in a big way, such as through multiple franchises, an area development agreement, or hotels and motels, funding from venture capital groups is usually a highly limited source. Yet, you might be able to tap into these sources in other ways.

Many private corporations and even state governments manage venture funds for investing in growth companies. One chief source for expanding franchisors is a Small Business Investment Company (SBIC). At the latest count, there is a network of 500 SBICs, which are mostly venture capital groups, investment firms, or other private financial organizations. All are licensed under the Small Business Investment Act of 1958 to borrow funds through the Small Business Administration (SBA) for reinvestment in small businesses. The government is a sort of silent partner in the investment, infusing capital through the SBIC licensed company. Some SBICs specialize in franchising, especially those franchisors that are very successful. Contact their national organization to obtain a list of SBICs.

National Association of Small Business Investment Companies
1199 North Fairfax, Suite 200
Alexandria, VA 22314
(703) 683-1601

SBICs make SBA loans with competitive interest rates, or they make direct investments by purchasing a percentage of the ownership. A pool of their investment company membership usually generates the funds. Currently, the debt-financing commitments, or loans, are increasing in number and dollar amount while equity-financing arrangements, or direct investments, are remaining stable.

One special version is a minority enterprise small business investment company (MESBIC) that focuses on businesses run by members of minority groups. In business, this includes women. A MESBIC may also be a subsidiary of the Minority Business Development Agency. Although similar to SBICs in that they make loans with competitive interest rates and direct investments, they sometimes grant subsidies to minority-owned businesses as well. They especially like franchises because of the high success rate. You can locate the MESBICs in your area by contacting your local or regional SBA office. A listing of the SBA's regional offices can be found in Appendix B.

The investment division of the Small Business Administration has a directory of available SBICs and MESBICs. In addition, the SBA publishes an update, the *SBIC Digest*, with additions and deletions to the directory.

Investment Division
Small Business Administration
409 3rd Street SW
Washington, DC 20416
(800) U-ASK-SBA

Capital Publishing Corporation is another source that keeps a record of venture capitalists, investors, and licensed SBICs.

Capital Publishing Corporation
125 South Wacker Drive
Chicago, IL 60606
(312) 214-2505

Today there is more venture capital available than there was in the early '90s. With such low interest rates from traditional investments in savings, money market accounts, Treasury bills, and tax-free bonds, and instability in the stock market and mutual funds, more venture capital is being channeled into strong, existing businesses and preferred franchising startups. Look for this to continue as the economy continues to improve. Strong growth companies always command a solid share.

Individual Investors

Because franchising is now a recognized method of business expansion, an increasing number of private investors make commitments of capital to approved prospective franchisees. "Angel" is the slang term for an individual or independent investor who provides money and support to a start-up franchise or other business, typically in exchange for equity interest (a portion of the ownership). Generally, retired or semiretired managers and executives have money to invest and would like to be a general partner or active member or owner through a limited liability company. They often want involvement in the operation and a management or director position. However, many investors would rather be limited partners, wishing to avoid liability beyond their own investment.

You can solicit potential partners in most states through advertising, but it is advisable to have your attorney review your ad copy first, because there are securities laws against advertising to sell corporate stock or to simply request money. It is better to advertise to fill a vacant director's or manager's position with the possibility of acquiring some ownership.

Besides advertising, the best resource for locating individual investors is a small business broker; however, you can put the word out with nearly anyone who meets and deals with these persons, such as attorneys, bankers, mortgage brokers, stockbrokers, and real estate brokers. Many others in business can direct you to a potential investor who might be interested in your specific type of business, especially if given an incentive and comfortably impressed with your business plan.

There Are More Alternatives

If you would rather explore other types of financing — as an alternative to equity financing — Chapter 13 discusses debt financing and Chapter 14 covers franchisor financing.

Sources for Debt Financing

Banking may well be a career from which no man really recovers.
— JOHN KENNETH GALBRAITH

After examining the various types of equity financing and weighing the burden that accompanies it, namely giving up some ownership interest, you may prefer to retain full ownership and attempt to get a loan. Debt financing is an alternative that does not involve a transfer of ownership.

Debt Financing

Debt financing is simply the acquiring of a loan and making principal and interest payments until it is paid. While simply stated, it is not so simple. Assuming you need financing and your franchise system is one of the 80 percent that doesn't provide it, the first step is to separate the amount to borrow into two categories:

- The amount needed for real estate and equipment representing fixed capital, or hard costs; and
- The amount needed for everything else, from supplies to working capital, or soft costs.

The hard costs are typically financed by long-term loans, while any portion of the soft costs, if financed, are usually handled through short-term loans. The lender may be the same for both.

What needs to be decided is the total amount you can afford, within your budget, in terms of payments for this financing. You can determine this with the help of your accountant. Try to establish the impact that payments for debt financing will have on your monthly cash flow during the first years of business and on the bottom line, your ability to make a profit.

Take the example of a franchise investment loan for debt financing in which the total investment needed is $600,000. The investment requirement is shown in the example.

A private money source offers to loan 65 percent of the total needed, structured under two loans.

- The first loan is long-term for $315,000, secured by the real estate and permanent improvements for 15 years at 10.75 percent fixed interest, with a monthly principal and interest payment of $3,521.
- The second loan is short-term for $75,000, to cover the soft costs set up for five years at 12 percent, with interest-only monthly payments of $750 and the entire principal due at the end.

The idea here is that at the end of five years, the franchisee is going to be well-heeled enough to pay off the $75,000 supplemental loan or have

Original Investment – Example			
Facility or site	$380,000		
Equipment and fixtures	65,000		
Signs	5,000		
Hard costs, subtotal		$450,000	
Miscellaneous deposits needed	2,000		
Product	35,000		
Supplies	12,000		
Initial fee	30,000		
Working capital to break even	71,000		
Soft costs, subtotal		$150,000	
Total investment, 100%			$600,000
Franchisee cash equity, 35%			(210,000)
Amount to finance, 65%			$390,000
Long-term loan, 70% LTV	$315,000		
Short-term loan, 50% LTV	75,000		
Total loans	$390,000		

the ability to refinance the debt. It represents risk for both parties, but the resulting combined monthly payment of $4,271 is the maximum payment the franchisee could manage.

As stated, the advantage of debt financing is that you maintain 100 percent ownership and full control of your business. The disadvantages, however, are that it is hard to find such funds if the need goes beyond the conventional real estate financing; and, if found, care must be exercised to keep from getting overleveraged.

In the example, if the lender had insisted on principal reductions of the supplemental short-term loan, the combined payment would not have worked within the budget of the franchisee. The real estate security represented tangible collateral, or hard collateral, for the long-term note. Other real estate, such as a second mortgage on your home, is another good source of hard collateral for additional funding if you cannot acquire an unsecured short-term note.

Some lenders will consider types of intangible collateral similar to lines of credit or specific insurance policies designating them as the beneficiary. For an established business, lenders have even assigned goodwill as intangible security for unconventional debt financing and some types of commercial loans.

Commercial Lending

What is a commercial lender? Most commercial lenders are banks. However, your local bank is probably a consumer bank, because there are only about 15,000 commercial banks in this country.

Commercial lending is a conventional type of debt financing for small business. These loans are primarily short term, as most of their business is in checking, savings, and time deposits, which means these funds can be withdrawn upon demand or with little notice, thus it is difficult for them to deal in long-term loans. From a commercial lending standpoint, however, franchising is still relatively new as a method of expanding a business. Because of this, these lenders generally want hard collateral as security, such as real estate, equipment, and inventory. If you are like most new franchisees, your problem with this is that even when this type of collateral is available, lenders expect you to allocate the borrowed proceeds primarily for the purchase of hard assets, whereas in reality, your needs are normally for soft costs such as for goods, supplies, salaries, advertising, and marketing costs. If you can overcome this obstacle, traditional bank loans from commercial lenders remain a viable source of capital for you.

Another common requirement for a commercial loan is equity participation. This means you have to participate in coming up with one-third to one-half of the loan on your own and still have sufficient collateral for the balance. For example, if your working capital need is $90,000, you will be required to have one-third down, $30,000, of your own funds for a loan of

$60,000 or one-half down, $45,000, for a loan of $45,000. In addition, you will have to secure the loan with collateral, such as a second mortgage on your house or some other asset.

When you negotiate a commercial loan or an operating line of credit, the chief considerations are the terms of the loan and the lender's requirement for its protection against loan default through collateral and personal guarantees or coveted control. Naturally, you want the best terms regarding loan fee, rate of interest, term of loan, and other costs. You also want to assign the least amount of collateral and yield the minimum level of coveted control. If you can, attempt to use a combination of tangible and intangible collateral and to reserve some unassigned collateral for emergency loans.

When you apply for a loan with a commercial lender, first find out what its parameters and guidelines are, to see if they answer your needs. It helps to talk to a loan officer before you formally apply, so you can structure your request to match the lender's criteria. This also makes the loan officer's job easier when your request is submitted.

The full cost of the loan may be somewhat obscure, even from the most reputable lenders. Whether intentionally or not, they camouflage these under direct and indirect costs. A direct cost is the loan fee, or cost-of-loan fee, which is a percentage of the total loan, called points — one and one-half percent is the same as one and one-half points. The indirect costs may cover any number of costs including closing costs, document preparation fees, processing fees, inspection fees, credit report fees, filing fees, appraisal costs, attorney or legal fees, and loan commitment fees. The loan commitment fee is an upfront fee, or deposit, charged at the time the lender issues a firm commitment to make the loan. This is customarily applied to, or credited against, the loan fee when the loan is executed.

When obtaining a commercial loan, look for another pending fee, a prepayment penalty. The lender adds one as a matter of course. If you think you may pay the loan off early, negotiate with the lender to release you from the prepayment penalty. Many times a conventional lender will waive this future fee as a concession in negotiation.

The rate of interest and term of the loan are sometimes negotiable. If you have the luxury of finding more than one lender interested in making you a commercial loan or line of credit, you can compare them for the most competitive terms. Frequently banks set these terms based on the prevailing market rates, your past relationship with them, your financial strength, and the extent of risk they establish for the proposed loan. Commercial lenders generally do not use fixed interest rates, favoring an adjustable rate based on prime plus some percentage that is set dependent on these other factors.

If you are seeking a loan from a commercial lender that is new to you, a gesture of good faith is to open other accounts and start doing business there to become an existing customer and to develop rapport. While this works best in a subtle and friendly manner, you can occasionally use a big deposit pointedly to negotiate better terms. Appendix A lists some commercial lending sources.

International Banks

If your franchisor is an established and well-known company, international banks may have some interest in making you a loan — especially banks from countries participating in the European Union, including the United Kingdom, Germany, the Netherlands, France, Belgium, Luxembourg, Italy, Denmark, Ireland, Greece, Portugal, Spain, Austria, Sweden, and Finland. Canadian banks and lenders in the Asian trade countries of Japan, Taiwan, and Hong Kong are also good sources. The catch is your business must be located in the service area of one of these banks. Any major cities along the East and West coasts, as well as those situated near the Canadian border, are good possibilities. To find these banks, check in the Yellow Pages or contact the local chamber of commerce. Appendix A has a listing of international banks that specialize in franchise financing.

The U.S. Small Business Administration

When you approach commercial lenders and attempt to obtain a small business loan, they will often mention SBA loans. SBA funds can be used for start-up capital, working capital, business expansion, real estate, construction or building conversions, equipment financing, or purchase of existing businesses.

The SBA offers two types of assistance. The first is a direct disbursement of funds — usually loans and on rare occasions grants or subsidies. The second is loans by private lenders backed by the SBA.

SBA Direct-disbursement Loans

The Small Business Administration is still in business; Congress created it specifically to help small businesspeople. In 1984, however, an effort was made to stop SBA programs. Although it failed, the effect made its impact and by 1985, funding was drastically reduced. While it is expected to remain this way until the government reduces the federal deficit, the new balanced budget includes an increase in the amount available.

Today, direct disbursement funds are only occasionally made available and then only for periods of three days or less. When the federal government announces that funds are available, regional offices distribute them quickly on a first-come-first-served basis to qualified applicants. The main advantage of this type of loan is the low interest rate, which is lower than any other type of debt financing. The disadvantage is the limited timing and the poor odds of getting one.

If you are a Vietnam or disabled veteran, you can be eligible for a direct SBA loan up to a maximum of $150,000. Every SBA office has a veterans affairs officer. As part of the eligibility requirements, you must be unable to get a guaranteed loan or other credit anywhere else. Unfortunately, the funds are available only two times a year. If you are on a waiting list and the funds come available but run out before they get to your request, you wait another six months with no guarantee.

SBA-backed Loans

The second and more realistic form of assistance from the SBA is the SBA-backed loan through a lender in the SBA participation program. (See Appendix A.) Their loans are made from their own funds, not federal government funds. But because they are SBA backed, the SBA guarantees the lender. If you default on the loan, the lender's loss is covered. An SBA-backed loan is guaranteed to 90 percent for loans up to $155,000 and 85 percent for loans of more than that amount. A two percent fee is charged, based on the amount guaranteed.

These loans have good interest rates, fixed or variable, set by the private lender participant but limited by a cap. Typically, SBA-backed loans are one of the few sources for commercial use in which you can borrow small amounts of under $100,000. A disadvantage is they usually require collateral, but the ratio of your collateral value to loan amount is much less than for a conventional loan, often as low as 50 percent. Personal guarantees are required.

It is interesting to note that in the six-year period from 1984 to 1989, the SBA guaranteed nearly 18,000 loans annually, averaging $175,000, with a maturity term of eight years. Still available on a limited basis, these are for start-up businesses and existing businesses for sustenance and expansion. However, for you to qualify, at least three conventional lenders must have turned you down first. When applying for an SBA-backed loan, if possible, go to an SBA certified lender in the program; there are about 500 of them in the country. They can help you complete the application, sometimes for a fee, and get it to the SBA with a much quicker response time. You can expect a reply within three days through a participating lender.

In addition to banks, various financial companies participate in this program. For more information on the Small Business Administration, refer to its publication, *SBA Business Loans, Publication No. OPI 15*. Appendix B features a list of all the SBA regional and field offices.

Just for Women

Because women comprise a minority in business, the Minority Business Development Agencies and Minority Enterprise Small Business Investment Companies, described earlier as investor sources for minorities, also include women. Besides these, other programs exist specifically for women.

In 1988, Congress enacted a ten-million-dollar grants program just for women as part of the Women Business Ownership Act (WBO). State and city women-in-business groups are the recipients of these. Look for one in your area under such titles as Women Economic Development Center or Women Business Development Venture. You can also contact your local SBA office for more details.

The federal government has established the Office of Women's Business Ownership (OWBO) through the SBA to develop a nationwide program to help women in business. This is set up to develop both government and private resources. The OWBO also monitors the SBA programs to ensure fairness for women business owners. Every field office of the SBA is supposed to have a WBO coordinator in their business development division. The regional SBA offices have OWBO regional coordinators. SBA regional offices are listed in Appendix B,

Other Forms of Financing

Besides traditional lenders and SBA-backed loans, you have other possible options for investment financing for small businesses. These are commercial finance companies, credit unions, investment clubs, life insurance companies, pension funds, Asian Kye money, and family trust funds. You can also consider private family and friends as potential sources.

Commercial Finance Companies

If you have collateral, commercial finance companies can set you up with a credit line. They use real estate, as well as equipment, for security. You can negotiate the terms, length of loan, or possibly a revolving credit line, but generally, interest rates are much higher than with commercial banks. A big advantage is they are much more flexible than conventional banks, not having the same regulatory controls.

Investment Clubs

Investment clubs are formed by a group of likeminded individuals who are interested in making investments via a pool of capital raised by modest monthly installments from the members. These are usually partnerships whose members take on the task of doing the research with their own resources.

There is a national association of investment clubs that publishes a directory of members; you can contact them to obtain a copy.

National Association of Investors Corporation
P.O. Box 220
Royal Oak, MI 48068
(248) 583-6242
FAX (248) 583-4880

Insurance Companies

While insurance companies deal mostly in large loans, you may need their assistance if you are involved in an area development agreement or are one of those entrepreneurial franchisees getting into multi-unit ownership. Insurance companies have loan officers and some already have programs in their portfolio set up to make loans to small business. These loans regularly start in the upper six-digit range at a minimum. If you have an existing operation that is strong, or your franchisor is firmly established, and you have a genuine need for this size loan, your chances can be good.

Pension funds belong in this category in that, similar to insurance companies, they prefer sizable loans. It takes as much staff to process and service a big loan as it does a small loan. Because of this, these companies usually choose to handle ten loans, each for one million dollars, than a hundred loans, each for one hundred thousand dollars; this is the way they usually look at it. If you do need a larger loan than the typical franchisee, contact an insurance company or one of the pension fund managers. Your commercial lenders have investment departments that may have access to these pools.

Small Business Development Centers

At the state and local government levels are agencies and committees whose objective is to bring new business into their area. Usually, the intent is to generate industrial and commercial tax revenues, such as property tax, sales tax, inventory tax, and excise tax, from the development of new businesses. In addition, their objective is often service-oriented — to provide a job base for those with different skill levels for the community. Whatever their reasons, they supply many business-related services and arrange for financing for new businesses. On the state level, a regional development company furnishes equity investments and long-term lending.

The Small Business Administration sponsors the Small Business Development Center (SBDC) program, a co-operative effort among states, colleges, and private enterprise. Small business loans and venture capital programs that are state or federally sponsored and managed are tracked with updated information in colleges and universities. Although about 500 SBDC centers exist throughout the country, certain lead offices administer the program. Appendix C lists a state university or college SBDC for each state, while Appendix D features a list of state economic and business development offices.

Less Conventional Financing Sources

Besides these traditional forms of financing, a wide range of less conventional sources exists for you to investigate. These encompass equipment leasing, trade credit, private investor participation, and factoring.

Sale and Leaseback Programs

If, in setting up your franchised unit, you locate one of those perfect, undeveloped corner sites, but you are unable to obtain a land loan, or the purchase ties up your cash and wipes out your working capital reserve, then a sale and leaseback program is a viable option. In these programs, you contact a sale and leaseback company, such as those listed in Appendix E, and execute a contingency agreement with them for your builder to use in getting a construction loan. The contingency agreement allows you to acquire the land, contract your building, and sell the developed site to the sale and leaseback company. The agreement also makes available to you a long-term net lease on the finished facility, normally for 15 to 40 years, with an option to buy it back during the term or at the end of the lease.

Rates are from three to five percent higher than a mortgage rate, but the advantage is that you can pull out most of your equity, which you then use for inventory and working capital needs.

Consumer Credit

For other sources of commercial lending, small businesses should consider consumer credit resources, such as credit cards, small commercial finance companies, and home equity loans. Also, don't overlook private investors who provide commercial lending as a debt financing source. Different from private venture capital in Chapter 13, these private investors require debt-service payments. Many private parties are looking to finance high-yield investments in small companies. This type of funding is not always recommended, because the interest rate is often too high to be supported by the narrow margins of the typical franchise.

One type of private party high-yield investment that works well is a quasi-partnership arrangement, differing from a partnership in that there is no formal partnership formed. In these cases, the capital is loaned, supported by a note, with a reasonable fixed rate of interest to be paid monthly as a portion of the investor's return. To complete the balance of this return, the investor receives a percentage of the franchisor's annual profit. This, in effect, is a profit-sharing agreement that should be reviewed by your attorney with respect to usury and partnership laws to meet legal requirements within your state.

Home Equity Loans

One of the basic loans, a home equity loan, is the easiest to obtain. If you own a home and have a first trust deed mortgage on it for substantially less than its value, you can opt to refinance the first mortgage upward to its maximum level, or take out a second loan behind the first. Typically, refinanced loans are available for as much as 80 percent of value, and in rare cases, higher. If the principle balance of your first mortgage is as low as 50 percent of your home's appraised value, you can refinance to the higher loan value or get a second for the 30 percent difference to total its 80 percent of value. Which way you go depends on the market rate of interest of your original loan, the current rate of your new loan, and the cost of loan fees involved. If you take out a home equity loan for your franchise business, make sure you can comfortably handle the increase in your monthly payment.

Equipment Leasing

In equipment leasing, nearly any capital asset can be leased. Other than real estate, which is leasable via other sources as discussed, all hard costs fall into this category, including:

- Vehicles;
- Equipment, such as copying machines, computers, cash registers, and specialty equipment for your industry;
- Fixtures;
- Furniture;
- Unattached leasehold improvements; and
- Signs.

Soft costs — such as working capital, salaries, inventory, supplies, grand opening expenses, and franchise fees — are not leasable.

In a typical equipment lease, the leasing company contracts with you, requiring you to grant it a waiver of rights. This means that if there is a problem with the equipment, the lessor wants you to take it up directly with the manufacturer or supplier with no right of action against the lessor. For a list of several full-service leasing companies, refer to Appendix E.

Generally, leasing is equivalent to 100 percent financing — you make monthly lease payments instead of debt service payments — but you sacrifice ownership. For new franchisees, this provides for operating with the same equipment and surroundings while having your investment capital available for other soft costs. An important consideration of leasing is that it does not involve liability — there is no altering of your equity-to-debt ratio, so your financial statement looks just as strong after the lease starts as before. Under the terms of most leases, you are responsible for loss or damage and all expenses relating to the equipment, including maintenance and insurance.

Some lessors adjust your lease payments to your business cash flow. If, for instance, your business is seasonal and you have a thriving motel business that does well six months of the year, these lessors accommodate you by scheduling your monthly lease payments to match. If supported by a realistic pro forma cash flow, lessors can grant this type of request.

Although commercial leasing underwriters usually only write loans for fixtures, equipment, and furniture, often real estate finish items can be added to obtain a higher ratio of loan to costs. Finish items include wall coverings, paneling, mirrors, light fixtures, flooring, carpet, and drapes. Usually, only those items not affixed to the real estate are leased.

For new or start-up businesses, a security deposit is required, but it's generally much less than the usual 25 percent down payment needed for most loans. In addition, approval is much easier to get because leasing is less regulated.

A final word of caution about full leases. Some established franchisors offer an entire franchise package on lease. This type of lease covers everything except product inventory. While very attractive for your capital requirements, these kinds of leases are adverse to the concept of franchised small business ownership. The franchisee, in this circumstance, has nothing to sell other than the franchise — and that is subject to the approval of the franchisor. The franchisor owns everything else. No tangible assets exist, there is nothing to build up, and the business becomes strictly a devise for providing its franchisee an income, with no appreciation and very little goodwill to show for the franchisee's efforts over time. In effect, the franchisee is merely renting the franchise.

Trade Credit

Although not a source of start-up capital, trade credit is another source of supplementing capital after your business is operating successfully. If you have established a good credit rating, frequently major suppliers offer to extend credit for prearranged terms to get your account. In your quest for expansion, this enables you to buy their products or services without the need to raise capital for that purpose. Your suppliers have strong economic incentives in assisting your growth, because it increases their business.

Factoring

Factoring is not a source of start-up capital either, but rather a source of raising additional capital for an established business that carries an accounts receivable. It is traditionally a method a company can use to sell its existing accounts receivable to a third party, the factor, for immediate cash at a discount. The third party has the responsibility for collections. In traditional factoring, the franchisee, that is the seller of the accounts, notifies the debtors, who are customers owing the accounts, to pay their obligations directly to the factor.

For obvious reasons, this does not meet with very sound business judgment as a good source for raising capital in the world of franchising. If you do this, customers see you as a weak business, at best, when you settle for discounted funds instead of waiting for uncollected profits. If you do plan to factor your accounts receivable, it is best if you personally notify your customers first, to explain your cash flow reasons for using this method, before they are surprised by the third party collector. Even then, if you elect to use factoring as a source of cash, rumors can cause problems with suppliers and referral customers.

You Have One More Option

For nonfranchised businesses, the search for financial assistance would end with the two chapters on equity and debt financing sources. For a franchise business, however, you have an additional and logical choice — franchisor financial assistance, discussed in Chapter 14.

Franchisor Financial Assistance

No bird soars too high if he soars with his own wings.
— WILLIAM BLAKE

So far, the only no-money-down financing discussed is the partnership or investor arrangement where you give up some ownership. In those cases, you typically do all the work in the developmental stages, putting together the business, acquiring the franchise, writing the business plan, and possibly selecting a site. Then your investor partner enters the picture, putting up funds in return for ownership. You are usually, at the minimum, a 50 percent owner and the operating member or partner, so you're in business with no money down.

In the case of some limited partnerships, especially with venture capital, the arrangement is such that your investor partners must sell their percentage back to you after they receive a certain return on their investments. You end up with full ownership of the business at the point of sale, again with no money down.

There is another way, however, to get into franchising with no money down. And that is through franchisor financing.

If you are working with an established franchiser, it may have this assistance available. One out of five franchisors provides financial help to start-up franchisees. Some of them furnish the financing directly; others arrange it through third parties, such as capital investment groups or leasing firms. They are all different. Some franchisors offer only small amounts of financial assistance, such as equipment leasing or franchisee fee financing, while others subsidize 100 percent of the financing. The few that do this make it possible for you to get into business with no money down. Appendix F is a listing of franchisors who have reported they offer some means of financial assistance. At this time, no one source explains the specific distinctions of what each franchisor will supply in it's financial assistance packages.

Research on the franchisors that do participate in financial assistance shows that a few have indicated they can provide full financing with fixed or adjustable interest rates for terms as long as 15 years. If you are fortunate enough to have one of the large, established franchisors that offers financing, you may be surprised to learn that a third party may arrange some or all of it.

Depending on what is financed, if it is part of the franchise fee, the franchisor is more than likely going to make the loan internally. If your lease is directly with the franchisor, it no doubt includes your leasehold improvements. These costs are then absorbed into the lease and become a part of your lease payment. If a third party source is used, it is mainly because of the financial strength of the franchisor. In most of these cases, the franchisor cosigns as an additional guarantor. The third party may be a supplier or manufacturer of fixtures or equipment or a lender that may have a complementary relationship with your franchisor. These lenders may be banks, insurance companies, or investment companies — wherever a strong banking or deposit relationship may exist.

This can be a win-win-win situation. The third party investor gets the depreciation and other benefits of capitalization; your franchisor expands its franchise with future royalties coming in; and you get your own business, sometimes with no money down.

How to Qualify for Franchisor Financing

The first step in getting financing is qualifying to be a franchisee in the system. If your franchisor furnishes financing and you fit the mold of the model franchisee profile, then it is not too difficult to obtain the financing.

What do they look for?

Besides their own criteria for an ideal franchisee, your references can reveal a history of certain traits that are weighed in your favor by the franchisors' reviewers. They generally look for honesty, motivation, ambition, persistence, and loyalty. And if you meet the qualifications for financing, past credit problems for certain conditions may not matter to the franchisor. In fact, franchisors report that individuals who have previously failed as small business owners often make excellent new franchisees, because they tend to trust the franchisor's training and advice over their own business judgment and, consequently, follow the proven business format of the franchise better than those who have not experienced a business failure.

Why a Franchisor Offers Financing

Franchisors subsidize financing for several different reasons. Many franchisors are sizeable corporations that have done so well in their relatively short period in the history of small business that they have great cash positions. Companies in this position have to look for the best ways to invest this cash; putting it into money market accounts or timed certificates of deposits does not offer good returns today when interest rates are so low. So financial officers are constantly looking for opportunities to invest their cash for a better return. What many franchisors have begun to realize is that infusing surplus funds into their own system by financing new outlets is an investment in their future that has a lucrative payoff.

Franchisors realize many qualified prospective franchisees could do very well running a franchise, but often do not have the necessary capital for start-up costs. When no financing is available, you do not get into the system; you do not add an outlet for the franchisor; and you do not contribute royalties.

On the other hand, well-qualified franchisees who do get loans not only pay them back with interest but also pay the ongoing royalties that the franchisor might not otherwise get. This also works great for you. Because the loan allows you to go into business, you are now actively working in the system. Monetarily, the franchisor can realize the interest return and the increase in quantities of outlets paying royalties, which increases its overall royalty revenue. If the financing is for equipment, the franchisor gets additional benefits from depreciation.

Probably the biggest incentive for franchisors, besides the instant monetary rewards, is the unquantified advantages gained by an increase in the number of outlets. Franchising is a numbers game, and franchisors who are more competitive are so because of increased royalties, more cooperative advertising funds, greater volume buying power, and better name recognition. All of the advantages of franchising are enhanced with higher numbers of outlets, for both the franchisor and you, and all these numbers are improved when financing is available for franchisees. If a franchisor has a strong cash position, there is no better place to invest the cash than back into the system, thus strengthening it both for short-term gains and for the long haul.

Now You Are Prepared

Armed with information on all of the different financing sources and ways to finance, you are now ready to select the avenues you want to pursue, then to make contact and to present your loan request or investment offering using your franchise business plan. Whichever direction you choose, make sure your business plan is tailored to your targeted reviewer and is up-to-date and presentable. Making your presentation is the subject of the next and final chapter.

Chapter 15

Presenting Your Business Plan

To the timid and hesitating everything is impossible because it seems so.
— SIR WALTER SCOTT

Now that you are familiar with the types and sources of financing available, you are ready to target one, or a combination, to obtain your capital requirement. Whether you feel you have time or not, make one trial run at the SBA. While Chapter 13 pointed out the poor odds of getting a direct SBA loan, take the time to prepare a cover letter. Call the field office in your area listed in Appendix B, and fill out an application. If the loan funds come available and you happen to be one of the few who attempts it, you may be fortunate enough to get one.

For all other sources, your goal is to submit copies of your business plan and, concurrently or by way of a follow-up appointment, to make a personal presentation of your loan request or investment offering.

Besides the SBA direct loans, compile a list of all those you think may be leads for your business plan. If you are looking for debt financing, pinpoint the different sources in your area that may have interest in your business plan including:

- Commercial lenders
- International banks
- SBA-backed lenders
- SBICs
- Local credit unions
- Investment clubs

If you don't mind giving up some ownership, then equity financing may be your best bet. Change section eight of your business plan from a loan request to an investment offering, structuring it along the lines pointed out in Chapter 12 for an investment capital group or partnership, then look for the sources to present it to, such as:

- Venture capital groups
- SBICs
- Independent investors

Don't hesitate to go for two or three sources in each of these nine financing categories. The more times you ask, the more likely you will get a "yes" to your financing request.

Submitting Your Business Plan

After you locate the sources in your area and separate your business plan into two types — for loan request and investment offering — you are ready to make telephone calls and prepare cover letters. For the telephone calls, try to talk directly to a loan officer, financial investments officer, or advisor. It helps if you can use a name as a reference; this is not very hard to do.

For example, suppose you are not familiar with any commercial lenders. Contact your consumer bank branch manager, Mike Harris, whom you know well, and ask him to help you find a local commercial lender and the name of a commercial loan officer. Because you are a good customer of his bank, Mr. Harris makes a call or two and then phones you with a commercial lender's name and the name of the loan officer, Jerry Clark. You then call Mr. Clark and tell the receptionist that Mike Harris of the local consumer bank referred you to Mr. Clark for your particular needs.

This is a standard method of introduction for a cold lender lead. Nearly every time, the loan officer will take your call, and then the rest is up to you. There are many better ways, but the relationships must be stronger for most of them, such as Mike Harris actually knowing Jerry Clark and calling him first for you.

When your call does reach the commercial loan officer, convey a sense of focus that you are seriously underway with your business plan and that financing is a detail that you have next to work out to continue with the schedule. If your parameters are within the scope of Mr. Clark's lending capabilities, he is more than likely going to welcome the submission of your business plan.

If not, you might want to rescue one last value of the call. In the event his bank or firm cannot help you, you can quiz him for other names or resources he might know, from his experience in financing, as sources for your type of loan or proposal. He may give you two or three leads; you can then ask for his permission to use his name when calling them. If he shares the names with you, most of the time he is going to grant permission.

If, on the other hand, he is interested in your deal, try to make an appointment to present your business plan in person. Some of the advantages to this are:

- You can set a strong first impression.
- Your business plan becomes more than a typed document among many sitting in a stack, because the loan officer can then connect a face with the paperwork.
- You get the opportunity to point out the most important features of your business and sell the person on you and the business venture.

Some lenders and investors have a policy against allowing you the opportunity to present your business plan. If they are going to accept it at all, they first want to review it independently of your sales pitch. Others gladly grant you an appointment if you sound like a good future customer.

Often, an invitation to lunch will provide the opportunity to meet with a loan officer who has a tight schedule. You might say, "Could I take you to lunch some day next week and present my business plan? It is involved, and I can shorten your review time by pointing out several of the highlights." If you make a date, it is a good idea to call the loan or investment officer's assistant the day before to confirm the lunch appointment date and time.

After your calls, and, hopefully, a successful appointment date, you still have some things you must do in preparation for the meeting; or, in lieu of a meeting, for sending in your business plan.

The Cover Letter

The first item in preparation is the cover letter. Even if you are going to present your business plan in person, a cover letter should accompany it. It is not advisable to use a form letter for your business plan. You should customize a cover letter for each financing source you contact. Call the bank or firm after your initial call and ask an assistant for the loan officer's full name, correct spelling, his or her title, and the correct spelling of the company name and address. Make sure all of this information is accurate on your cover letter.

Even when you make a personal presentation, the cover letter is essential because the loan or investment officer may hand your business plan over to some other staff director who is going to read your cover letter later. The purpose of the cover letter is to catch the reviewers' attention and make them want to open the plan and review the abstract.

A successful cover letter touches on the main points, without totally duplicating the abstract. It should be about three paragraphs long and no more than four. It needs to be on quality letterhead stationery, preferably of the business you are trying to fund. This indicates to the reviewer you are progressing and already investing in yourself and your business.

Sample Cover Letter

Your Letterhead

Date

Loan officer's full name
His or her title
Company name and address

Dear Mr. Clark:

Thank you for taking my telephone call. Per our conversation, I am submitting the enclosed copy of my business plan for Equipment Hut in Waterford, California.

You may not know that Equipment Hut is the fastest growing equipment-rental service franchise in the United States. Our franchisor has an extensive training program, a complete support service, and the franchise advantages of national advertising and volume purchasing power. This allows the franchisees to rent equipment at more competitive rates than any other nonfranchised equipment rental business.

You'll find in this business plan a business summary, franchise background, our target market, marketing plan, management qualifications, and thorough pro forma financial information. Among the exhibits is a copy of my franchise agreement. Please direct your attention to the résumé of my Operations Director who, you will see, is highly qualified for the job.

[Conclusion]

I am looking forward to our lunch on February 16 and will be eager to answer any questions you might have. If you would like to ask anything before then, please feel free to reach me at the number above. Thanks again for your interest.

Closing,

Your signature

[or]

Thank you again for your consideration. If you have any questions, I am available any time during the week of February 22 through February 27. It would be my pleasure to take you to lunch or to come in and answer any questions you may have.

Closing,

Your signature

Personalize the salutation with the officer's name.

First, state your purpose for writing.

Then write a short summary of your business, the franchise system, your product or service, and your market.

Next, present a short overview of your business plan. Mention anything that separates you or your business as outstanding.

Finally, generate a response. If you have an appointment, include a reminder of its date.

If your letter is going to a person who did not permit the personal presentation, ask again for an appointment.

Finally, the closing should be warm and personal, such as "Very truly yours." The closings, "Sincerely yours" or simply "Sincerely" are not as well-received, and "Best regards" is often considered too casual.

The Appointment

Just as you would before exam day, get a good night's sleep the night before the appointment. Review your business plan before the appointment to make sure you are familiar with it and can answer questions about it, especially as to numbers.

Dress sharply though, it is normally best to dress conservatively. While this is a matter of taste, the old adage that it is better to be overdressed than underdressed applies. If there is appropriate attire for your business, then dress accordingly. Most lenders do not expect any business manager to be wearing radically trendy clothes unless you are in a trendy franchise; even then, you are advised to tone it down for this appointment.

It is universally good advice to be on time.

From your perspective, you want to sell the lenders on your business, your franchise, and your qualifications to run the business. These are the goals to have in mind when preparing for your appointment.

A common mistake many inexperienced applicants make is expecting the appointment to be one-sided, to focus only on going over the business plan. But loan officers may feel it is their opportunity to sell you on them. In nearly every case, if the lenders or investors are interested, they want to chat to you about themselves and their business. Allowing your interviewers the opportunity to talk about their business gives you the chance to be personable and to learn something that may be of value. Many references advise you to be personable, without defining what that means. Because everyone likes to talk about themselves, being personable is usually no more than allowing this to happen, asking questions about them, and allowing them to get as personal as they wish. It can be an unnerving experience to remain confident, friendly, and open-minded during a disarming conversation; but, if you carefully prepared your business plan and are intimately familiar with it, you will convey an assurance that your business plan is a great blueprint for a successful business.

To add to this confidence, take along any additional materials that show that you are sincere, determined, and moving forward in carrying out your business plan. If you have any new supporting data not included in your business plan, take it with you if it is significant. If you have time, incorporate the new material into your business plan and change the appropriate pages. If you don't have time, take it anyway and tell your reviewers that the material is so new it isn't in your business plan, so you will send them an updated version. Sometimes, to convey a personal touch, you can casually work into the conversation little extras, such as the forms with your business logo and address you just received from the printer.

Once you are past the first impression stage, and the lenders or investors seem positive about going forward, take the opportunity to find out some serious information about their company. If they have financed anyone else in similar circumstances to yours, see if you can find out who or get references. Try to discover the terms of recent loans or other deals like it. If they were equity financing arrangements, find out if the investors became involved or played a role in the businesses and how the paybacks were structured.

The initial appointment should lead to others. The interviewer(s) may want you to meet with their next-in-line up the chain of command, a committee, or a board of directors. Between interviews, try to find out as much as you can about the lenders or investors so you can ask informed questions about them and their businesses during follow-up meetings.

From this point forward, tenacity is your greatest ally. Make notes and follow-up lists and continue to pursue all lender and investor leads until their termination or until one meets your criteria. It takes marathon-like personal energy to locate the sources, submit copies of your plan, and make presentations; but if you are organized, it doesn't take as much time as you might think. For instance, if you make two applications to the nine financial sources listed in this chapter, you have only 18 applications to deal with. Many of these presentations require only about an hour of your time, maybe two hours at the most.

A few places accept business plans but never follow up with you for a personal presentation. However, if your business plan is complete and is constructed and assembled professionally, most sources take calls and allow appointments for the personal touch. If your list of sources is organized correctly, you can get through the process in three or four weeks.

To reach success, you are going to have to repeat the presentation process several times. Even though it takes a lot of energy, do not give up during the slow times or slack off when your hopes are elevated by one lead. Just remember:

The deal isn't done until the funds are won.

A Final Comment

Franchising has proved to be a viable and lucrative system for business expansion over the last forty years. Despite its short history, today franchising comprises over one third of all small business in the United States, and by all accounts, economists anticipate this trend to continue — even to surpass one half of all sales of small business by the year 2010.

You may remember from the introduction, the statistics of "the franchise advantage": that 80 percent of all small businesses within the United States fail within the first three years of business, most within the first year, while for franchised businesses, less than 3 percent fail within the first ten years of business. As a small business owner, there is no question that jumping on board with a successful franchise and opening your own franchised outlet — as opposed to owning a nonfranchised business — is a surety for success.

After you have discovered which industry you are most interested in and narrowed the field to the best franchise for your chosen location, the biggest hurdle in opening any new business, for most entrepreneurs, is attracting the capital required.

By examining your financial picture and understanding your capital requirements — types of vesting and financing options — you can see your position as lenders and investors will, so you can establish a realistic, achievable goal. While preparing your business plan for acceptance by lenders or investors, you carefully map out your business venture with realistic objectives and forecasts. In addition to funding, this activity provides the basis of a management plan that can insure the successful operation of your business once it is opened.

After you have completed your business plan, be sure to have it reviewed by your proofreader, attorney, and accountant before your presentation, so you will have the benefit of their expertise in creating the most successful presentation possible. Even after your plan is completed, you may receive additional information — such as, during your interviews with lenders — which you can use to further fine tune it.

Now you are prepared to tenaciously search out your financing, through as many sources as it takes, to afford you the opportunity of reaching out and grabbing hold of the new American dream — owning, opening, and operating your chosen franchise venture. To achieve it, be guided by the slogan:

The one who gets the most *nos* also gets the most *yeses*.

Effort is rewarded.

Success is a journey, not a destination.
— H. Tom Collard

Appendices

Debt Financing Sources

SBA Participating Banks

American National Bank
5603 Ridge Road
Parma, OH 44129-2699
(440) 884-1112

Central Progressive Bank (CPB)
111 North Oak Street
P.O. Drawer 1299
Hammond, LA 70404
(504) 542-2040

City Bank
116 North College Street
Cordell, OK 73632-4822
(580) 832-3322

Eldorado Bank
19200 Von Karman Avenue,
    Suite140
Irvine, CA 92612-1540
(714) 756-1919

Farmers & Merchants State Bank
209 North 12th Street
Boise, ID 83702-5609
(208) 343-7848

Frontier Bank SBA Dept
21992 Cayuga Lane
Lake Forest, CA 92630-2303
(714) 454-1945

Nations Bank
2401 Harrison Street
Batesville, AR 72501-7422
(870) 698-2590

Peoples Bank
301 Main Street
Tallassee, AL 36078-1936
(334) 283-6594

Pioneer National Bank
402 East Yakima Avenue
Yakima, WA 98901-2760
(509) 575-6300

SBA Participating Lenders

AT&T Small Business Lending
1660 Highway 100 South, Suite 428
St. Louis Park, MN 55416-1533
(612) 525-0380

Business Loan Center
415 Beckrich Road, Suite 250
Panama City, FL 32407
(904) 234-5056

Commercial Capital Corporation
50 Albany Turnpike
Canton, CT 06019
(860) 693-3667

Deseret Certified Development Co.
7050 Union Park Center
Midvale, UT 84047
(801) 566-1163

GE Capital Small Business
635 Maryville Centre Drive, Suite 120
St. Louis, MO 63141-5822
(314) 205-3500

Heller First Capital Corp.
717 North Harwood Street, Suite 1150
Dallas, TX 75201-6538
(214) 220-7550

Money Store Investment Corp.
1603 Farnam Street
Omaha, NE 68102-2101
(402) 341-2232

WinStar Commercial Funding
Cornell Business and Technology
  Park, Suite 244
Ithaca, NY 14850
(888) 946-9994

Zions Small Business Finance
401 North 31st Street, Suite 770
Billings, MT 59101-1200
(406) 255-7479

Other Franchise Lenders

Atherton Capital Corporation
1001 Bayhill Drive, Suite 155
San Bruno, CA 94066
(650) 827-7800

AT&T Small Business Lending
200 Broadhollow Road
Melville, NY 11747-4806
(516) 271-8468

Citibank
4041 North Central Avenue, Suite 300
Phoenix, AZ 85012-3303
(602) 631-4131

Commercial Capital Corp
8000 Bonhomme Avenue, Suite 217
St. Louis (Clayton), MO 63105
(314) 721-3131

Pacific Northwest Bank
111 3rd Avenue, Suite 250
Seattle, WA 98101-3207
(206) 624-0609

PMC Capital, Inc.
1150 Lakehearn Drive, Suite 200
Atlanta, GA 30342
(404) 250-3226

International Lenders for Franchises

International:

International Franchise Capital
3900 5th Avenue, Suite 340
San Diego, CA 92103
(619) 260-6000

United Kingdom:

National Westminster Bank PLC
Franchise Section, 8th Floor
Finsbury Court
101/117 Finsbury Pavement
London EC2 England

Canada:

Bank of Montreal
Commercial Banking
First Canadian Place, 18th Floor
Toronto, Ontario
M5X 1A1, Canada
(416) 867-5050

**Canadian Imperial Bank of
  Commerce**
Commerce Court
Toronto, Ontario
M5L 1A2, Canada
(416) 980-2211

The Propexx Group
#1 843 Yates Street
Victoria, British Columbia
V8W 1M1, Canada
(250) 413-3132

Royal Bank of Canada
Royal Bank Plaza, Suite 1200
South Tower
Toronto, Ontario
M5J 2J5, Canada
(416) 974-3940

SBA Offices by Region

Region 1

Connecticut, Maine, Massachusetts, New Hampshire, Rhode Island, and Vermont

Connecticut
330 Main Street, 2nd Floor
Hartford, CT 06106
(203) 240-4700

1441 Main Street, Suite 410
Springfield, MA 01103
(413) 785-0268

Maine
40 Western Avenue, Room 512
Augusta, ME 04330
(207) 622-8378

New Hampshire
143 North Main Street
Concord, NH 03301
(603) 225-1400

Massachusetts
Regional Office
10 Causeway Street
Boston, MA 02222-1093
(617) 565-8415

Rhode Island
380 Westminster Mall, 5th Floor
Providence, RI 02903
(401) 528-4562

10 Causeway Street, Room 265,
 10th Floor
Boston, MA 02222
(617) 565-5590

Vermont
Federal Building
87 State Street
P.O. Box 605
Montpelier, VT 05602
(802) 828-4422

Region 2

New Jersey, New York, Puerto Rico, and Virgin Islands

New Jersey
Two Gateway Center, 4th Floor
Newark, NJ 07102
(973) 645-2434

New York
Federal Building, Room 1311
111 West Huron Street
Buffalo, NY 14202
(716) 551-4301

333 East Water Street, 4th Floor
Elmira, NY 14901
(607) 734-8130

35 Pine Lawn Road, Suite 207W
Melville, NY 11747
(516) 454-0750

Regional Office
26 Federal Plaza, Suite 3108
New York, NY 10278
(212) 264-1450

26 Federal Plaza, Suite 3100
New York, NY 10278
(212) 264-2454

Federal Building, Room 601
100 State Street
Rochester, NY 14614
(716) 263-6700

401 South Salina Street, 5th Floor
Syracuse, NY 13202
(315) 471-9393

Puerto Rico
252 Ponce De Leon Avenue
Hato Rey, PR 00918
(809) 766-5572

Virgin Islands
3013 Golden Rock
St. Croix, VI 00820
(809) 778-5380

3800 Crown Bay
St. Thomas, VI 00802
(809) 774-8530

Region 3

Delaware, District of Columbia, Maryland, Pennsylvania, Virginia, and West Virginia

Delaware
824 North Market Street
Wilmington, DE 19801-3011
(302) 573-6294

District of Columbia
1110 Vermont Avenue, NW
Washington, DC 20005
(202) 606-4000

Maryland
10 South Howard Street
Baltimore, MD 21201-2525
(410) 962-4392

Pennsylvania
100 Chestnut Street, South,
  Suite 309
Harrisburg, PA 17101
(717) 782-3840

900 Market Street, 5th Floor
Philadelphia, PA 19107
(215) 580-2722

Regional Office
1000 Liberty Avenue, Room 1128
Federal Building
Pittsburgh, PA 15222-4004
(412) 395-6560

20 North Pennsylvania Avenue
Wilkes-Barre, PA 18701-3589
(717) 862-6497

Region 3 (continued)

Virginia	1504 Santa Rosa Road Dale Building, Suite 200 Richmond, VA 23229 (804) 771-2400	**West Virginia**	405 Capitol Street, Suite 412 Charleston, WV 25301 (304) 347-5220 168 West Main Street Clarksburg, WV 26301 (304) 623-5631

Region 4

Alabama, Florida, Georgia, Kentucky, Mississippi, North Carolina, South Carolina, and Tennessee

Alabama	2121 8th Avenue North, Suite 200 Birmingham, AL 35203-2398 (205) 731-1344	**Kentucky**	600 Drive M. L. King Jr. Pl., Room 188 Louisville, KY 40202 (502) 582-5971
Florida	100 South Biscayne Boulevard, 7th Floor Miami, FL 33131 (305) 536-5521 7825 Bay Meadows Way, Suite 100-B Jacksonville, FL 32256-7504 (904) 443-1900	**Mississippi**	2909 13th Street, Suite 203 Gulfport, MS 39501-1949 (228) 863-4449 Federal Building, Suite 400 100 West Capitol Street Jackson, MS 39201 (601) 965-4378
Georgia	**Regional Office** 1720 Peachtree Road, NW South Tower, Suite 496 Atlanta, GA 30309-2482 (404) 347-4999 1720 Peachtree Road, NW, 6th Floor Atlanta, GA 30309-2482 (404) 347-4147	**North Carolina**	200 North College Street, Suite A2015 Charlotte, NC 28202-2137 (704) 344-6563
		South Carolina	1835 Assembly Street, Room 358 Columbia, SC 29201 (803) 765-5377
		Tennessee	50 Vantage Way, Suite 201 Nashville, TN 37228-1500 (615) 736-5881

Region 5

Illinois, Indiana, Michigan, Minnesota, Ohio, and Wisconsin

Illinois

Regional Office
500 West Madison Street
Chicago, IL 60661-2511
(312) 353-5000

500 West Madison Street
Chicago, IL 60661-2511
(312) 353-4528

511 West Capitol Avenue
Springfield, IL 62704
(217) 492-4416

Indiana

429 North Pennsylvania Avenue
Indianapolis, IN 46204-1873
(317) 226-7272

Michigan

McNamara Building, Room 515
477 Michigan Avenue
Detroit, MI 48226
(313) 226-6075

501 South Front Street
Marquette, MI 49855
(906) 225-1108

Minnesota

610C Butler Square
100 North 6th Street
Minneapolis, MN 55403-1563
(612) 370-2324

Ohio

525 Vine Street
Cincinnati, OH 45202
(513) 684-2814

1111 Superior Avenue
Cleveland, OH 44114-2507
(216) 522-4180

2 Nationwide Plaza
Columbus, OH 43215-2592
(614) 469-6860

Wisconsin

212 East Washington Avenue, Room 213
Madison, WI 53703
(608) 264-5261

310 West Wisconsin Avenue, Suite 400
Milwaukee, WI 53203
(414) 297-3941

Region 6

Arkansas, Louisiana, New Mexico, Oklahoma, and Texas

Arkansas

2120 Riverfront Drive
Little Rock, AR 72202
(501) 324-5278

Louisiana

365 Canal Street
New Orleans, LA 70130
(504) 589-6685

New Mexico

625 Silver Avenue, SW
Albuquerque, NM 87102
(505) 766-1870

Oklahoma

210 Park Avenue, Suite 1300
Oklahoma City, OK 73102
(405) 231-5521

Texas

606 North Carancahua
Corpus Christi, TX 78476
(512) 888-3331

Regional Office
4300 Amon Carter Boulevard
Dallas/Ft. Worth, TX 76155
(817) 885-6581

4300 Amon Carter Boulevard
Dallas/Ft. Worth, TX 76155
(817) 885-6500

10737 Gateway West, Suite 320
El Paso, TX 79935
(915) 540-5676

Region 6 (continued)

Texas (cont.)   222 East Van Buren Street, Suite 500
Harlingen, TX 78550
(956) 427-8625

9301 Southwest Freeway
Houston, TX 77074-1591
(713) 773-6500

1205 Texas Avenue, Suite 408
Lubbock, TX 79401-2693
(806) 742-7462

727 East Durango
San Antonio, TX 78206
(210) 472-5900

Region 7

Iowa, Kansas, Missouri, and Nebraska

Iowa   215 4th Avenue SE
Cedar Rapids, IA 52401-1806
(319) 362-6405

210 Walnut Street
Des Moines, IA 50309
(515) 284-4422

Kansas   110 East English Street
Wichita, KS 67202
(316) 269-6616

Missouri   Regional Office
323 West 8th Street, Suite 307
Kansas City, MO 64105-1500
(816) 374-6380

323 West 8th Street, Suite 501
Kansas City, MO 64105-1500
(816) 374-6708

620 South Glenstone Street
Springfield, MO 65802-3200
(417) 864-7670

815 Olive Street
St. Louis, MO 63101
(314) 539-6600

Nebraska   11145 Mill Valley Road
Omaha, NE 68154
(402) 221-4691

Region 8

Colorado, Montana, North Dakota, South Dakota, Utah, and Wyoming

Colorado   Regional Office
721 19th Street, Suite 500
Denver, CO 80202
(303) 844-0500

721 19th Street, Suite 400
Denver, CO 80201
(303) 844-3984

Montana   301 South Park, Room 528
Helena, MT 59626
(406) 441-1081

North Dakota   Federal Building, Room 218
657 2nd Avenue North
Fargo, ND 58108
(701) 239-5131

South Dakota   101 South Phillips Avenue
Sioux Falls, SD 57102
(605) 330-4231

Utah   Federal Building, Room 2237
125 South State Street
Salt Lake City, UT 84138
(801) 524-5800

Wyoming   Federal Building, Room 4001
100 East B Street
Casper, WY 82602
(307) 261-6500

Region 9

Arizona, California, Hawaii, Nevada, and Guam

Arizona
2828 North Central Avenue
Phoenix, AZ 85004-1025
(602) 640-2316

California
2719 North Air Fresno Drive, Suite 200
Fresno, CA 93727-1547
(209) 487-5791

330 North Brand Boulevard
Glendale, CA 91203-2304
(818) 552-3210

660 J Street, Suite 215
Sacramento, CA 95814-2413
(916) 498-6410

550 West "C" Street, Suite 550
San Diego, CA 92101-3500
(619) 557-7250

Regional Office
455 Market Street, Suite 2200
San Francisco, CA 94105
(415) 744-2118

455 Market Street, 6th Floor
San Francisco, CA 94105-2445
(415) 744-6820

200 West Santa Ana Boulevard, Suite 700
Santa Ana, CA 92701
(714) 550-7420

Hawaii
300 Ala Moana Boulevard, Room 2213
Honolulu, HI 96850-4981
(808) 541-2990

Nevada
301 East Stewart Street, Room 301
Las Vegas, NV 89125-2527
(702) 388-6611

Guam
400 Route 8, Suite 302
Mongmong, GU 96927
(671) 472-7277

Region 10

Alaska, Idaho, Oregon, and Washington

Alaska
222 West 8th Avenue
Anchorage, AK 99513-7559
(907) 271-4022

Idaho
1020 Main Street, Suite 290
Boise, ID 83702
(208) 334-1696

Oregon
1515 SW Fifth Avenue
Portland, OR 97201-5494
(503) 326-2682

Washington
Regional Office
1200 6th Avenue, Suite 805
Seattle, WA 98101-1128
(206) 553-5676

1200 6th Avenue, Suite 1700
Seattle, WA 98101-1128
(206) 553-7310

West 601 First Avenue
Spokane, WA 99204-0317
(509) 353-2829

Small Business Development Centers

Alabama

University of Alabama at Birmingham
School of Business
1717 Eleventh Avenue South, Suite 419
Birmingham, AL 35294-4410
(205) 934-7260

Alaska

University of Alaska – Anchorage
430 West 7th Avenue, Suite 110
Anchorage, AK 99501
(907) 274-7232

Arizona

Arizona SBDC Network
2411 West 14th Street, Suite 132
Tempe, AZ 85281
(602) 731-8720

Arkansas

University of Arkansas – Little Rock
100 South Main Street, Suite 401
Little Rock, AR 72201
(501) 324-9043

California

Napa Valley College
1556 First Street, Suite 103
Napa, CA 94559
(707) 253-3210

Colorado

Community College of Denver
1445 Market Street
Denver, CO 80202
(303) 620-8076

Connecticut

University of Connecticut
2 Bourn Place, U-94
Storrs, CT 06269-5094
(860) 486-4135

Delaware

University of Delaware
Purnell Hall, Suite 005
Newark, DE 19716-2711
(302) 831-1555

District Of Columbia

Howard University
2600 Sixth Street, NW, Room 125
Washington, DC 20059
(202) 806-1550

Florida

University of West Florida
Downtown Center
19 West Garden Street
Pensacola, FL 32501
(904) 444-2060

Georgia

University of Georgia
1180 East Broad Street
Chicopee Complex
Athens, GA 30602-5412
(706) 542-6762

Hawaii

University of Hawaii at Hilo
200 West Kawili Street
Hilo, HI 96720-4091
(808) 974-7515

Idaho

Boise State University
College of Business
1910 University Drive
Boise, ID 83725
(208) 426-1640

Illinois

University of Illinois
Urbana ITC
428 Commerce West
1206 South 6th Street
Champaign, IL 61820
(217) 244-1585

Indiana

Purdue University
Business and Industrial Development Center
1220 Potter Drive
West Lafayette, IN 47906
(317) 494-5858

Iowa

Iowa State University
Chamberlynn Building
137 Lynn Avenue
Ames, IA 50014
(515) 292-6351

Kansas

Wichita State University
1845 Fairmont, Clinton Hall
Wichita, KS 67260-0148
(316) 978-3193

Kentucky

University of Kentucky
Center for Business Development
225 Business and Economics Building
Lexington, KY 40506-0034
(606) 257-7668

Louisiana

Northeast Louisiana University
College of Business Administration, Room 2-57
Monroe, LA 71209
(318) 342-5506

Maine

University of Southern Maine
96 Falmouth Street
P.O. Box 9300
Portland, ME 04101
(207) 780-4420

Maryland

University of Maryland
Dingman Center for Entrepreneurship
College Park, MD 20742-1815
(301) 405-2144

Massachusetts

University of Massachusetts – Amhurst
205 School of Management
Amherst, MA 01003
(413) 545-6301

Michigan

Wayne State University
2727 Second Avenue
Detroit, MI 48201
(313) 964-1798

Minnesota

University of Minnesota – Duluth
Ten University Drive
Duluth, MN 55812-2496
(218) 726-8758

Mississippi

University of Mississippi
Old Chemistry Building, Suite 216
University, MS 38677
(601) 232-5001

Missouri

University of Missouri
300 University Place
Columbia, MO 65211
(573) 882-7096

Montana

Flathead Valley Community Co9llege
777 Grandview Drive
Kalispell, MT 59901
(406) 756-8333

Nebraska

University of Nebraska at Omaha
Administration Building, Room 407
60th and Dodge Streets
Omaha, NE 68182-0248
(402) 554-2521

Nevada

University of Nevada Reno
College of Business Administration, Room 411
1664 North Virginia Street
Reno, NV 89557-0100
(702) 784-1717

New Hampshire

University of New Hampshire
108 McConnell Hall
Durham, NH 03824-3593
(603) 862-2200

New Jersey

Rutgers University
180 University Avenue, 3rd Floor
Ackerson Hall
Newark, NJ 07102
(201) 648-5950

New Mexico

Santa Fe Community College
P.O. Box 4187
Santa Fe, NM 87502-4187
(505) 438-1362

New York

State University of New York
SUNY Plaza, Draper Hall, Room 107
135 Western Avenue
Albany, NY 12222
(518) 442-5577

North Carolina

University of North Carolina
333 Fayette Street Mall, Suite 1150
Raleigh, NC 27601
(919) 715-7272

North Dakota

University of North Dakota
118 Gamble Hall
University Station Box 7308
Grand Forks, ND 58202-7308
(701) 777-3700

Ohio

Ohio University
20 East Circle Drive
Athens, OH 45701
(614) 593-1797

Oklahoma

Southeastern Oklahoma State University
517 University, Station A, Box 2584
Durant, OK 74701
(405) 924-0277

Oregon

Lane Community College
44 West Broadway, Suite 501
Eugene, OR 97401-3021
(541) 726-2250

Pennsylvania

University of Pennsylvania
423 Vance Hall
Philadelphia, PA 19104-6374
(215) 898-1219

Puerto Rico

University of Puerto Rico
Oficina Estatal
P.O. Box 364984
San Juan, PR 00936-4984
(809) 250-0000

Rhode Island

Bryant College
1150 Douglas Pike
Smithfield, RI 02917
(401) 232-6111

South Carolina

University of South Carolina
College of Business Administration
Columbia, SC 29208
(803) 777-4907

South Dakota

University of South Dakota
School of Business
414 East Clark Street
Vermillion, SD 57069
(605) 677-5498

Tennessee

University of Memphis
South Campus, Building #1
Memphis, TN 38152
(901) 678-2500

Texas

University of Texas
1222 North Main, Suite 450
San Antonio, TX 78212
(210) 458-2460

Utah

Salt Lake Community College
1623 State Street
Salt Lake City, UT 84115
(801) 957-3480

Vermont

Vermont Technical College
P.O. Box 422
Randolph Center, VT 05060-0422
(802) 728-9101

Virginia

James Madison University
College of Business
Zane Showker Hall, Room 523
Harrisonburg, VA 22807
(703) 568-3227

Virgin Islands

University of the Virgin Islands
8000 Nisky Center, Suite 202
Charlotte Amalie, St. Thomas
U.S. Virgin Islands 00802
(809) 776-3206

Washington

Washington State University
College of Business, 135 Kruegel Hall
Pullman, WA 99164-4727
(509) 335-1576

West Virginia

West Virginia University
P.O. Box 6025
Morgantown, WV 26506
(304) 293-5839

Wisconsin

University of Wisconsin
432 North Lake Street, Room 423
Madison, WI 53706
(608) 263-7794

Wyoming

University of Wyoming
P.O. Box 3622
Laramie, WY 82071-3622
(307) 766-3505

State Economic Development Offices

Alabama

Alabama Development Office
401 Adams Avenue
Montgomery, AL 36104
(334) 242-5525

Alaska

Department of Commerce and Economic Development
Division of Trade and Development
3601 C Street, Suite 700
Anchorage, AK 99503-5934
(907) 269-8110

Arizona

Department of Commerce
1700 West Washington
Phoenix, AZ 85007
(602) 280-1480

Arkansas

Arkansas Economic Development Commission
1 State Capitol Mall, 4C-300
Little Rock, AR 72201
(501) 682-1121

California

Trade and Commerce Agency
Division of Economic Development
801 K Street, Suite 1700
Sacramento, CA 95814
(916) 322-0089

Colorado

Office of Business Development
1625 Broadway, Suite 1710
Denver, CO 80202
(303) 892-3809

Connecticut

Department of Economic and Community Development
505 Hudson Street, 4th Floor
Hartford, CT 06106
(860) 270-8033

Delaware

Economic Development Office
99 Kings Highway
Dover, DE 19901
(302) 739-4271

District of Columbia

Financial Responsibility and Management Assistance
 Authority
1 Thomas Circle, Suite 900
Washington, DC 20005
(202) 504-3400

Florida

Department of Commerce
Division of Economic Development
107 Gaines Street, Suite 524-I
Tallahassee, FL 32399-2000
(904) 488-5507

Georgia

Department of Community Affairs
Office of Economic Development
60 Executive Park, NE
Atlanta, GA 30329-2231
(404) 679-1587

Hawaii

Department of Business, Economic Development, and
 Tourism
No. 1 Capitol District Building
250 South Hotel Street
Honolulu, HI 96813
(808) 586-2423

Idaho

Department of Commerce
Division of Economic Development
700 West State Street
P.O. Box 83702
Boise, ID 83720-0093
(208) 334-2470

Illinois

Department of Commerce and Community Affairs
620 East Adams Street, 3rd Floor
Springfield, IL 62701
(217) 524-0171

Indiana

Indiana Economic Development
One North Capitol, Suite 420
Indianapolis, IN 46204
(317) 264-6871

Iowa

Department of Economic Development
Small Business Assistance
200 East Grand Avenue
Des Moines, IA 50309
(512) 242-4831

Kansas

Department of Commerce and Housing
Business Development Division
700 SW Harrison Street, Suite 1300
Topeka, KS 66603-3712
(785) 296-5298

Kentucky

Cabinet for Economic Development
500 Mero Street
Frankfort, KY 40601
(502) 564-7670

Louisiana

Department of Economic Development
P.O. Box 94185
Baton Rouge, LA 70804-9185
(504) 342-3000

Maine

Department of Economic and Community Development
Office of Business Development
59 State House Station
Augusta, ME 04333
(207) 287-3153

Maryland

Department of Economic Development
217 East Redwood Street, 10th Floor
Baltimore, MD 21202
(410) 333-6552

Massachusetts

Department of Economic Development
1 Ashburton Place, Room 2101
Boston, MA 02108
(617) 727-8380

Michigan

Department of Consumer and Industry Services
Financial Institutions Bureau
333 South Capitol Avenue, Suite A
Lansing, MI 48909
(517) 373-3460/9808

Minnesota

Department of Trade and Economic Development
500 Metro Square
121 Seventh Place East
St. Paul, MN 55101-2146
(612) 297-5770

Mississippi

Department of Economic and Community Development
1200 Walter Sillers Building
Jackson, MS 39205
(601) 359-3449

Missouri

Department of Economic Development
HST Room 680
Jefferson City, MO 65102
(573) 751-4962

Montana

Department of Commerce
1424 Ninth Avenue
Helena, MT 59620
(406) 444-4780

Nebraska

Department of Economic Development
Small Business Division
301 Centennial Mall South
P.O. Box 94666
Lincoln, NE 68509-4666
(800) 426-6505

Nevada

Commission on Economic Development
State Capital Complex
Carson City, NV 89710
(800) 336-1600

New Hampshire

Department of Resources and Economic Development
172 Pembroke Road
P.O. Box 1856
Concord, NH 03302-1856
(603) 271-2341

New Jersey

Department of Commerce and Economic Development
P.O. Box 820
Trenton, NJ 08625
(609) 984-2333

New Mexico

Department of Economic Development
Joseph M. Montoya Building
1100 St. Francis Drive
P.O. Box 20003
Santa Fe, NM 87504-5003
(505) 827-1734

New York

Department of Economic Development
One Commerce Plaza
Albany, NY 12245
(518) 474-6950

North Carolina

Department of Commerce
301 North Wilmington Street
Raleigh, NC 27601
(919) 733-4962

North Dakota

Department of Economic Development and Finance
1833 East Bismarck Expressway
Bismarck, ND 58504-6708
(701) 328-5300

Ohio

Department of Development
77 South High Street, 28th Floor
Columbus, OH 43266-0101
(614) 466-2711

Oklahoma

Department of Commerce
900 North Stiles
P.O. Box 26980
Oklahoma City, OK 73126-0980
(405) 815-6552

Oregon

Department of Economic Development
775 Summer Street, NE
Salem, OR 97310
(503) 986-0123

Pennsylvania

Community and Economic Development
100 Pine Street
Harrisburg, PA 17101
(717) 787-3405

Rhode Island

Business Development Company of Rhode Island
40 Westminster Street, Suite 702
Providence, RI 02903
(401) 351-3036

South Carolina

Department of Commerce
Division of Business Development
P.O. Box 927
Columbia, SC 29202
(803) 737-0439

South Dakota

Governor's Office of Economic Development
711 East Wells Avenue
Pierre, SD 57501-3369
(800) 872-6190

Tennessee

Department of Economic and Community Development
320 6th Avenue North, 7th Floor
Nashville, TN 37243-0405
(615) 741-3282

Texas

Department of Economic Development
Small Business Division
1700 Congress Avenue, Suite 1146
Austin, TX 78701
(512) 936-0223

Utah

Department of Community and Economic Development
324 South State Street, Suite 500
Salt Lake City, UT 84111
(801) 538-8700

Vermont

Department of Economic Development
Pavilion Office Building
109 State Street, 4th Floor
Montpelier, VT 05609-0501
(802) 828-3211

Virginia

Department of Economic Development
901 East Byrd Street, Suite 1800
Richmond, VA 23219
(804) 371-8253

Washington

Department of Community, Trade and Economic
  Development
906 Columbia Street, SW
P.O. Box 48300
Olympia, WA 98504-8300
(360) 753-7426

West Virginia

Governor's Office of Development
950 Kanawha Boulevard East
Charleston, WV 25301
(304) 558-2960

Wisconsin

Department of Commerce
Division of Economic Development
201 West Washington Avenue
Madison, WI 53707
(608) 266-0562

Wyoming

Department of Commerce
Economic and Community Development
Herschler Building
122 West 25th Street
Cheyenne, WY 82002
(307) 777-7284

Leasing Companies

Sale and Leaseback Companies

Allbex Financial Partners
3355 Via Lido Drive, Suite 355
Lido Building
Newport Beach, CA 92663
(949) 673-7220

Carey Diversified LLC
50 Rockefeller Plaza, 2nd Floor
New York, NY 10020-1605
(212) 492-1100

Dana Commercial Credit
1801 Richards Road
P.O. Box 906
Toledo, OH 43697-0906
(419) 322-7400

New Millennium Financial Corp
150 West 96th Street, 9th Floor
New York, NY 10025
(212) 665-4550

Full-service Leasing Companies

Captec Financial Group, Inc.
24 Frank Lloyd Wright Drive
Ann Arbor, MI 48105-9755
(734) 994-5505

Comprehensive Leasing Service
8767 Satyr Hill Road
Parkville, MD 21234-2825
(410) 882-7800

GE Capital Credit Service
7222 West Cermak Road
Riverside, IL 60546-1422
(708) 442-5891

Stearns Financial Service, Inc.
131 Fifth Street, P.O. Box 540
Albany, MN 56307-8438
(320) 845-2149

Franchisors Providing Some Financial Assistance

This appendix is an alphabetical list of all of the franchises that report they provide some level of financial assistance to franchisees. The list was compiled from responses to data collection questionnaires for *The Franchise Redbook* — to be published in 1999 by The Oasis Press — where current addresses and contact numbers for these businesses will be included. Until its release, you can get information on a specific company on the Internet or, since most of them are members of the International Franchise Association (IFA), you can get their addresses and telephone numbers, by contacting:

International Franchise Association
1350 New York Avenue, NW Suite 900
Washington, D.C. 20005-4709
(202) 628-8000
FAX (202) 628-0812
Internet: http://www.franchise.org
e-mail: ifa@franchise.org

A

1 Potato 2

2001 Flavors Plus Potatoes

7-Eleven Food Stores

A Buck or Two Stores

A. J. Barnes Bicycle Emporium

A. L. Van Houtte

Aamco Transmission, Inc.

Aaron's Rental Purchase

ABC Seamless

Academy for Mathematics & Science

Accountax Services

Accounting Business Systems

Acctcorp

Ace America's Cash Express

Ace Personnel

Active Green + Ross Tire & Automotive Centre

Admiral Subs

Adventures in Advertising

Aerowest & Westair Sanitation Services

Aim Mail Centers

Airbag Options

Airbag Service

Aire-Master of America

AJ Texas Hots

Almost Heaven, Ltd.

Aloette Cosmetics

Alphagraphics Printshops of the Future

Altracolor Systems

Ambic Building Inspection Consultants

Ameci Pizza & Pasta

American Brake Service

American Institute of Small Business

American Leak Detection

American Mobile Sound

American Poolplayers Association

American Sign Shops

American Speedy Printing Centers

American Transmissions

Americinn International

Amigo Mobility Center

Apparelmaster USA

Apple Auto Glass

Appletree Art Publishers

Arabica Coffeehouse

Archadeck

Arrow Prescription Center

Ashbury Suites & Inns

Ashley Averys Collectables

ASI Sign Systems, Inc.

The Athlete's Foot

ATL International

Atlanta Bread Company

ATS Personnel

Atwork Personnel Services

Auto Accent Centers

AWC Commercial Window Coverings

B

B-Dry System

Baby's Away

Back Yard Burgers, Inc.

Bagelz – The Bagel Bakery

Bahama Buck's Original Shaved Ice Co.

Baker Street Artisan Breads & Cafe

Baker's Dozen Donuts

Baldinos Giant Jersey Subs

Balloons & Bears

Barbizon Schools of Modeling

Bassett's Original Turkey

Bathcrest

BCT

Beneficial Health & Beauty

Better Homes & Gardens Real Estate Service

Better Homes Realty

Between Rounds Bagel Deli & Bakery

Beverly Hills Weight Loss & Wellness

Bevinco

Big O Tires

Bike Line

Bingo Bugle Newspaper

Bladerunner Mobile Sharpening

Blimpie Subs and Salads

Blue Chip Cookies

Bobby Rubino's Place for Ribs

Boomerang Gameware

Borvin Beverage

Boston Pizza

Brake Centers of America

The Brake Shop

Breadsmith

Bresler's Ice Cream & Yogurt Shops

Brew Thru

The Brickkicker

Brite Site

Buck's Pizza

Buddy's Bar-B-Q Franchise, Inc.

Budget Blinds

Budget Car & Truck Rental

Buffalo's Cafe

Building Services of America

Bullwinkle's Restaurant & The Family Fun Centers

Buns Master Bakery Systems

Buscemi's International

Business Information International, Inc.

Butterfields, Etc.

The Buyer's Agent

C

CA$H Plus

Caffe Appassionato

California Closet Company

Candleman Corporation

Candy Bouquet

Candy Express

Cap'n Taco

Capital Carpet Cleaning

Captain Tony's Pizza & Pasta Emporium

The Car Wash Guys/Gals

Car-X Muffler & Brake/Speedy Muffler King

Carpet Master

Carpet Network

Carpetmate

Cartex Limited

Carvel Ice Cream Bakery

Castles Unlimited

CD Warehouse

CGI Worldwide Express Services

Champion Auto Stores

Champion Cleaners Franchise, Inc.

Charlie Barlie's

Checkcare Systems

Chem-Dry Carpet/Drapery/Upholstery

Chem-Dry Carpet/Upholstery (Canada)

Chemstation

Chico's Tacos

Children's Orchard

Chip King

Churchs Chicken

Cici's Pizza

Cinema Grill

Citizens Against Crime

Classy Maids USA

Clean 'N' Press America

The Cleaning Authority

Cleannet USA

Clintar Groundskeeping Services

The Closet Factory

Closettec

Cluck-U Chicken

The Coffee Beanery

Coit Services

Coldwell Banker Residential Affiliates

Color Me Mine

Colors on Parade

Colortyme

Colter's Bar-B-Q

Comet One-Hour Cleaners

Complete Music

Computemp, Inc.

Computertots

Condotels

Connect Ad

Conroys 1-800-Flowers

Cottagecare

Cottman Transmission

Country Inns & Suites by Carlson

Cousins SUBS

Coustic-Glo International

Coverall Cleaning Concepts

Craters & Freighters

Creative Cakery

Creative Colors International

Crestcom International, Ltd.

Criterium Engineers

Critter Care Of America

Croissant + Plus

Crown Trophy

Cruise Holidays International

Cruise Vacations

Cruiseone

Cut Only

Cyber Exchange Software and Computers

D

Dairy Queen

Dairy Queen Canada

Dealer Specialties International, Inc.

Decor-At-Your-Door International

Decorating Den Interiors

Denny's, Inc.

Dent Doctor

Dentpro

Diamond Dave's Mexican Restaurants

Dickey's Barbecue Pit Restaurants

The Different Twist Pretzel Co.

Discount Car & Truck Rentals

Diversified Dental Services

Dog N' Suds Drive-In Restaurants

Dollar Discount Stores

Dollar Rent A Car

Dollar Rent A Car (Canada)

Donut Delite Cafe

Doubledave's Pizzaworks Restaurant

Dr. Vinyl & Assoc.

Drapery Works Systems

Dreamcatcher Learning Centers

Dry Cleaning Station

Ductbusters

Dunhill Staffing Systems

Dunkin' Donuts

Duraclean International

Dynamark Security Centers

E

E.P.I.C. Systems

Eagle Cleaners

East Of Chicago Pizza Company

Ecomat

Econotax

Ecosmarte Planet Friendly

EDO Japan

El Pollo Loco

Electronic Tax Filers

Elliott & Company Appraisers

Emerald Green Lawn Care

Empire Business Brokers

Endrust Auto Appearance Centers

English Butler Canada

Envirofree Inspections

Erbert & Gerbert's Subs & Clubs

Estrella Insurance

Executrain

Express Mart Convenient Store

Express Oil Change

Express One

Express Personnel Services

Expressions in Fabrics

F

Fabri-Zone Cleaning Systems

Family Pizza

Famous Sam's, Inc.

Fantastic Sams

Faro's Franchise Systems

Fastframe USA

Fastsigns

FCI Franchising, Inc.

Field of Dreams

Figaro's Italian Kitchen

Fire Defense Centers

First Choice Haircutters

First Optometry Eye Care Centers

Firstat Nursing Services

Flamers Charbroiled Hamburgers & Chicken

Floor Coverings International

Fortune Personnel Consultants

Four Star Pizza

The Fourth R

Fox's Pizza Den

Framing & Art Centres

Frank & Marvin's More Than Bagels

Franklin Traffic Service

Friendly's Ice Cream Corporation

Frozen Fusion Fruit Smoothies

Frullati Cafe

Furniture Medic

G

Gateway Newstands

GCO Carpet Outlet

Gelato Amare

General Nutrition Centers

Genius Kid Academy

Glamour Shots

Glass Magnum

Gloria Jean's Gourmet Coffees

Goldberg's New York Bagels

Golden Corral Franchising Systems, Inc.

Gold's Gym

Good for You! Yogurt

Grandma Lee's Bakery Cafe

Grease Monkey International

The Great Canadian Bagel

Great Clips, Inc.

Great Earth Vitamins

The Great Frame Up

The Great Wilderness Company, Inc.

Group Trans-Action Brokerage Services

Guardsman Woodpro

Gwynne Learning Academy

H

Handle With Care Packaging Store

Handyman Connection

Happy Joe's Pizza & Ice Cream Parlor

Happydays Handbag & Luggage Company

Harvey Washbangers

Hauntrepreneurs, Ltd.

Head Over Heels

Health Force

Heaven's Best

Heavenly Ham

Heel Quik

The Hemorrhoid Clinic

Her Real Estate

High Touch-High Tech

Ho-Lee-Chow

Hobbytown USA

Hogi Yogi Sandwiches & Frozen Yogurt

Holiday Hospitality

Hollywood Weight Loss Centre

Homewatch International, Inc.

Hoop Mountain

Hospitality International

Hot Sam's Pretzel Bakery

Houlihan's Restaurant Group

Hubb's Pub

Hudson's Grill of America

Hungry Howie's Pizza & Subs

Huntington Learning Center

Hydro Physics Pipe Inspection

I

Ice Cream Churn

Iclean America

IMBC

Impressions On Hold

Inches A Weigh

Indy Lube

Inhouse Travel Group LLC

Insulated Dry Roof Systems

Interim Healthcare

International Golf

International News

J

J. D. Byrider Systems

Jackson Hewitt Tax Service

Jan-Pro Franchising International, Inc.

Jani-King International

Jantize America

Jay Roberts & Associates

JDI Cleaning Systems

Jerry's Subs & Pizza

Jet-Black Sealcoating & Repair

Jiffy Lube International, Inc.

Joe Loue Tout Rent All

Juice Connection

Juice World

Jumbo Video

Just Legs

Just-A-Buck

K

K-Bob's Steakhouses

Kampgrounds of America, Inc.

Kelsey's Restaurants

Kiddie Academy International

Kiddie Kobbler

Kids R Kids Quality Learning Centers

Kinderdance International

King Bear Auto Service Centers

Kirby Tours

Kitchen Tune-Up

Kitchen Wizards

Knowledge Development Centers, Inc.

Kohr Bros. Frozen Custard

Koya Japan

Kwik Dry International

Kwik-Kopy Printing

L

L.A. Smoothie Healthmart & Cafe

Lady of America

Langenwalter Carpet Dyeing

Larry's Giant Subs

Las Vegas Discount Golf & Tennis

Laser Chem Advanced Carpet & Upholstery Dryclean

Lawcorps

Lawn Doctor

Lazerquick

Le Print Express

Leadership Management, Inc.

Learning Express

Ledgerplus

Lee Myles Transmission

Lemon Tree – A Unisex Haircutting Establishment

Lentz USA Service Centers

Lindy – Gertie's

Link Staffing Services

Liqui-Green Lawn & Tree Care

The Little Gym

Little King

Little Professor Book Centers

Longbranch Steakhouse & Saloon, Inc.

Look No-Fault Auto Insurance Agencies

Lord's & Lady's Hair Salons

Lube Depot

M

M & M Meat Shops

Maaco Auto Painting & Bodyworks

Macbirdie Golf Gifts

The Mad Science Group

Madame Et Monsieur

Magis Fund Raising Specialists

Maid Brigade Services

Maid to Perfection

Maidpro

The Maids

Mail Boxes Etc.

Mail Boxes Etc. (Canada)

Maintain Cleaning Systems

Mamma Ilardo's

Management Recruiters

Manchu Wok (U.S.)

Manhattan Bagel Company

Marble Renewal

Marblelife

Marco's Pizza

Master Care

The Master Mechanic

Matco Tools

Maxcare Professional Cleaning Systems

Mazzio's Pizza

McBeans

McCoy's Cake & Pie Shop

Medicap Pharmacy

Medichair

The Medicine Shoppe

Meineke Discount Mufflers

Merkinstock

Merle Norman Cosmetics

Merlin's Muffler & Brake

Microplay Video Games

Mikes Restaurants

Minuteman Press International

Miracle Auto Painting & Body Repair

Miracle Ear Hearing Systems

Miracle Method

Mirage Tanning Centers

Mister Mobile On-Site Oil Changes

Mister Money – USA

Mister Transmission

Mmmarvellous Mmmuffins

Moe's Italian Sandwiches

Morrone's Italian Ices

Mountain Mike's Pizza

Mr. Front-End

MR. GOODCENTS Subs & Pasta

Mr. Hero

Muffin Break

N

Nach-O Fast

Naked Furniture

National Maintenance Contractors

National Property Inspections

National Tenant Network

Nationwide Floor/Window Coverings

Naturalawn of America

The Nature of Things Store

Naut-A-Care Franchising Inc.

New Horizons Computer Learning Center

New York Burrito-Gourmet Wraps

Nitro-Green Professional Lawn & Tree Care

Norrell Services

Norwalk – The Furniture Idea

Novus Windshield Repair

Nu-Look 1-Hr. Cleaners

Nursefinders

Nutri-Lawn, Ecology-Friendly Lawn Care

Nutter's Bulk and Natural Foods

O

O.P.E.N. Cleaning Systems

Oil Butler International

Oil Can Henry's International

One-Hour Martinizing

One Hour Motophoto & Portrait Studio

One Hour Motophoto & Portrait Studio (Canada)

Open Pantry Food Marts

Outdoor Connection

P

P.A.M.'S Coffee & Tea Co.

Paceco Financial Services

Pack Mart

Packaging and Shipping Specialist

Padgett Business Services

Pak Mail Centers (Canada)

Pak Mail Centers of America

Papa John's Pizza

Papa Murphy's

Papyrus

Paradise Bakery & Cafe

Parcel Plus

Payless Car Rental System

PC Professional Computer Training & Repair

Pearle Vision Center

Penn Station Inc.

Pepe's Mexican Restaurants

Permacrete Systems

Personet – The Personnel Network

Pestmaster Services

Pet Habitat

Pet-Tenders

Petland

Petrucci's Dairy Barn

Peyron Tax Service

Pillar To Post

Pizza Delight

Pizza Man – He Delivers

The Pizza Ranch

Planet Earth Recycling

Pony Mailbox & Business Centers

Pool Franchise Service (PFS)

Port of Subs

Postal Annex+

Postnet Postal & Business Centers

Power Smoothie

Practical Rent A Car

Pre-Fit

Precision Tune Auto Care

Pressed 4 Time, Inc.

The Pretzel Twister

Pretzelmaker

Pridestaff

Primrose School Franchising Co.

Pro-Cuts

Pro-Tect

Professional Dynametric Programs/PDP

Professional House Doctors

Professional Polish

Proforma

Profusion Systems

Proshred Security

Puckmasters Hockey Training Centers

Purified Water To Go

Q

Q Lube

Quizno's Classic Subs

R

Racs International

Radio Shack International

Rainbow International Carpet Care & Restoration

Re-Bath

Re/Max International

Red Hot & Blue

Remedy Intelligent Staffing

Rennsport

Rent-A-Wreck Of America

Rent-A-Wreck of Canada

Renzios

Riders Hobby Shop

Rita's Italian Ice

Robin's Donuts

Rocky Mountain Chocolate Factory

Rodan Jewellers/ Simply Charming

Ronzio Pizza

Room-Mate Referral Service Centers

Rynker Ribbon Xchange

S

Saf-T Auto Centers

Sales Consultants

Sandler Sales Institute

Sanford Rose Associates

Sangsters Health Centres

Sanibrite

Schlotzsky's Deli

Schumacher Garage Door Franchise

Scooter's Place

Screen Printing USA

The Screenmobile

Scrubway

Sealmaster

Select Sandwich

Serv U-1st

Service Center

Service One

Service-Tech Corporation

Servicemaster Caring Companions

Servicemaster Residential/ Commercial

Servpro

Showhomes of America

Shred-It

Sign-A-Rama

Signal Graphics Printing

Signs by Tomorrow

Signs & More in 24

Signs Now

Sir Speedy (Canada)

Slats Blind Cleaning

The Sleeping Giant Within, Inc.

Slimmer Image Weight Loss Clinics

Smitty's

Snap-On Tools

Snelling Personnel Services

Snip N' Clip Haircut Shops

Sonic Drive-In

Sparkle Wash

Speedy Auto Service

Speedy Printing Centers

Speedy Transmission Centers

Sport Clips

The Sports Section

Spot-Not Car Washes

Spring Crest Drapery Centers

Stanley Steemer Carpet Cleaner

Star Mart

The Steak Escape

Steak-Out

Steam Brothers Professional Cleaning & Restoration

Steamatic

Sterling Optical

Straw Hat Pizza

Strokes

Sub Station II

Submarina

Subs Plus

Subway Restaurants

Sunbanque Island Tanning

Sunbelt Business Brokers

Sunshine Cafe

Super Lawns

Superglass Windshield Repair

Superior Walls of America

Surface Specialists Systems

Swisher Hygiene

Sylvan Learning Centers

T

The Taco Maker

Taco Mayo

Taco Villa

Techstaff

Tenniskids

Terra Systems Franchise Corp

Terri's Consign & Design Furnishings

TFM/ Top Forty

Thrifty Car Rental

Thrifty Rent-A-Car

Tilden for Brakes Car Care Centers

Tim Hortons

Tire Time Rentals

Together Dating Service

Tony Maroni's Famous Gourmet Pizza

Top Value Exhaust Systems

Totally Wireless

Tower Cleaning Systems

TPI Travel Services

Tradebank International

Training Experience International

Travel Network

TRC Staffing Services

Treats International, Inc.

Tri-Color Carpet Dyeing and Cleaning

Triple Check Income Tax Service

Tropi-Tan, Inc.

Tropik Sun Fruit & Nut

Truck Options

Truly Nolen

Tubby's Submarines

Tuffy Auto Service Centers

Tutor Time Child Care Learning Center

Two Men and a Truck

U

U.S. Franchise Systems

U.S. Lawns

U-Save Auto Rental of America Inc.

U-Wash Doggie

UncleSam's Convenient Store

Unishippers Association

United Check Cashing

United Consumers Club

United Energy Partners

United Printing Unlimited

United States Seamless

V

Val-Pak Direct Marketing

Valet Express

Value Line Maintenance Systems

Valvoline Instant Oil Change

Victory Lane Quick Oil Change

Video Data Services

Video Impact

Villa Pizza

Vinylgraphics Custom Sign Centres

The Visual Image

W

We Care Home Health Services

Wetzel's Pretzels

Wheelchair Getaways

White Hen Pantry

Wicks 'N' Sticks

Wienerschnitzel

Wild Bird Center/Wild Bird Crossing

Wild Bird Marketplace

Wild Birds Unlimited

Window Perfect

Window Works

Wine Not

Wing Machine

Woody's Wood Shops

World Inspection Network

World Trade Network

X

X-Bankers Check Cashing

Y

Yipes Stripes

Yogen Fruz Worldwide

Yogi Bear Jellystone Park Camp-Resorts

Your Office USA

Z

Z Land

Zero's Subs

Ziebart Tidycar

Zuzu Mexican Food

Bibliography

Baumback, Clifford M. *How to Organize and Operate a Small Business, 7th Ed.* Old Tappan, NJ: Prentice-Hall, 1985.

"Entrepreneur 19th Annual Franchise 500." *Entrepreneur* (January 1998).

Foster, Dennis L. *Franchising for Free. Owning Your Own Business Without Investing Your Own Cash.* New York: John Wiley & Sons, 1988.

Franchise Opportunities, 22nd Edition. New York: Sterling Publishing Company, Inc., 1991.

Franchise Opportunity Guide. (Fall/Winter, 1998–1999).

"Franchising." *Small Business Reporter* (1994).

Keup, Edwin J. *Franchise Bible.* Grants Pass, OR: The Oasis Press, 1995.

Mancuso, Joseph. *How to Write a Winning Business Plan.* New York: Simon & Schuster, 1985.

Modica, Alfred J. *Franchise Encyclopedia.* Dobbs Ferry, NY: ADA Publishing, 1986.

Modica, Alfred J. *Franchising.* Dobbs Ferry, NY: Quick Fox, 1981.

Modica, Alfred J. and Anthony F. Libertella. *Franchise Manual.* White Plains, NY: The National/International Institute for Franchise Research and Development, 1986.

Posner, Bruce G. "How To Finance Anything." *Inc. Magazine* (February 1993).

Rule, Roger C. *The Franchise Redbook.* Grants Pass, OR: The Oasis Press, to be published October 1999.

Scherer, Donald J. *Financial Security and Independence through a Small Business Franchise.* Babylon, NY: Pilot Industries, Inc., 1976.

Seltz, David D. *Complete Handbook of Franchising. The.* Reading, MA: Addison-Wesley, 1981.

Serif, Med. *Business Building Ideas for Franchises and Small Business.* New York: Pilot Industries, Inc., 1985.

Tol Broome, J. Jr., "How To Write A Business Plan." *Nation's Business, 81,* no. 2.

Other Resources:

Caplan, Suzanne and Thomas M. Nunnally. *The Insider's Guide to Bankers*. Grants Pass, OR: The Oasis Press, 1997.

Frigstad, David B. *Know Your Market: How to Do Low-cost Market Research*. Grants Pass, OR: The Oasis Press, 1994.

Placencia, José, et al. *Business Owner's Guide to Accounting and Bookkeeping*. Grants Pass, OR: The Oasis Press, 1997.

Salvaneschi, Luigi. *Location, Location, Location*. Grants Pass, OR: The Oasis Press, 1996.

Index

U

UFOC, Uniform Franchise Offering Circular. *See also* disclosure document, 18, 43, 45, 51–52, 54–55, 68, 106–107, 111, 158
  introduced, 17–18
  item 13, 54
  item 14, 54
  item 19, 54
  item 20, 19, 54
  item eight, 53, 62
  item eleven, 45, 53
  item five, 53
  item nine, 53, 62
  item one, 52
  item seven, 17–18, 20, 24, 53
  item six, 53
  item twelve, 54, 68
  item two, 53, 106, 111
  items 1–23, 52
U.S. Bureau of Labor Statistics, 5, 58
U.S. Bureau of the Census, 58, 156
  regional offices, 58
U.S. Department of Commerce, 2, 4, 58–59
U.S. Government Printing Office, 58
U.S. Industrial Outlook, 59
U.S. Small Business Administration. *See also* SBA, 177
up-front money, 5
use of funds, 34, 40
utilities, 20–21, 23, 28, 125, 127

V

value
  cost-basis, 130
  fair-market, 130, 153
variable costs, 17, 22, 25–26, 28, 90, 119–121, 126
  advertising, 23, 90
  commissions, 23
  costs of goods sold, 22
  royalties, 23
  supplies, 22
venture capital, 145, 168–171, 180–181, 185, 190
venture capital groups, 145, 168–170, 190
Venture Capital OnLine, 169
Venture Capital Resource Library, 169
vesting, 42–43, 145–146, 148, 195
veteran, 177
vocabulary, 160
volume
  advertising plans, 92
  buying, 3, 187

W

Wall Street Journal, The, 92
warrants, 170
web page, 114
Wilson, Woodrow, 41
Women Business Ownership Act (WBO), 178–179
Women Economic Development Center, 179
worker's compensation, 159
working capital
  calculations, 26, 136
  definition of, 25
  example of, 128
  ratio. *See also* ratio, working capital, 142
  through commercial lending, 175–176
  through leaseback companies, 181
  through SBA, 177
working-capital requirement, 24–27, 128

Y

Yellow Pages, 11, 79, 87, 91, 93, 95, 97, 177

Z

zone, retail trade, 78

ESTABLISH A FRAMEWORK
FOR EXCELLENCE
WITH THE OASIS PRESS ®

OASIS PRESS BOOKS & SOFTWARE
Celebrating 25 Years

THE OASIS PRESS'
PSI RESEARCH
P.O. BOX 3727
CENTRAL POINT, OR
97502-0032

Fastbreaking changes in technology and the global marketplace continue to create unprecedented opportunities for businesses through the '90s and into the new millennium. However with these opportunities will also come many new challenges. Today, more than ever, businesses, especially small businesses, need to excel in all areas of operation to compete and succeed in an ever-changing world.

The Successful Business Library takes you through the '90s and beyond, helping you solve the day-to-day problems you face now, and prepares you for the unexpected problems you may be facing down the road. With any of our products, you will receive up-to-date and practical business solutions, which are easy to use and easy to understand. No jargon or theories, just solid, nuts-and-bolts information.

Whether you are an entrepreneur going into business for the first time or an experienced consultant trying to keep up with the latest rules and regulations, The Successful Business Library provides you with the step-by-step guidance, and action-oriented plans you need to succeed in today's world. As an added benefit, PSI Research/The Oasis Press® unconditionally guarantees your satisfaction with the purchase of any book or software application in our catalog.

More than a marketplace for our products, we actually provide something that many business Web sites tend to overlook... useful information!

It's no mystery that the World Wide Web is a great way for businesses to promote their products, however most commercial sites stop there. We have always viewed our site's goals a little differently. For starters, we have applied our 25 years of experience providing hands-on information to small businesses directly to our Web site. We offer current information to help you start your own business, guidelines to keep it up and running, useful federal and state-specific information (including addresses and phone numbers to contact these resources), and a forum for business owners to communicate and network with others on the Internet. We would like to invite you to check out our Web site and discover the information that can assist you and your small business venture.

ALL MAJOR CREDIT CARDS ACCEPTED

CALL TO PLACE AN ORDER
— or —
TO RECEIVE A FREE CATALOG
1-800-228-2275

International Orders (541) 479-9464   *Fax Orders* (541) 476-1479
Web site http://www.psi-research.com   *Email* sales@psi-research.com

PSI Research P.O. Box 3727 Central Point, Oregon 97502 U.S.A.

The Oasis Press Online
http://www.psi-research.com

From The Leading Publisher of Small Business Information
Books that save you time and money.

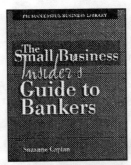

In business, the banker and the institution they represent are often perceived as opponents to your business' success. Shows why business owners should take a leading role in developing and nurturing a worthwhile and lasting partnership with their banker. This inside look will help new and seasoned business owners develop a functional understanding of how the banking industry operates, how to speak their language, and how to turn your banker into an advocate for the growth and success of your small business.

Small Business Insider's Guide to Bankers   **Pages: 176**
Paperback: $18.95   **ISBN: 1-55571-400-5**

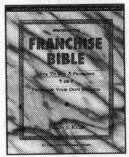

A franchise attorney developed this up-to-date guide for prospective franchises or for those who want to franchise their own business. Includes sample documents, such as the latest FTC-approved offering circular, plus worksheets for evaluating franchise companies, locations, and organizing information before seeing an attorney. A valuable resource for lawyers as well as their clients.

Franchise Bible   **Pages: 300**
Paperback: $24.95   **ISBN: 1-55571-367-X**

There are numerous intangible factors that influence the valuation of an enterprise, including asset variables, operating income, the buyer's income, and return on investment. *The Secrets to Buying and Selling a Business* approaches the transition from the viewpoints of both seller and buyer, giving you a very practical and balanced overview of the process. Covers financing, protecting investments, how to construct a deal, as well as other key points. Includes sample forms, checklists, and worksheets.

Secrets to Buying & Selling a Business   **Pages: 300**
Paperback: $24.95   **ISBN: 1-55571-398-X**

Makes understanding the economics of your business simple. Explains the basic accounting principles that relate to any business. Step-by-step instructions for generating accounting statements and interpreting them, spotting errors, and recognizing warning signs. Discusses how creditors view financial statements.

Business Owner's Guide to Accounting & Bookkeeping Pages: 172
Paperback: $19.95   **ISBN: 1-55571-381-5**

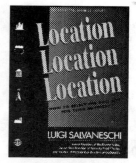
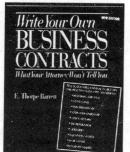

Call, Mail, Email, or Fax Your Order to: PSI Research, P.O. Box 3727, Central Point, OR 97502
Order Phone USA & Canada: +1 800 228-2275   Email: sales@psi-research.com   Fax: +1 541 476-1479

Includes
Titles Through
Winter 1999

TITLE	✔ BINDER	✔ PAPERBACK	QUANTITY	COST
Advertising Without An Agency: A Comprehensive Guide to Radio, Television, Print...		❑ $19.95		
Bottom Line Basics: Understand and Control Your Finances	❑ $39.95	❑ $19.95		
BusinessBasics: A Microbusiness Startup Guide		❑ $16.95		
The Business Environmental Handbook	❑ $39.95	❑ $19.95		
Business Owner's Guide to Accounting & Bookkeeping		❑ $19.95		
businessplan.com: how to write a web-woven strategic business plan		❑ $19.95		
Buyer's Guide to Business Insurance	❑ $39.95	❑ $19.95		
California Corporation Formation Package		❑ $29.95		
Collection Techniques for a Small Business	❑ $39.95	❑ $19.95		
A Company Policy and Personnel Workbook	❑ $49.95	❑ $29.95		
Company Relocation Handbook	❑ $39.95	❑ $19.95		
CompControl: The Secrets of Reducing Workers' Compensation Costs	❑ $39.95	❑ $19.95		
Complete Book of Business Forms		❑ $19.95		
Connecting Online: Creating a Successful Image on the Internet		❑ $21.95		
Customer Engineering: Cutting Edge Selling Strategies	❑ $39.95	❑ $19.95		
Develop & Market Your Creative Ideas		❑ $15.95		
Developing International Markets: Shaping Your Global Presence		❑ $19.95		
Doing Business in Russia: Basic Facts for the Pioneering Entrepreneur		❑ $19.95		
Draw The Line: A Sexual Harassment Free Workplace		❑ $17.95		
Entrepreneurial Decisionmaking: A Survival Manual for the Next Millennium		❑ $21.95		
The Essential Corporation Handbook		❑ $21.95		
The Essential Limited Liability Company Handbook	❑ $39.95	❑ $21.95		
Export Now: A Guide for Small Business	❑ $39.95	❑ $24.95		
Financial Decisionmaking: A CPA/Attorney's Perspective		❑ $19.95		
Financial Management Techniques for Small Business	❑ $39.95	❑ $19.95		
Financing Your Small Business: Techniques for Planning, Acquiring, & Managing Debt		❑ $19.95		
Franchise Bible: How to Buy a Franchise or Franchise Your Own Business	❑ $39.95	❑ $24.95		
Friendship Marketing: Growing Your Business by Cultivating Strategic Relationships		❑ $18.95		
Funding High-Tech Ventures		❑ $21.95		
Home Business Made Easy		❑ $19.95		
Information Breakthrough: How to Turn Mountains of Confusing Data into Gems of Useful Information		❑ $22.95		
Improving Staff Productivity: Ideas to Increase Profits		❑ $16.95		
The Insider's Guide to Small Business Loans		❑ $19.95		
InstaCorp – Incorporate In Any State (Book & Software)		❑ $29.95		
Joysticks, Blinking Lights and Thrills		❑ $18.95		
Keeping Score: An Inside Look at Sports Marketing		❑ $18.95		
Know Your Market: How to Do Low-Cost Market Research	❑ $39.95	❑ $19.95		
The Leader's Guide: 15 Essential Skills		❑ $19.95		
Legal Expense Defense: How to Control Your Business' Legal Costs and Problems	❑ $39.95	❑ $19.95		
Legal Road Map for Consultants		❑ $18.95		
Location, Location, Location: How to Select the Best Site for Your Business		❑ $19.95		
Mail Order Legal Guide	❑ $45.00	❑ $29.95		
Managing People: A Practical Guide		❑ $21.95		
Marketing for the New Millennium: Applying New Techniques		❑ $19.95		
Marketing Mastery: Your Seven Step Guide to Success	❑ $39.95	❑ $19.95		
The Money Connection: Where and How to Apply for Business Loans and Venture Capital	❑ $39.95	❑ $24.95		
Moonlighting: Earn a Second Income at Home		❑ $15.95		
Navigating the Marketplace: Growth Strategies For Your Business		❑ $21.95		
No Money Down Financing for Franchising		❑ $19.95		
People Investment: How to Make Your Hiring Decisions Pay Off For Everyone	❑ $39.95	❑ $19.95		
Power Marketing for Small Business	❑ $39.95	❑ $19.95		
Profit Power: 101 Pointers to Give Your Business a Competitive Edge		❑ $19.95		
Proposal Development: How to Respond and Win the Bid	❑ $39.95	❑ $21.95		
Public Relations Marketing: Making a Splash Without Much Cash		❑ $19.95		
Raising Capital: How to Write a Financing Proposal		❑ $19.95		
Renaissance 2000: Liberal Arts Essentials for Tomorrow's Leaders		❑ $22.95		
Retail in Detail: How to Start and Manage a Small Retail Business		❑ $15.95		
Secrets of High Ticket Selling		❑ $19.95		
Secrets to Buying and Selling a Business		❑ $24.95		
Secure Your Future: Financial Planning at Any Age	❑ $39.95	❑ $19.95		
Selling Services: A Guide for the Consulting Professional		❑ $18.95		
The Small Business Insider's Guide to Bankers		❑ $18.95		

BOOK SUB-TOTAL (Additional titles on other side)

TITLE	✔ BINDER	✔ PAPERBACK	QUANTITY	COST
SmartStart Your (State) Business... series		❏ $19.95		
Please specify which state(s) you would like:				
Smile Training Isn't Enough: The Three Secrets to Excellent Customer Service		❏ $19.95		
Start Your Business (Also available as a book and disk package, see below)		❏ $ 9.95 *(without disk)*		
Successful Network Marketing for The 21st Century		❏ $15.95		
Surviving Success: Managing the Challenges of Growth		❏ $19.95		
TargetSmart! Database Marketing for the Small Business		❏ $19.95		
Top Tax Saving Ideas for Today's Small Business		❏ $16.95		
Twenty-One Sales in a Sale: What Sales Are You Missing?		❏ $19.95		
Which Business? Help in Selecting Your New Venture		❏ $18.95		
Write Your Own Business Contracts		❏ $24.95		
BOOK SUB-TOTAL (Don't forget to include your amount from the previous side)				

OASIS SOFTWARE   Please specify which computer operating system you use (DOS, Mac OS, or Windows)

TITLE	✔ Windows	✔ Mac OS	QUANTITY	COST
California Corporation Formation Package ASCII Software	❏ $ 39.95	❏ $ 39.95		
Company Policy & Personnel Software Text Files	❏ $ 49.95	❏ $ 49.95		
Financial Management Techniques (Full Standalone)	❏ $ 99.95			
Financial Templates	❏ $ 69.95	❏ $ 69.95		
The Insurance Assistant Software (Full Standalone)	❏ $ 29.95			
Start Your Business (Software for Windows™)	❏ $ 19.95			
The Survey Genie - Customer Edition (Full Standalone)	❏ $199.95 (WIN)	❏ $149.95 (DOS)		
The Survey Genie - Employee Edition (Full Standalone)	❏ $199.95 (WIN)	❏ $149.95 (DOS)		
Winning Business Plans in Color (MS Office Addition)	❏ $ 39.95			
SOFTWARE SUB-TOTAL				

BOOK & DISK PACKAGES   Please specify which computer operating system you use (DOS, Mac OS, or Windows)

TITLE	✔ Windows	✔ MacOS	✔ Binder	✔ Paperback	QUANTITY	COST
The Buyer's Guide to Business Insurance w/ Insurance Assistant	❏		❏ $ 59.95	❏ $ 39.95		
California Corporation Formation Book & Text Files	❏	❏		❏ $ 59.95		
Company Policy & Personnel Book & Software Text Files	❏	❏	❏ $ 89.95	❏ $ 69.95		
Financial Management Techniques Book & Software	❏		❏ $129.95	❏ $ 119.95		
Start Your Business Paperback & Software (Software for Windows™)	❏			❏ $ 24.95		
BOOK & DISK PACKAGE SUB-TOTAL						

SOLD TO: Please give street address for shipping.

Name:

Title:

Company:

Street Address:

City/State/Zip:

Daytime Phone: Email:

SHIP TO: If different than above, please give alternate street address

Name:

Company:

Street Address:

City/State/Zip:

Daytime Phone:

GRAND TOTAL

SUB-TOTALS *(from other side)* $

SUB-TOTALS *(from this side)* $

SHIPPING (see chart below) $

TOTAL ORDER   **$**

If your purchase is:	Shipping costs within the USA:
$0 - $25	$5.00
$25.01 - $50	$6.00
$50.01 - $100	$7.00
$100.01 - $175	$9.00
$175.01 - $250	$13.00
$250.01 - $500	$18.00
$500.01 +	4% of total merchandise

**You can also order online
24-hours a day and 7 days a week at
http://www.psi-research.com**

PAYMENT INFORMATION: *Rush service is available, call for details.*
International and Canadian Orders: *Please call 1-541-479-9464 for quote on shipping.*
Please indicate a method of payment below:

❏ **CHECK** *Enclosed, payable to PSI Research*   ❏ **VISA**   ❏ **MASTERCARD**   ❏ **AMEX**   ❏ **DISCOVER**

Card Number: Expires:

Signature: Name On Card: